MODERN CAMBRIDGE ECONOMICS

SOCIALIST PLANNING

MODERN CAMBRIDGE ECONOMICS

Editors Phyllis Deane
Gautam Mathur
Joan Robinson

Also in the series

Phyllis Deane
The Evolution of Economic Ideas

Joan Robinson
Aspects of Development and Underdevelopment

SOCIALIST PLANNING

Michael Ellman
Professor of Economics
University of Amsterdam

CAMBRIDGE UNIVERSITY PRESS

CAMBRIDGE
LONDON NEW YORK NEW ROCHELLE
MELBOURNE SYDNEY

Published by the Press Syndicate of the University of Cambridge
The Pitt Building, Trumpington Street, Cambridge CB2 1RP
32 East 57th Street, New York, NY 10022, USA
296 Beaconsfield Parade, Middle Park, Melbourne 3206, Australia

First published 1979
Reprinted 1980, 1982

Printed in Great Britain at the
University Press, Cambridge

Library of Congress Cataloguing in Publication Data
Ellman, Michael.
Socialist planning.

(Modern Cambridge economics series)
Bibliography: p.
Includes index.
1. Economic policy. 2. Comparative economics. 3. Marxian economics. I. Title
HD82.E52 335·43 78-57757
ISBN 0 521 22229 X hard covers
ISBN 0 521 29409 6 paperback

SERIES PREFACE

The modern Cambridge Economics series, of which this book is one, is designed in the same spirit as and with similar objectives to the series of Cambridge Economic Handbooks launched by Maynard Keynes soon after the First World War. Keynes' series, as he explained in his introduction, was intended 'to convey to the ordinary reader and to the uninitiated student some conception of the general principles of thought which economists now apply to economic problems'. He went on to describe its authors as, generally speaking, 'orthodox members of the Cambridge School of Economics' drawing most of their ideas and prejudices from 'the two economists who have chiefly influenced Cambridge thought for the past fifty years, Dr Marshall and Professor Pigou' and as being 'more anxious to avoid obscure forms of expression than difficult ideas'.

This series of short monographs is also aimed at the intelligent undergraduate and interested general reader, but it differs from Keynes' series in three main ways: first in that it focuses on aspects of economics which have attracted the particular interest of economists in the post Second World War era; second in that its authors, though still sharing a Cambridge tradition of ideas, would regard themselves as deriving their main inspiration from Keynes himself and his immediate successors, rather than from the neoclassical generation of the Cambridge school; and third in that it envisages a wider audience than readers in mature capitalist economies, for it is equally aimed at students in developing countries whose problems and whose interactions with the rest of the world have helped to shape the economic issues which have dominated economic thinking in recent decades.

Finally, it should be said that the editors and authors of this Modern Cambridge Economics series represent a wider spectrum of economic doctrine than the Cambridge School of Economics to which Keynes referred in the 1920s. However, the object of the series is not to propagate particular doctrines. It is to stimulate students to escape from conventional theoretical ruts and to think for themselves on live and controversial issues.

PHYLLIS DEANE
GAUTAM MATHUR
JOAN ROBINSON

'... our task is to study the state capitalism of the Germans, to spare *no effort* in copying it and not to shrink from adopting dictatorial methods to hasten the copying of it. Our task is to hasten this copying even more than Peter hastened the copying of Western culture by barbarian Russia, and did not refrain from using barbarous methods in fighting barbarism.'

V. I. LENIN

(*'Left wing' childishness and the petty-bourgeois mentality*)

CONTENTS

Tables and figures

Figures

PREFACE

The purpose of this book is to provide a clear and simple introduction to the economics of planning in state socialist countries. The book differs from most of the literature on economic planning and comparative economic systems published in the Anglo-Saxon world in two respects. It does not take general equilibrium theory as the standard by which economic systems should be judged, and it takes Marxist ideas seriously. It differs from most of the literature on economic planning and comparative economic systems published in the state socialist countries in that it treats Marxism as a science whose conclusions can be modified, or rejected, on the basis of experience. It does not treat it as a dogma which is always true and whose precise content from time to time is defined by Authority.

The book attempts to summarise in a short space the experience of many countries and six decades. It also covers a large number of subjects. Hence it has been impossible to treat any single topic in depth, or to treat all aspects of the subject, or to provide anything like an exhaustive survey of the literature. In a number of places I have been guilty of oversimplification. The book concentrates on two countries, the USSR and China, and has little to say about the interesting experiences of countries such as the German Democratic Republic, Cuba and Vietnam. This results from shortage of space. I have concentrated on the USSR and China because they are the most important of the state socialist countries. The USSR was the first country to introduce socialist planning, its experiences have had a world wide impact, numerous countries have modelled their institutions on the USSR, and there is a world wide political movement that regards Soviet planning as a model. China is the most populous country in the world. For those who wish to pursue further the topics raised, a list of suggested further reading is appended to each chapter.

The reader may wonder how it is possible to write a serious book on this subject in view of the inadequate statistics and the bias of most authors. It is true that the availability of statistics leaves much to be desired. For China many key time series (e.g. for the population and for agricultural output) have wide margins of error. It is in many important cases only possible to indicate the main areas of ignorance. As for the USSR, while some data (such as that on industrial diseases and accidents, on crime and on prices at the collective farm markets in recent years) are lacking, on the whole there is an abundance of data. It is of course true that it has to be approached critically. For example, the data on Soviet defence expenditures during the First Five Year Plan and on serious diseases in the 1930s are known to have been faked in order to create a misleading impression abroad. In addition, some Soviet statistics of agricultural output appear to be non-comparable with similar statistics for other countries. Nevertheless, there are some first class Soviet statistical data, such as the material product accounts for 1928–30 which are a landmark in the history of national income accounting. As far as bias is concerned, this is not really a serious problem, since in many authors it is so obvious as to be merely funny. In addition, in recent years a number of monographs and scholarly papers have been published in several countries whose authors have added substantially to understanding. I am much indebted to these authors, without whose work this book would have been impossible. I hope that by carefully sifting through the currently available material it has been possible to illuminate the topics chosen for discussion in this book. Because of data limitations, this book is only an interim study and leaves open many areas for further investigation. They include, the calculation of standardised inter-system social indicators; improved grain, population, distribution of income and nutritional data for China; industrial safety data for the state socialist countries; and comparative international studies of labour morale.

The author has benefited greatly from repeated discussions with colleagues. Particularly helpful were the comments, criticisms and suggestions made by Mahmoud Abdel-Fadil, Wlodzimierz Brus, Chris Davis, Phyllis Deane, Hans van den Doel, Patricia Ellman, Stanislaw Gomulka, Jack Gray, Philip Hanson, Christopher Howe, Ruud Knaack, Michael Masuch, Alec Nove, Joan Robinson, Sandy Smith and Roger Tarling. In addition, I am very grateful to the Director, staff and library of the Centre for Russian and East European Studies, Birmingham University, the Director, staff and library of the East European Institute of the University of Amsterdam, and the Economics Faculties of Cambridge and Amsterdam Universities, for the stimulus, assistance and encouragement which they have provided.

Unfortunately there is no neutral terminology for discussing the topics treated in this book. In the USSR the world is considered to be divided into 'socialist' and 'capitalist' countries. In China it is considered to be divided into three, the imperialist (USA) and social imperialist (USSR) countries, the second-rate capitalist countries (Western Europe and Japan) and the third world (Asia less Japan, Africa and Latin America). In the West, as in the USSR, it is considered to be divided into two, only the names are different. Instead of 'capitalist' and 'socialist' the terms 'mixed economies' and 'centrally planned/managed' are used. In this book the convention is adopted according to which the world is divided into 'capitalist' and 'state socialist' economies. (The latter term is borrowed from David Lane. In the text it is sometimes shortened to 'socialist'. This is purely an abbreviation and has no theoretical significance.) This is an imperfect terminology, but seems less so than other possible conventions.

Part of chapter 3 was first published in *Oxford Economic Papers* and I am grateful to the editors for permission to reprint it.

MICHAEL ELLMAN

Amsterdam University
January 1978

GLOSSARY

The administrative economy The term used by the author to describe the economic mechanism (q.v.) which has existed in the USSR since 1929. It corresponds to model 1 in the classification of allocation models by Margolis and Trzeciakowski, and to Kornai's 'suction economy'. The distinguishing feature of the administrative economy is *current planning* (q.v.).

CC The Central Committee of the Communist Party.

CCP Chinese Communist Party.

Classical Marxism Marxism 1881–1914.

CMEA The Council for Mutual Economic Assistance (often known as Comecon). Its members are, Bulgaria, Cuba, Czechoslovakia, the German Democratic Republic (GDR), Hungary, Mongolia, Poland, Romania, Vietnam and the USSR.

CPSU The Communist Party of the Soviet Union.

Current planning The system under which enterprises receive instructions as to which products they should produce in the current period (quarter, half year or year) and quotas for the materials which are to be used to meet the production targets, and other instructions concerning their activities in the current period. To be contrasted with long-term planning, medium-term planning, and regional planning.

Economic mechanism The relationship between the parts of the economic system, such as the role of the banks and the existence of allocation or of wholesale trade, which together form a system, such as *War Communism* (q.v.), *NEP* (q.v.) or the administrative economy. In theoretical analysis referred to as the ownership and allocation model.

The 11th Congress The 11th Congress of the CCP was held in 1977. This Congress confirmed the appointment of Hua Kuo-feng as Party Chairman, of Teng Hsiao-ping as one of the Vice-Chairmen, and the condemnation of the 'gang of four' (q.v.).

Gang of four Wang Hung-wen, Chang Chun-chiao, Chiang Ching (Mao Tse-tung's fourth and last wife) and Yao Wen-yuan. Fell from power after Mao Tse-tung's death in 1976.

GLF Great Leap Forward.

Gosplan The State Planning Commission, the central planning organ.

Great Patriotic War The Soviet term for the Soviet–German war 1941–45.

GPCR The Great Proletarian Cultural Revolution.

Narodniks The original 'Narodniks' were intellectuals in nineteenth century Russia who advocated policies in the interests of the peasantry. They were the intellectual ancestors of the Socialist Revolutionary Party, a political party which played an important role in Russia in 1905–1918, the 'green' parties of inter-war Eastern Europe, and the pro-peasant intellectuals and political parties in contemporary third world countries. In this book the word 'Narodnik' is used by extension to apply to the whole pro-peasant political tendency of which these intellectuals and political parties are particular manifestations.

NEM The New Economic Mechanism introduced in Hungary from 1 January 68. The distinguishing feature of the NEM is the absence of current planning.

NEP The New Economic Policy is the term used to describe the economic mechanism which existed in the USSR in the 1920s.

OGAS 'Nation-wide automated management system for the gathering and processing of information for accounting, planning and control of the national economy', i.e departmental management information and control systems which are compatible with one another.

Productive forces The technology, skills and resources available to society.

Productive relations The relationship between people in the process of production, e.g. the exploitation of the workers by the capitalists in the Marxist model of capitalism.

Taylorism Organisation of the labour process which separates planning from execution. Founded by US engineer F. W. Taylor. Basis of 'scientific management'.

R & D Research and Development.

The 20th Congress The 20th Congress of the CPSU was held in 1956. At this Congress the First Secretary made a report 'On the personality cult and its consequences'.

The 22nd Congress The 22nd Congress of the CPSU was held in 1961. At this Congress a resolution was passed to remove the body of J.V. Stalin from the Lenin mausoleum.

War Communism Term used to describe the economic mechanism which existed in the USSR in 1918–21.

IMPORTANT DATES

15th century	Portuguese ships enter the Indian Ocean. Spanish assault on the Americas begins.
16th century	Growth of Portuguese trade with Africa, Ceylon, Indonesia and Brazil. Portuguese Empire created. Spain conquers Mexico, Peru and the Philippines. Demographic catastrophe in Mexico.
1568–1648	1st bourgeois revolution. United Provinces becomes an independent state. Amsterdam becomes the commercial capital of the world.
1640–1688	2nd bourgeois revolution. England prepared for commercial expansion.
18th century	Heyday of the slave trade. Britain overtakes the United Provinces.
1688–1815	Britain and France struggle for commercial mastery of the world. Britain emerges victorious. British rule established in India, Canada, Australia, New Zealand and South Africa.
1776	Continental Congress issues Declaration of Independence.
1787	United States Constitution drafted.
1789	1st pure bourgeois revolution begins in France.
1780–1820	Industrial revolution in Britain.
1815–1914	Industrial revolution spreads across Europe and North America. Transcontinental railways built. Industrialisation of war. Conquest by European countries and the United States of Central Asia, Vietnam, nearly all Africa and the remainder of North America.
1839–42	1st Opium War.
1848	*Communist Manifesto* published. Year of revolutions.
1856–60	2nd Opium War.
1861–65	US Civil War.
1867	*Capital* vol. 1 published.
1868	Meiji Restoration.
1917	October Revolution.
1918–20	Russian civil war.
1921–22	Famine in Russia.
1921–28	New Economic Policy in Russia.

1928–	Five Year Plans in USSR.
1929–53	Stalin's dictatorship in USSR.
1929–32	Collectivisation of agriculture in the USSR.
1932–33	Bottom of the Great Depression. Mass unemployment in Europe and North America. Ruin of many primary producers. Widespread bank closures in the USA. Victory of National Socialism in Germany. Famine in USSR.
1937–38	Mass arrests in USSR.
1937–45	Japanese–Chinese war.
1941–45	Second World War.
1945–	Decline of Britain.
1945–49	Division of Europe into US and Soviet spheres.
1946–47	Last famine in USSR.
1947–55	USA establishes world-wide network of military bases.
1947	Britain withdraws from India.
1948	Soviet–Yugoslav split.
1949	People's Republic of China established.
1950	Korean war begins.
1950–52	Land reform in China.
1952–73	Cyclical boom in capitalist world.
1953–57	First Five Year Plan in China.
1953	USA overthrows Mossadeq regime in Iran.
1954–73	Volume and price of oil exports develop satisfactorily for importers.
1956	20th Congress of the CPSU. Anglo-French-Israeli invasion of Egypt. Soviet invasion of Hungary.
1957	USSR launches world's first artificial satellite. 100 flowers movement in China.
1958	Great Leap Forward in China.
1959	Victory of Castro in Cuba.
1959–61	Economic crisis in China. Three bad harvests, famine and industrial recession.
1960	USSR withdraws technicians from China.
1961	22nd Congress of the CPSU.
1961–73	USA wages war in Vietnam, Laos and Cambodia.
1962–66	Socialist education movement in China.
1964–66	Debate on alternative economic mechanisms in Cuba.
1965–66	White terror in Indonesia.
1966–68	Cultural Revolution in China.
1966–70	Maoist–Guevarist economic mechanism in Cuba.
1968	NEM introduced in Hungary. USSR invades Czechoslovakia.
1968–	Liberal opposition in USSR.
1969	Serious Sino-Soviet border clashes.
1970s	Extensive imports of technology from capitalist world by state socialist countries. Development of East–West production cooperation agreements. Creation of trans-ideological enterprises.

1973	Internal opposition and the USA successfully destabilise *Unidad Popular* in Chile. Murder of Allende.
1975	Bottom of recession in capitalist world. Victory of state socialism in South Vietnam, Laos and Cambodia. Mass sending down in Cambodia. Disintegration of Portuguese Empire.
1976	Death of Mao Tse-tung and defeat of 'gang of four'.
1977	11th Congress of the CCP. New economic management system introduced in Cuba.
1977–78	Serious Kampuchean (Cambodian)–Vietnamese border clashes.

1

THE NEED FOR PLANNING

The reasons for state control and direction of the economy can conveniently be considered under two heads, theoretical and empirical.

THEORETICAL CONSIDERATIONS

The relationship between the individual and society, and the role of the state in economic activity, has of course been a central issue for a whole school of economists, sometimes referred to as 'orthodox'. This, however, is a misleading terminology. 'Orthodoxy' varies substantially between places and over time. What is 'orthodox' at the ancient university of Cambridge is very different from what is 'orthodox' at the ancient university of Cracow. What is 'orthodox' in China in 1978 is very different from what was 'orthodox' in China in 1968. Another adjective which is often used to describe this school is 'bourgeois'. In view of the fact that in the twentieth century this term has often been used, not as an instrument of class-historical analysis, but as a piece of vulgar abuse accompanying arrest and preceding incarceration in a concentration camp, I find this terminology rather distasteful. Accordingly I will use a geographical terminology and refer to the 'Western' school of economists. This school has its roots in the eighteenth century but still flourishes today.

The Western view

An outstanding early representative of the school was Mandeville. The conclusion of his famous (1724) was that the book had demonstrated

that neither the friendly qualities and kind affections that are natural to man, nor the real virtues he is capable of acquiring by reason and self-denial, are the foundations of society: but that what we call evil in the world, moral as well as natural, is the grand principle that makes us sociable creatures, the solid basis, the life and support of all trades and employments without exception: that there we must look for the true origin of all arts and sciences, and that the moment evil ceases the society must be spoiled, if not totally dissolved.

He expressed this thought both in prose and also in verse, in his well known description of the hive, analogous to human society:

There every part was full of vice
Yet the whole mass a paradise.
Such were the blessings of that state
Their crimes conspired to make them great.

This idea played a major role in Adam Smith's great work *The Wealth of Nations.* There is the well-known passage in which Smith argued that 'It is not from the benevolence of the butcher, the brewer or the baker that we expect our dinner, but from their regard to their own interest. We address ourselves, not to their humanity but to their self love, and never talk to them of our own necessities but of their advantage.' At another point he refers to the 'invisible hand' which ensures that individuals pursuing their own selfish ends collectively act in a socially rational way. From Adam Smith's day to the present a large part of the teaching of elementary economics has been devoted to explaining and expounding this doctrine of the strange virtues of private vices. Traditionally students have come along to lectures on economics concerned about the great problems of poverty, inequality and unemployment. Their teachers have taught them to readjust their vision, and instead of these evils to see in the market system a socially rational process for combining individually rational decisions into socially rational ones.

En passant, one should note that the process by which the acceptance of a new theory replaces what one previously 'saw' by an entirely new set of observations, is not the absurdity that it might seem at first sight. After all, a central part of Marxist economics is concerned with replacing one vision of the labour contract by another. Before studying the Labour Theory of Value one may 'observe' a mutually beneficial process whereby a worker obtains a wage in exchange for working a certain number of hours for an employer. After one has learned the Labour Theory of Value one 'sees' a process of exploitation whereby the worker sells his labour power and the employer obtains surplus value. Such a transformation may seem odd to a vulgar positivist, who imagines that there exist so called 'facts' independent of our theories. On the other hand, to someone who accepts the doctrine of Sextus Empiricus and of Popper according to which 'there are no empirical propositions, only theoretical ones' it seems entirely normal.

In some quarters there appears to lurk the view that Ricardo was some kind of 'progressive', a proto Marx. After all, we are told, his theory of the rate of profit is different from, and free from the justificationist bias of, later writers. In addition his theory recognised the class nature of capitalist society and the reality and importance of class conflict. All this is undoubtedly true. It is very important to bear in mind, however, that this same David Ricardo fully accepted Adam Smith's doctrine of the invisible hand. If one looks, for example, at the chapter on wages in *The Principles* one finds the proposition that 'Like all other contracts, wages should be left to the free and fair competition of the market, and should never be controlled by the interference of the legislature.' This certainly contrasts dramatically with Marx's analysis of the 10 hours Act!

In the late nineteenth century the classical economists, with their concern with growth and distribution, gave way to the neoclassical economists, with their concern with the efficient allocation of resources and the mathematical demonstration both of the invisible hand doctrine and also of the 'exceptions' to it.[1] One of the most eminent of the neoclassical economists was Walras, whose views on this matter are clearly set out in the following extract from *The principles of pure economics* (1954 edn p. 255 italics added):

> *Production in a market ruled by free competition is an operation by which services can be combined and converted into products of such a nature and in such quantities as will give the greatest possible satisfaction of wants* within the limits of the double condition, that each service and each product have only one price in the market, namely that price at which the quantity supplied is equal to the quantity demanded, and that the selling price of the products be equal to the cost of the services employed in making them.

Besides their 'rigorous', mathematical 'proof', of the invisible hand doctrine, the masters of the neoclassical school, such as Marshall and Pigou, were, of course, very much concerned with the 'exceptions' to the general rule that leaving things to the

[1] Generations of economics students have been taught both the 'proof' of laissez faire doctrines and the standard list of 'exceptions'. How many of the teachers have explained how it is possible to 'prove' a doctrine which is obviously false?

market is best, such as monopoly, increasing returns, consumer's surplus and externalities.

In the 1930s there took place what, in Cambridge England, is known as the 'Keynesian revolution'.[2] The incorporation of Keynes' teaching within the accepted corpus of economic theory led to the well-known division of economic theory into two halves, *micro* and *macro*. What does *micro* economics teach? That the price mechanism leads to the efficient allocation of resources, of course. What does *macro* economics teach? That unless the Government pursues just the right sort of stabilisation policy either we will have serious unemployment, or serious inflation, or possibly both together. What is the relationship between *micro* and *macro*? Well...This curious coexistence of *micro* and *macro* reflects a society in which the overall regulation of the economy is in the hands of the state, whereas concrete production and distribution decisions are in the hands of private firms. *Macro* economics performs the technocratic role of discussing some aspects of the central regulation of the economy. *Micro* economics continues the very important ideological role which invisible hand doctrines have had since Adam Smith incorporated Mandeville's paradoxical notion into his powerful analysis of original accumulation. It is used to adjust the vision of those who are so benighted that they 'observe' poverty, inequality and unemployment.

A standard exposition of the Western position, as it seemed to an intelligent English economist of the early 1950s, is set out in Crossland (1956). This book was the classic 'Revisionist' text, i.e. the authoritative statement of the views of the Right Wing of the Labout Party, of those who wanted to 'modernise' the Labour Party by expunging from its creed the view that capitalism suffers from serious economic problems. It argued that if the state ensured full employment and growth by Keynesian *macro* economic policies, the *micro* allocation of resources (except in a few special cases where externalities were important) could be left to market forces. The conclusion of the book was that this happy combination of *micro* and *macro* would ensure the achievement of the *economic* goals of the socialist movement, and that socialists should increasingly concentrate on the non-economic quality of life. The development and popu-

[2] This phrase is used to describe the emergence and acceptance of the doctrines of Keynes' *General Theory*, although adherents of Hobson, Myrdal, Kalecki and Currie might dispute their originality, and Marxists, or indeed anyone living outside the very cloistered world of Cambridge in the 1920s and 1930s, their 'revolutionary' character.

larity of revisionist ideas reflected, in part, the great boom (1952–73) in the capitalist world, and reads very oddly in the Britain of the 1970s!

Besides developments in the material world, there are also two developments in the intellectual world which have emphasised the special case nature of the invisible hand doctrine. I have in mind developments within game theory and within general equilibrium theory.

Von Neumann and Morgenstern in their (1944) opened up a new field of theoretical investigation in economics, game theory.[3] Subsequent research in this field uncovered a far-reaching proposition which, from an invisible hand point of view, appeared a paradox. Under certain circumstances the interaction of isolated individuals, each making individually rational decisions, may result in a situation which is not only socially irrational but also worse for each individual than an alternative which was open to him but which he consciously declined! In textbooks of mathematical economics this proposition is known, for reasons which will appear shortly, as 'The prisoners' dilemma'. The simplest method of explaining it is by way of example.

Consider the following situation. Two suspects have been arrested. The police have enough evidence to ensure that each one would receive on trial a light sentence, e.g. one year. They would very much like, however, to strengthen their case by obtaining confessions. Accordingly they decide to interrogate each prisoner separately and offer him the following deal. If he confesses, they tell him, and the other prisoner does not, then the prisoner who does confess will receive only three months. If he does not confess, and the other prisoner does, then the prisoner who did not confess will get ten years. If he confesses and so does the other, he gets five years. The situation is set out in figure 1.1.

Take prisoner 1 (the situation is symmetrical for both prisoners). If he does not confess, the worst possible outcome for himself would be that he would receive a ten year sentence (in the event that 2 caves in). If he does confess, the worst possible outcome for himself is that he receives a five year sentence (if 2 also confesses). Accordingly, if prisoner 1 is a cautious person

[3] Whereas the 'marginalist revolution' had been concerned with applying seventeenth-century mathematics to economics, the 'von Neumann revolution' applied twentieth-century mathematics to economics.

Figure 1.1 *The prisoners' dilemma*

		Prisoner 2	
		Not confess	Confess
Prisoner 1	Not confess	1 year each	10 years for 1 and 3 months for 2
	Confess	3 months for 1 and 10 years for 2	5 years each

who when making choices chooses the least bad of the worst possible outcomes, he will confess. The same argument applies to prisoner 2. Accordingly, the outcome will be that each prisoner will receive a five year sentence. In the event, however, that neither prisoner had confessed, each would have received only a one year sentence (because of the lack of evidence). Each decision maker has made an individually rational decision, but as a result both are worse off than if they had both made an alternative decision which each one considered and rejected. Each individual prisoner would be better off if some force other than his own immediate self interest (such as Republican Loyalty, Working Class Solidarity, the State, or belief in the Golden Rule) compelled him not to confess. This 'paradoxical' situation has resulted from a combination of the decision rule adopted (striving to avoid the worst possible outcomes, i.e. the maximum criterion), the fact that the decisions are made in isolation (i.e. that it is a non-cooperative game), and that the total sentence received depends very much on the decisions made (i.e. that it is a non-constant-sum game).

This startling (from an invisible hand point of view) result has been interpreted by Runciman & Sen (1965) as an elucidation of Rousseau's concept of the 'general will' and his idea of the advantages to the members of society of their being 'forced to be free'. Many writers have found Rousseau's concepts absurd or meaningless, but the prisoners' dilemma is a situation in which the general will is clearly distinct from and superior to the outcome that would result from atomistic decision making. Pursuing this line of argument, one can say that if Mandeville's doctrine is the 'liberal paradox', the prisoners' dilemma is the 'totalitarian paradox'. From this point of view one can say that the difference between 'liberal democracy' and 'totalitarian democracy' (Carr 1945 pp. 5–19, Talmon 1952, 1957 and 1960) is that, while both make the value judgement that social choices ought to be based on individual preferences, liberal democracy assumes that individual preferences are both unconcerned with, and independent of, the choices of other individuals whereas totalitarian democracy assumes that the decision making process normally corresponds to the 'prisoners' dilemma' situation.

If the first internal intellectual discovery which undermined invisible hand doctrines was in the field of game theory, the second was in the field of general equilibrium theory, the branch of economics which was widely assumed to have demonstrated in a 'rigorous', 'scientific' way the validity of the assertion by Walras quoted above. During the 1950s and 1960s there was a great deal of research into general equilibrium theory. According to two leading workers in this field (Arrow & Hahn 1971 p. vii) the purpose of this research was to ascertain the conditions under which Adam Smith's assertion about the invisible hand is valid. The main result of this immense body of research has been to emphasise how very stringent these conditions are. The general equilibrium model focuses attention on trade rather than production; ignores the central role of labour; treats prices as guides to efficient allocation rather than as a reflection of the mode of production, the distribution of the national income and the methods of production; treats competition as a socially rational process for ensuring efficient allocation rather than as a mechanism for fostering technical progress or as a cost-increasing factor; emphasises the equilibrating role of markets and neglects the disequilibrating role of markets; ignores information other than price information; approaches all decision making from the standpoint of maximisation; focuses attention on the combination of individually rational choices into socially rational choices while neglecting the possibility of individually rational choices combining into socially irrational choices; neglects the role of increasing returns in manufacturing; concentrates on auction markets; treats the quantity of resources and the effectiveness with which they are used, rather than the level of effective demand, as the determinants of the level of output; considers an economy without a past and with a certain future; plays down the difference between a barter and a monetary economy... Indeed, according to Hahn (1974 p. 36), an eminent general equilibrium theorist often referred to as a supporter of 'orthodox' or 'neoclassical' economics, general equilibrium theory, by emphasising the stringency of the conditions necessary for Mandeville's doctrine to hold, has demonstrated that the Mandeville–Smith world 'cannot serve as a description of an actual economy in which prices are never fully known and economic agents are ceaselessly adjusting to new circumstances'. The same author has also argued in his (1973 p. 330) that 'the vulgarizations of General Equilibrium theory [i.e. the view that General Equilibrium theory is a descriptive theory of the world in which we live and hence that Mandeville's doctrine is valid in our world] which are the substance of most textbooks of economics are both scientifically and politically harmful'. Furthermore, he has stated (Hahn 1974 p. 37) that the conclusion of Western theory is that, 'the Government can in principle always do as well and often better than the market'. Hence it is no accident that economists steeped in the Western tradition are busily engaged in theorising about the operation of planned economies (Heal 1973, Weitzmann 1974).

The Marxist view

The Marxist analysis of capitalism stresses two advantages which a planned socialist economy has over an unplanned capitalist economy. First, the absence of the anarchy of production, and secondly the absence of class conflict. On the first point a standard Marxist text, Bukharin & Preobrazhensky (1969 edn pp. 88–9), argues that

> under capitalism the production and distribution of goods is quite unorganized; 'anarchy of production' prevails. What does this mean? It means that all the capitalist entrepreneurs (or capitalist companies) produce commodities independently of one another. Instead of society undertaking to reckon up what it needs and how much of each article, the factory owners simply produce upon the calculations of what will bring them most profit and will best enable them to defeat their rivals in the market. The consequence often is that commodities are produced in excessive quantities... There is no sale for them. The workers cannot buy them, for they have not enough money. Thereupon a crisis ensues. The factories are shut down, and the workers are turned out into the street. Furthermore, the anarchy of production entails a struggle for the market; each producer wants to entice away the others' customers, to corner the market. This struggle assumes various forms: it begins with the competition between two factory owners; it ends in the world war, wherein the capitalist states wrestle with one another for the world market. This signifies, not merely that the parts of capitalist society

interfere with one another's working, but that there is a direct conflict between the constituent parts.

The first reason, therefore, for the disharmony of capitalist society is the anarchy of production, which leads to crises, internecine competition, and wars.

In this connection one should note that Marxists have traditionally ignored the problem, central to the Western economic tradition, of actually calculating and implementing a plan for the efficient allocation of a nation's resources. For example, Bukharin and Preobrazhensky in their (1969 pp. 114–15) wrote that under socialism

society will be transformed into a huge working organization for cooperative production. There will then be neither disintegration of production nor anarchy of production. In such a social order, production will be organised. No longer will one enterprise compete with another; the factories, workshops, mines, and other productive institutions will all be subdivisions, as it were, of one vast people's workshop, which will embrace the entire national economy of production. It is obvious that so comprehensive an organization presupposes a general plan of production. If all the factories and workshops together with the whole of agricultural production are combined to form an immense cooperative workshop, it is obvious that everything must be precisely calculated. We must know in advance how much labour to assign to the various branches of industry; what products are required and how much of each it is necessary to produce; how and where machines must be provided. These and similar details must be thought out beforehand, with approximate accuracy at least; and the work must be guided in accordance with our calculations. This is how the organisation of communist production will be effected. Without a general plan, without a general directive system, and without careful calculation and book-keeping, there can be no organization. But in the communist social order, there is such a plan.

About the difficulties involved in calculating and implementing it, not a word. This is entirely natural in a book written under difficult conditions, during a civil war, at a time when there was virtually no experience of planned economies. The present book is concerned precisely with what the experience of six decades and many countries has indicated about the possibilities, and difficulties, of a planned economy.

On the second point the same text (pp. 89 and 119–20) explains that a major

Reason for the disharmony of capitalist society is to be found in the class structure of that society. Considered in its essence, capitalist society is not one society but two societies; it consists of capitalists, on the one hand,

and of workers and poor peasants, on the other. Between these two classes there is continuous and irreconcilable enmity; this is what we speak of as the *class war*...[Under socialism, on the other hand] there will have ensued the liberation of the vast quantity of human energy which is now absorbed in the class struggle. Just think how great is the waste of nervous energy, strength, and labour – upon the political struggle, upon strikes, revolts and their suppression, trials in the law-courts, police activities, the State authority, upon the daily effort of the two hostile classes. The class war now swallows up vast quantities of energy and material means. In the new system this energy will be liberated; people will no longer struggle one with another. The liberated energy will be devoted to the work of production.

It is for these two reasons, to overcome the anarchy of production and class struggle characteristic of capitalism, that socialists have traditionally argued for a planned economy.

EMPIRICAL CONSIDERATIONS

The division between advanced and backward countries has been a major feature of the world economy since West European military technology overtook and surpassed that of all other parts of the world in the sixteenth century (Cipolla 1965). This division widened still more after the industrial revolution. The advanced countries were in Western Europe and subsequently in certain overseas territories which they colonised. The backward countries comprised the rest of the globe. Historically speaking, this division is very recent. When Marco Polo visited China he was most impressed by Chinese civilisation, which manifestly compared extremely favourably with that of mediaeval Western Europe. Within a historically very short period the Europeans used their military superiority to overrun what is now Latin America, and colonise Africa and much of Asia. China probably only escaped colonisation because of rivalries between the potential conquerors.

This predatory behaviour by the advanced countries aroused intense anxiety in the surviving independent countries, the leaders of which realised that if they were to retain their independence it was necessary for them to catch up with the advanced countries. This fact was keenly appreciated by Japan's rulers after the Meiji restoration and by Russia's rulers during Witte's tenure of office.

This historical background is absolutely indispensable for understanding the nature of economic planning in the state socialist countries. With some exceptions (such as the GDR and the Czech lands) the socialist countries are backward countries, and a major task of their economic institutions and policies has been to facilitate the essential task of catching up with the advanced countries.

The fact that they are backward countries is not an accident but has a definite theoretical explanation. According to classical Marxism, the socialist revolution is a result of the contradictions of capitalist society. Hence, those people and political parties which wished to organise socialist revolutions in pre-capitalist societies, simply showed their ignorance of the laws of motion of society discovered by Marx. This view was made explicit in Plekhanov's famous polemic with the narodniks in the 1880s. Nevertheless, the Bolsheviks, and all subsequent Communists ultimately came in practice to accept the view that Communists should strive for power and build socialism even in countries which were not yet developed capitalist countries, i.e. the theory of the 'permanent revolution'. The significance of this theory, as explained by its chief theorist (Trotsky 1930 p. 15) is that it

> demonstrated that the democratic tasks of backward bourgeois nations in our epoch lead to the dictatorship of the proletariat, and that the dictatorship of the proletariat places socialist tasks on the agenda. This was the central idea of the theory. If the traditional view held that the road to proletarian dictatorship ran through a lengthy democratic period, the doctrine of permanent revolution asserted that *for the backward countries the road to democracy leads through the dictatorship of the proletariat.*

This analysis makes it clear that Communist dictatorship is only relevant for backward countries and quite irrelevant to the advanced industrial countries. It also explains why the Eurocommunist parties, which operate in advanced industrial countries, have abandoned the aspiration to establish dictatorships of the proletariat. Since they operate in advanced countries which already have democracy, policies advocated for pre-democratic backward countries are absolutely irrelevant. Whether in fact the route advocated by Trotsky leads to the goal he postulated, is considered in chapter 10.

The fact that the state socialist countries are backward countries desperate to catch up, explains why it is that instead of executing the legacy of Marx, of constructing an egalitarian, non-market, society with a truly human organisation of the labour process and an end to the division of labour and the exploitation of man by man, they have in fact been mainly concerned with executing the legacy of Peter the Great and the Meiji reformers. That is to say, with the accelerated import of foreign techniques in order to preserve national independence, and, in the words of Lenin which have been taken as a motto for this book, of 'using barbarous methods in fighting barbarism'. The reasons why socialist planning has not come about in the advanced industrial countries are twofold. First, in those countries capitalism has led to a huge and historically unprecedented increase in real wages, a development not foreseen by Marx. Secondly, the experience of socialist planning has not appeared markedly superior to that of capitalism. This book considers, implicitly throughout, and explicitly in the final chapter, whether the latter view is in fact correct.

The fact that Soviet economic policy was largely concerned with catching up, for military reasons, was clearly explained by Stalin at the very beginning of socialist planning. In a famous speech delivered in 1931 and reprinted in his (1955b pp. 40–1) he explained the imperative need to press on with rapid industrialisation regardless of the obstacles.

It is sometimes asked whether it is not possible to slow down the tempo somewhat, to put a check on the movement. No, comrades, it is not possible! The tempo must not be reduced! On the contrary, we must increase it as much as is within our powers and possibilities. This is dictated to us by our obligations to the workers and peasants of the USSR. This is dictated to us by our obligations to the working class of the whole world.

To slacken the tempo would mean falling behind. And those who fall behind get beaten. But we do not want to be beaten. No, we refuse to be beaten! One feature of the history of old Russia was the continued beatings she suffered because of her backwardness. She was beaten by the Mongol khans. She was beaten by the Turkish beys. She was beaten by the Swedish feudal lords. She was beaten by the Polish and Lithuanian gentry. She was beaten by the British and French capitalists. She was beaten by the Japanese barons. All beat her – because of her backwardness, because of her military backwardness, cultural backwardness, political backwardness, industrial backwardness, agricultural backwardness. They beat her because to do so was profitable and could be done with impunity. You remember the words of the pre-revolutionary poet: 'You are poor and abundant, mighty and impotent, Mother Russia.' Those gentlemen were quite familiar with the verses of the old poet. They beat her, saying: 'You are abundant', so one can enrich oneself at your expense. They beat her, saying: 'You are poor and impotent', so you can be beaten and plundered with impunity. Such is the law of the exploiters – to beat the backward and weak. It is the jungle law of capitalism. You are backward, you are weak – therefore you are wrong; hence you can be beaten and enslaved. You are mighty – therefore you are right; hence we must be wary of you.

That is why we must no longer lag behind.

In the past we had no fatherland, nor could we have had one. But now that we have overthrown capitalism and power is in our hands, in the hands of the people, we have a fatherland, and we will uphold its independence. Do you want our socialist fatherland to be beaten and to lose its independence? If you do not want this, you must put an end to its backwardness in the shortest possible time and develop a genuine Bolshevik tempo in building up its socialist economy. There is no other way. That is why Lenin said on the eve of the October Revolution: 'Either perish, or overtake and outstrip the advanced capitalist countries.'

We are fifty or a hundred years behind the advanced countries. We must make good this distance in ten years. Either we do it, or we shall go under.

Ten years later the USSR was invaded for the second time.

This view of Stalin's is also orthodox in China. In a speech of 9 May 1977 at the national conference on learning from Taching in industry, Hua Kuo-feng stated that

The question of the speed of construction is a political rather than a purely economic question. When viewed in the light of the international class struggle, the political nature of the question stands out still more sharply. By their very nature, imperialism and social-imperialism mean war. We must definitely *be ready for war.* We cannot afford to let time slip through our fingers, as it waits for no one. Every Communist, every revolutionary and every patriot should be clear about the situation, seize the present opportune moment, strive to work well and make our country strong and prosperous as soon as possible.

Many features of the state socialist economies, from their degree of centralisation, via the share of accumulation in the national income, to their regional policies, can only be understood if their need to catch up with the advanced countries is appreciated.

SUMMARY

From the eighteenth century onwards a central feature of what was to become Western economic theory was the view that a decentralised market economy was bound to be more efficient than a state directed economy. As a result of internal intellectual developments taking place during the elaboration of the theory, this view was transformed into its opposite. Adherents of Western orthodoxy came round to the view that, 'the Government can in principle always do as well and often better than the market'. Marxists have traditionally argued in favour of planning on the grounds that this enables society to overcome both the anarchy of production and the class war inherent in the capitalist mode of production. Existing state socialist economies have to be seen against the background both of Marxist theory and of the imperative need to catch up with the most advanced countries, especially in the crucial field of military technology.

SUGGESTIONS FOR FURTHER READING

C. Bliss, 'Prices, Markets and Planning', *Economic Journal* (March 1972).

W. J. Baumol, *Welfare economics and the theory of the state* (London 1952).

W. G. Runciman and A. K. Sen, 'Games, Justice and the General Will', *Mind* (1965).

M. Ellman, 'Individual preferences and the market', *Economics of Planning*, no. 3 (1966).

N. Bukharin and E. Preobrazhensky, *The ABC of Communism* (Penguin edn with introduction by E. H. Carr) (London 1969).

J. Stalin, 'The tasks of business executives', *Works* vol. 13 (Moscow 1955).

J. Berliner, 'The economics of overtaking and surpassing', H. Rosovsky (ed.) *Industrialisation in two systems* (New York 1966).

2

COMPILING THE PLAN

Leaders must combine revolutionary enthusiasm with businesslike sense. They must be able not only to put forward high targets but also to adopt effective measures in time to ensure the realization of the targets. They must not indulge in empty talk and bluff. The targets we put forward should be those which can be reached with hard work. Do not lightly publicise or plan that which is not really obtainable, lest failure dampen the enthusiasm of the masses and delight the conservatives.

Liu Shao-chi (Speech at the Second Session of the 8th Congress of the CCP, May 1958)

The process by which plans are drawn up has varied substantially between the state socialist countries and over time. It has depended on the internal political situation; the international situation; the relative importance of the various sectors (such as agriculture and foreign trade); the statistics, staff and data processing facilities available; and the complexity of the economy. What is common to planning in all the state socialist countries, is the use of state ownership of the means of production, national economic planning, and political dictatorship, in the attempt to mobilise all the resources available to society and use them in the interests of national economic objectives. These normally include, rapid economic growth and in particular rapid industrialisation, an egalitarian income distribution, and the development of the armed forces.

This chapter provides a brief outline of the contemporary plan compilation process in the two chief state socialist countries, the USSR and China. First the situation in the USSR is described, and then those features of the Chinese situation that differ significantly from it.

PLAN COMPILATION IN THE USSR

Basic ideas

General background. In the USSR the theory of economic planning is derived from the political economy of socialism. The latter is one of the branches, together with party history and historical and dialectical materialism, of the official doctrine of the USSR, Marxism–Leninism. The derivation of Soviet planning theory from Marxism–Leninism has a number of important consequences.

First, in Marxist–Leninist theory economic growth is a process in which both the forces of production and the relations of production are developed. Hence, socialist planning concerns itself not just with purely production problems, but also with such questions as ownership and the distribution of income. As Stalin (1929) put it, on the eve of the fateful decision to collectivise agriculture: 'We do not need just any growth of productivity of the people's labour. We need a *definite* growth of productivity of the people's labour, namely the growth which ensures a *systematic preponderance* of the socialist sector of the economy over the capitalist sector.'

Secondly, in Marxist–Leninist theory, economic growth is a unified process of production, distribution, exchange and consumption, in which the decisive phase is production. The starting point of socialist planning is the decisive role of production.

Thirdly, in Marxist–Leninist theory, although all kinds of socially useful labour are equally necessary, nevertheless, the basis and condition for the existence of the entire national economy is the production of material goods, created by labour in the productive sphere (industry, agriculture, construction, freight transport). Accordingly, it is a basic principle of socialist planning that the only source of the national income is labour in the productive sphere. Expansion in the non-productive sphere is only possible on the basis of the growth of the productive sphere. National income accounting takes the form of MPS (material product system) accounting rather than SNA (system of national accounts) accounting.

Fourthly, in Marxist–Leninist theory, under socialism the growth process takes place simultaneously in physical and money (price) terms. Hence, planning must be in both physical and money units. In the higher phase of communism, however, money will become redundant and goods will circulate on the basis of direct product exchange.

Specific principles. The following specific ideas in Soviet planning thought seem to me particularly important. They are partymindedness, directive character, one-man management, scientific analysis, balance method, address principle, leading links and commercial accounting. Consider each in turn.

The principle of partymindedness means that the plan is a concrete expression of party policy. It must look at all problems from a party point of view. This principle is of great importance in all the state socialist countries. A major reason why economic reform, in the sense understood by some economists in the USSR and by many Western commentators, was not implemented in the USSR in the 1960s was precisely because, as one State Planning Commission official put it (Krylov 1969), 'in practice it means a weakening of the role of the socialist state and the party of the working class in the management of the economy'.

Characterising Soviet planning, Stalin long ago observed that 'our plans are not forecasts but instructions'. Whereas in capitalist countries, planning often takes an 'indicative' form, or is merely political or external (as when it is intended merely to impress external aid givers), in the USSR it takes the form of instructions binding on the participants in the economy.[1] In some quarters, a 'planned' economy is understood as one which attains the objectives of the plan. In the USSR, however, the mark of 'planning' is thought to be that economic activity proceeds in accordance with instructions from above.

The Leninist principle of one-man management is very important in Soviet planning. It means that in each economic unit decisions are made, not by a committee, but by one man. He has the authority to take decisions and is responsible to his superiors for the execution of orders.

Soviet plans are intended to embody not the subjective decisions of this or that official or organisation, but a scientific analysis of the problems confronting society. Hence, an impor-

[1] This is why Western 'indicative' planning is sometimes contrasted with Soviet 'imperative' planning.

tant role in the planning process is played by scientific organizations. For example, consumption planning is partly based on scientific consumption norms worked out by the relevant organisations (see chapter 8 below). To improve the planning techniques there is a continuous process of cooperation between scientific research institutes and the planning organisations. When plans are drawn up, numerous scientific research organisations take part on a consultancy basis. They prepare reports on issues ranging from the location of particular industrial plants to long-term forecasts of scientific–technical progress.

The balance principle refers to the basic method of Soviet planning, double-entry book keeping in physical or value (price) units. Balances are the main method used in the attempt to ensure that the plans are consistent. There are material balances for the production and distribution plans, labour balances for the labour plan, fuel–energy balances for the plans of the energy sector and financial balances for the financial plan. A major innovation in Soviet planning in the 1960s involved the introduction into planning work of a new type of integrated balances, input–output.

The address principle means that to each target there corresponds an organisation, or address, responsible for carrying it out. If that were not so, then Soviet plans might be merely the inaccurate forecasts that are known as 'plans' in many capitalist countries.

The leading links principle is that, at any given moment, the efforts of the planners, and the allocation of material and human resources, are directed to achieving the plan goals in certain priority sectors, the leading links. Precisely which sectors are the leading links naturally varies over time. In the USSR, in the 1930s the leading links were iron and steel and heavy engineering, in the 1940s armaments, in the 1950s steel, coal and oil, in the 1960s chemicals and natural gas, and in the 1970s agriculture and electronics.

The principle of commercial accounting (*khozraschet*) is that each economic unit, e.g. an enterprise or association, should have its own profit and loss account and be run in a businesslike way. Enterprises and associations should pay attention not only to their physical results (e.g. output in tons) but also to their financial results. In general, all efficient enterprises and associations should show a profit. The aim of this is to stimulate efficiency and prevent waste and bureaucratisation.

Organisational aspects

The central planning organ in the USSR is the State Planning Commission (Gosplan). Gosplan is responsible for working out production plans and passing them to the relevant organisations (e.g. Ministries) for execution. For working out plans for the distribution of commodities, the central organisation is the State Committee on Material–Technical Supplies (Gossnab). There are also other important central organisations, e.g. the State Committee on Prices which is responsible for working out the price determination methods, and also for confirming all prices. The central bodies in labour matters are the State Committee on Labour and Social Questions and the all-Union Central Council of Trade Unions. In foreign trade the central body is the Ministry of Foreign Trade and its specialised corporations. For R & D it is the State Committee on Science and Technology.

The actual productive units in the economy are enterprises or associations. Enterprises, generally one factory, farm, building organisation, mine or shop, are the traditional basic units of the Soviet economy. In the 1970s a merger movement led to their being grouped into production associations (see chapter 3 below). In each industry there is a Ministry, responsible for the operational leadership and medium- and long-term planning of the industry. (Industry investment planning is discussed in chapter 5 below.) Traditionally, the Ministries were subdivided into Chief Administrations (*glavki*) each responsible for one branch of the industry. In the 1970s, many of these chief administrations were transformed into industrial associations (see chapter 3 below).

Besides the all-Union organisations (i.e. organisations concerned with the Union of Soviet Socialist Republics as a whole), there are also Republican, regional and local planning and administrative bodies. For example, there are Republican ministries, city plans and local branches of Gossnab. For regional economic planning there is a central organ, the Council for the Study of the Productive Forces (SOPS) attached to the USSR Gosplan. Until 1969 there were also local organs for regional economic planning, the planning commissions of sixteen of the big economic regions and the Gosplans of the two Republics (Byelorussia and Kazakhstan) which are also big economic regions.[2]

For checking on the fulfilment of the plan two important organisations are the Central Statistical Administration (TsSU) and the State Bank. All the enterprises, associations and Ministries have to report regularly their plan fulfilment data to TsSU, which also conducts regular censuses (e.g. of the capital stock) and spot checks (e.g. on inventories). All organisations keep their accounts with the State Bank, the officials of which can check the financial side of their activities. Other organisations concerned with checking up on plan fulfilment are the Committee of People's Control, the Ministry of Finance and the party. The party committees at all levels play a very important role. Their functions range from making appointments to, and deciding on dismissals from, all important positions; via coordinating all the other organisations; to (piece) rate busting (see chapter 6 below).

The above is a brief and extremely simplified picture of the situation with respect to the state sector. There is also a cooperative sector (mainly the collective farms)[3] and a private sector (the private plots of the collective farmers and others and the illegal economy).[4]

Stages of the planning work

The calculation of the plans can be split up conceptually into the following eight stages (Bor 1971 pp. 46–7).

First, the elaboration of the forms, tables and indices of the plan and of methodological instructions relating to them. For example, for the national plan Gosplan USSR published *Methodological instructions for the compilation of the state plan for the development of the national economy of the USSR* in 1969 and a revised edition of it in 1974. There are analogous official documents relating to the compilation of other types of plan, e.g. for optimal industry investment plans (see chapter 5 below).

[2] Regional economic planning in the USSR is much complicated by the fact that it is a multi-national state. The republics, whose boundaries are determined by ethnic, historical and political considerations, have considerable power but no interest in regional planning. The big economic regions, which do have appropriate boundaries for regional economic planning, have little power.

[3] See chapter 4 below.

[4] See chapters 8 and 10 below.

Most of the planning work is similar to that of clerks in income tax offices in the West, i.e. filling in figures in official forms in accordance with established procedure.

Secondly, studying the results, and analysing the fulfilment, of the previous plan. Plans are normally based on the outcome of the previous period with a few per cent added on.

Thirdly, working out the main outlines of the plan in the light of the plan fulfilment data for the previous period and current party objectives.

Fourthly, on the basis of the main outlines, working out preliminary production and investment targets and using them to calculate preliminary orientations, or control figures, for the lower levels of the hierarchy.

Fifthly, working out draft plans for the enterprises, associations, ministries, republics and the national economy as a whole. These plans are worked out by a process of planning and counter planning, i.e. of administrative iteration. The centre issues control figures, the periphery receives the control figures and on their basis submits plan suggestions to the centre. In the light of these suggestions the centre issues revised control figures. Having received them, the periphery submits revised suggestions, and so on. Besides administrative iteration of this sort, confined to the planning and administrative hierarchy, there is also an iterative process initiated and supervised by the party committees. This is aimed at overcoming the notorious tendency for lower level units to strive, during the process of planning and counter planning, for slack plans (see chapter 3 below). It tries to overcome this tendency by the use of moral incentives, by mobilising the masses. (Moral incentives are discussed in general in chapter 6 below.) During the Ninth Five Year Plan (1971–75), it became customary for enterprise (or association) collectives to adopt counter plans tauter than those originally agreed between the higher organs and the enterprises, as a result of uncovering possibilities for greater efficiency. A counter (*vstrechnyi*) plan is a revised plan worked out on the initiative of the enterprise or association collective on the basis of uncovering and using additional productive possibilities of the plants and people of an enterprise. Counter plans provide mainly for an increase in output, a widening of the assortment, a raising of quality and an increase in the growth rates of labour productivity. The widespread adoption of this type of counter plan revived a practice which had been important during the First Five Year

Plan (1928–32). The pioneer in the ninth plan was the Ivanovo textile trade. The adoption of counter plans is often linked with socialist competition. This stress on moral incentives and the party hierarchy is part of the reaction against material incentives and the ministerial hierarchy which characterised the 1970s. It is also an example of the control by the party mentioned above.

Sixthly, confirming the national economic plan. This is done by the central party and state bodies.

Seventhly, passing down the relevant parts of the confirmed national economic plan to the appropriate republics, ministries, departments, associations and enterprises.

Finally, working out the final plans for the development of the republics, regions, counties, ministries, departments, associations and enterprises.

The planning process is an endless one (like painting a big bridge). Once the plans are finalised, which should be before the beginning of the planned period but which is often delayed, it is necessary to supervise the operational fulfilment of the plans (this may involve altering them during the planned period), to check up regularly on the degree of plan fulfilment, and to prepare the plans for the following period.

Periodisation of plans

One can distinguish between three periods for which plans are drawn up: fifteen or twenty years (long-term plans), five years (five year plans) and one year (annual plans). The last are the most operational, the first have often been abandoned quite soon after compilation (see chapter 3 below).

Long-term plans. An example of a long-term plan is the Soviet plan for 1976–90. This was intended to set out the strategy of development of the USSR over this fifteen year period. It was the first Soviet work on long-term planning since the compilation of the Party programme and the decisions of the XXII Congress (1961). The relationship between the various stages of compiling the long-term plan are set out in figure 2.1.

The figure shows how, starting from forecasts and policy conceptions, programmes for the solution of major problems and plans for particular industries and regions are worked out. For example, starting from forecasts of the economic and political situation in the CMEA countries, and the policy of bringing the

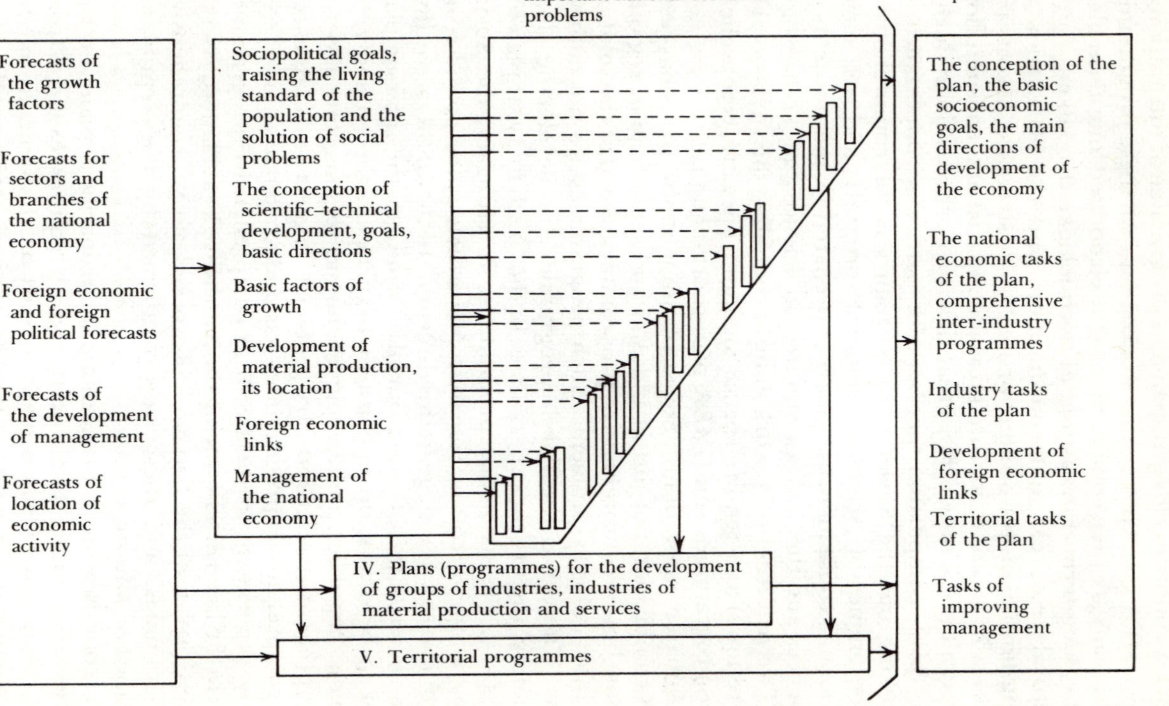

Figure 2.1 The process of compiling the long-term national economic plan.
Source: Kirichenko (1974a) p. 69.

CMEA countries closer together, a programme of integration of the CMEA countries can be worked out. All these programmes and plans are then combined into the elaborated long-term plan. The long-term forecasting of technology, the labour force, natural resources and consumption, and the elaboration of long-term plans for production (its branch structure, its costs and prices, its location, its foreign trade aspects) and consumption, were all areas in which a great deal of work was done during the plan compilation period. Of particular importance in working out the Soviet 1976–90 plan was the comprehensive programme of scientific–technical progress and its socio-economic consequences. This was prepared by the Academy of Sciences and the State Committee on Science and Technology.

Two features of the work done in compiling the 1976–90 plan were novel and require special mention. They are, comprehensive programmes and CMEA plan coordination.

A major innovation in Soviet planning in the 1970s has been the compilation not just of industry and republican or regional plans, but of comprehensive programmes aimed at the solution of inter-industry problems. Such programmes are not entirely new. There was the Polish programme for developing ship-building, the urgent programmes in the Czech five year plan for 1971–75, the six major programmes in Hungary, the Soviet programme of cosmic research. Nevertheless, the period from 1976 marks a new stage in this direction. In the USSR, according to a decree of the CC and Council of Ministers, the 1976–90 plan had to be drawn up not just by branches of the economy, by Union Republics and by big economic regions, but also for comprehensive inter-industry problems. A great deal of research on comprehensive programmes was undertaken in 1971–75. An early experiment in the USSR in comprehensive programmes was in the Latvian SSR during the Ninth Five Year Plan (1971–75). The Gosplan of the Latvian SSR worked out 52 comprehensive programmes, and these were confirmed by the Republican Council of Ministers.

A comprehensive programme is primarily a plan for the achievement of a certain objective which requires resources from several industries, has a major impact on the structure of the economy and which may extend over a period of more than five years. The importance of comprehensive programmes largely arises from the fact that the achievement of a particular goal in one sector can have a major impact on many other sectors of the economy. This must be taken into account if disproportions are to be avoided. For example, according to calculations made some years ago by Gosplan's Chief Computing Centre and Scientific Research Institute, the full investment cost of the Tol'yatti car plant (i.e. allowing for investment in component production, living facilities for the workers, servicing and repair facilities for the cars, road building and maintenance, etc.) would be more than ten times its direct investment cost. Particularly important in the USSR are regional comprehensive programmes. These are aimed at the full utilisation of the resources of particular regions, e.g. the West Siberian and South Tadzhik regions.

In his speech at the 25th Congress (1976), the Chairman of the USSR Council of Ministers stated that

> In the tenth five-year period, [1976–80] Gosplan should elaborate comprehensive programmes in line with the sectoral and territorial aspects of the national economic plan. Among the priority tasks is the elaboration of a programme for developing the production base of atomic energy, a programme for mechanising manual and arduous physical labour, and programmes for shaping large-scale territorial and production complexes.

In Hungary, during the 1971–75 plan, six comprehensive programmes were being realised. They were, the utilisation of natural gas, the development of petro-chemistry, the development of the aluminium industry, the modified development programme of road transport vehicles, the promotion of the utilisation of computers and their domestic production and the promotion of complex construction technology using light-weight structures.

Experience with comprehensive programmes has shown that they have not only advantages but also problems. First, comprehensive programmes usually embrace a number of large investment projects. These often take long periods to complete and deliver their fruits at quite distant periods. Small investment projects, which can often be brought onto production soon, also have an important role to play in the national economy. Secondly, comprehensive programmes require special efforts for their preparation, supervision and coordination. This special effort is only rational if the goals of the programme can not be attained by normal planning methods. Thirdly, the comprehensive programmes have considerable priority. This priority, however, tends to be dissipated if there are too many of them. Fourthly, if there are too many comprehensive programmes there is a tendency to replace planning by a mass of comprehensive programmes. These may be poorly coordinated and thus disorganise the economy and cause waste. For these reasons, the orthodox view in Hungary in the mid 1970s was that it was useful and desirable to have five or six simultaneously operating comprehensive programmes, but undesirable to have more or to move in the direction of replacing national economic planning by a mass of comprehensive programmes.

CMEA plan coordination is just one aspect of CMEA integration (see chapter 9 below). Coordination of the five year plans of the CMEA members for 1971–75 was at a qualitatively new level compared with previous experience. The coordination began in good time, almost three years before the beginning of the five year plan, and continued up till the signing in 1971 of intergovernmental protocols on plan coordination. In addition, for the first time not only national Gosplans took part, ,but also Ministries and departments and working groups of experts. Since 1974, the annual, five year and long-term plans worked out by Gosplan USSR have had a special section dealing with CMEA integration. The preparation of the 1976–80 plans of the CMEA members was also coordinated, in accordance with the decisions of the XXVI session of CMEA held in 1972 and the work of the CMEA committee on cooperation in the field of planning. On their basis the long-term trade agreements between the CMEA countries were signed in 1975. In addition, at the XXIX session of CMEA in 1975 a plan for multilateral integration measures for 1976–80 was confirmed.

The 1976–90 long-term plans of the CMEA members were also coordinated. At the end of 1970 the CMEA organised a meeting of specialists from the Gosplans of the member countries to exchange experiences in the field of elaborating and using long-term forecasts. In July 1971 in accordance with the work plan of the Economic Commission of the CMEA an international scientific conference was held in Prague to exchange experiences in the working out of economic forecasts. In July 1976, the XXX session of CMEA, meeting in Berlin, agreed to five CMEA comprehensive programmes to be implemented in a 10–15 year period. They were, programmes for cooperation in the fuel-energy and raw material industries, cooperation in the production of basic foodstuffs, expanding output and trade of consumer goods, and cooperating in the development of transport.

Five-year plans. In Soviet planning theory, the basic plan is the five year plan. It is this which is intended to shape the structure of the economy, focus the work of all persons in the economy, and make substantial progress in achieving the objectives of the party. Great efforts were made in the 1970s to ensure that this was actually so. (Traditionally, the main operational plans have been the annual plans and those for shorter periods such as quarters, months, ten days, and 24 hours.)

Physically, a five year plan is a book containing several hundred pages of text and plan targets. For example, the Soviet Ninth Five Year Plan (1971–75) contains chapters on, the chief objectives of the plan, industry, agriculture, forestry, transport and communications, investment, geographical location of activity, raising living standards, foreign economic relations, and about a hundred pages of plan targets.

An important innovation of the Soviet ninth plan was that it was broken down by years. This made possible the compilation of five year plans for lower level units such as enterprises. An enterprise (or association) five year plan has eleven interrelated sections and can be represented graphically as in figure 2.2. The main advantages of enterprise five year plans are twofold. First, they make possible the calculation of stable norms (e.g. those relating the incentive funds to the fund-forming indices). This is important because it reduces one of the incentives (desire to obtain a soft plan for the following period) enterprises have traditionally had to work at less than 100 per cent efficiency. Secondly, they facilitate long-term relationships between producers and consumers which is a major way of improving the functioning of the supply system.

Five year plans for associations or enterprises were also drawn up for the tenth five year plan. Their compilation took place in two stages. First, the working out of preliminary suggestions for the basic directions (control figures) of development of production and their discussion with the higher organs. Secondly, the working out, starting from these basic directions (control figures) of a draft five year plan with a distribution of tasks by year. The annual tasks of an enterprise's or association's five year plan are the basis for working out each annual plan.

Annual plans. Annual plans are worked out in great detail for all units in the economy. Extensive efforts are devoted both to

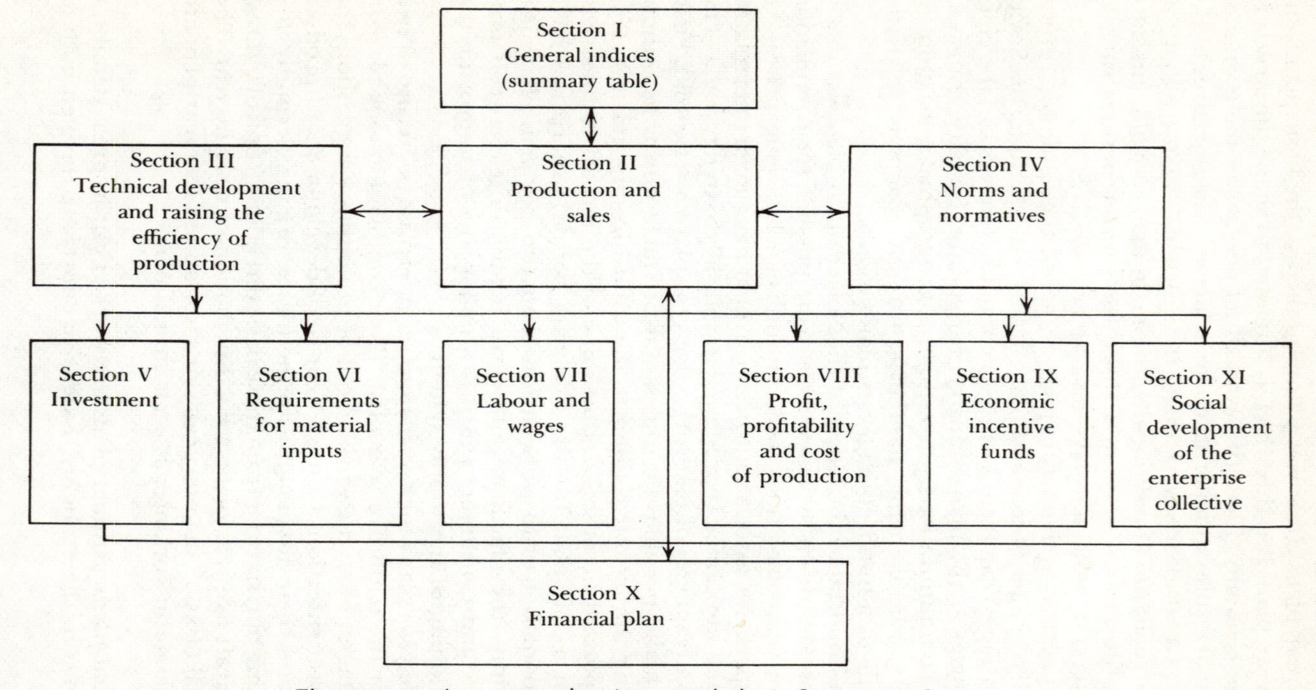

Figure 2.2 An enterprise (or association) five year plan.
Source: Kovalevskii (1973) p. 29.

their compilation and also to checking up on their fulfilment. They are intended to be detailed breakdowns of the relevant part of the five year plan. This is often not so in the later years of the five year plan as the original version of the five year plan has been outdated by new developments.

PLAN COMPILATION IN CHINA

When planning began in the People's Republic of China it was modelled on the institutions and practices of the USSR. This was entirely natural since the Chinese had no other experience to learn from, and Soviet experience was regarded by all Communist Parties (except the Yugoslav) and many others as *the* model of how socialist planning should be organised. Hence, the Chinese First Five Year Plan, 1953–57, was modelled on Soviet experience. This applies both to its strategy (emphasis on heavy industry) and to the principles underlying its methods of implementation (e.g. one-man management). Experience of the application of the Soviet model to China, however, soon led the Chinese leadership to the view that it was not wholly suitable for China.

The first major expression of the view that it was necessary to develop a new type of planning relevant to the conditions of China, was in Mao Tse-tung's speeches of 1955–56. A classic text is his famous 1956 speech *On the ten major relationships.* It reflected both China's experience with Soviet-style planning and also the reaction of the Chinese leaders to the twentieth congress. In it Mao argued, inter alia, that it was necessary for China to pay greater attention to agriculture and light industry, not to squeeze the peasants too hard, to give greater power to local organs, make less use of repression, not to slavishly copy the USSR and to admit weaknesses. Subsequently China embarked on the Great Leap Forward (1958), went through the economic crisis which followed (1959–61), experienced the Great Proletarian Cultural Revolution (1966–68), the political struggles which followed it and the policies of Chairman Hua (from 1976). For many years now, in the Chinese media the Soviet economic system has been showered with abuse and treated as entirely unsuitable as a model of how a socialist economy should be organised – the mirror image of the situation prevailing in the early 1950s. A description of the evolution of the Chinese planning system between 1949 and the mid 1960s is in Donnithorne (1967 ch. 17). A description of the system existing in the early 1970s can be found in Eckstein (1977 chs. 2, 3 and 4) Robinson (1976 ch. 3) and Howe (1978 ch. 2). Many of the differences between planning in China and the USSR result from the different environments in which the two systems exist, for example, the much smaller importance of agriculture in the USSR than in China,[5] and the smaller proportion of qualified planning and statistical staff in the population in China than in the USSR. The chief differences between the Chinese planning system as it existed in the early 1970s and the Soviet model are set out below.

First, Chinese planning is based not on Marxism–Leninism but on Marxism–Leninism–Mao Tse-tung Thought, the official doctrine in China. This has had numerous important consequences, ranging from a non-extractive type of collectivisation (see chapter 4) via the obligation of all administrative personnel to undertake manual labour (see chapter 10) and the extensive use of mass campaigns (such as the Great Leap Forward and the Cultural Revolution) to develop socialist relations of production, to a non-bureaucratic attitude to data collection and policy formation. In the Marxist–Leninist–Mao Tse-tung Thought tradition, leaders do not reach decisions simply by studying incoming statistics, reports and computer printouts. They go out into the field to collect information by personal observation. The classic example of this field work approach to data collection and policy formation is Mao Tse-tung's 1927 *Report on an investigation of the peasant movement in Hunan* based on a five week stay in Hunan villages. A contemporary example is the T'aoyüan Experience of Wang Kuang-mei (the wife of Liu Shao-chi) in 1963–64 during the Socialist Education Movement.[6] It is in the villages, not in libraries or offices, that a Maoist leader comprehends reality. Similarly, the Chinese Communist Party, unlike other Communist Parties, often holds its CC meetings outside the capital.

[5] As a result of the much greater importance of agriculture in China than in the USSR, when the Chinese Third Five Year Plan (for 1966–70) was being drawn up, Mao advocated basing the output targets on probable grain output. Instead of the Soviet method of starting planning work from targets for key industrial intermediate products such as steel, the correct approach he asserted (Howe 1977 p. 214) was to base the Plan on probable grain output, to be estimated by assuming one good, two average and two poor harvests every five years.

[6] She spent five months in T'aoyüan production brigade, Funing County, Hopei as chief of the work team dispatched there. On the basis of her experience she made a very critical report.

Secondly, Chinese industrial planning has been characterised by an incessant groping for a suitable industrial planning system. This has been caused by the failure to find a model suitable for Chinese conditions combined with the pragmatism of the Chinese leaders. (In agriculture, on the other hand, the system has been basically unchanged since 1962.) In the USSR, the traditional Soviet planning system was adopted in 1930–34 in a haphazard unplanned way as a reaction to the economic crisis of 1931–33 and as a tool of rapid industrialisation. Once adopted, however, it remained basically unchanged for decades. It succeeded the moneyless, fully planned model of 1929–30, which in turn had succeeded the mixed economy model of the 1920s. Since 1934 it has remained largely unchanged, although it has developed. For example, since 1956 inequality has been much reduced (see chapter 7), in the 1960s the techniques of planning became much more sophisticated and in the 1970s industry was organised into associations (see chapter 3). One major institutional change, however, the dissolution of the industrial ministries and their replacement by regional organisations in 1957, was subsequently reversed (in 1965). China, on the other hand, has been characterised by permanent changes in the industrial planning system, which have been associated with perpetual political struggle.

The traditional Soviet model was rejected in 1956–58. In 1957 there was decentralisation of industry on the lines of the contemporary Soviet reorganisation and also a CC decree stressing the need for cadres to participate in manual labour. During the GLF there was a virtual end to national planning, a strengthening of the position of the party committees at all levels, a weakening of functional departments, an increase in the autonomy of production groups within factories and attacks on piece work and bonuses. The early 1960s saw considerable differences about economic organisation (e.g. whether or not to decentralise to industrial enterprises or trusts as in contemporary Soviet and East European discussion and whether or not to develop industry along the lines of the 'Seventy Articles').[7] During and after the Cultural Revolution there was, less

[7] The 'Seventy Articles' was a set of regulations for industrial management adopted in 1961 during the crisis which followed the GLF and the withdrawal of Soviet experts. It came under fire during the Cultural Revolution because it favoured material incentives, reliance on qualified engineers, recognition of the need for authority in industry and the need for the party to focus on the achievement of production targets.

piecework and individual cash bonuses, devolution of initiatives to provinces and lower-level local authorities and emphasis on horizontal integration of the economy and local self-sufficiency, a reduction in the number of ministries and other central bodies, despecialisation of production, attacks on rules and regulations and managerial authority, attacks on cadres and formation of revolutionary committees, and stress on workers' control. After the downfall of the 'gang of four' in 1976, there was renewed stress on the need for discipline, authority, hierarchy, specialisation and centralisation, and on the importance of production, its profitability, quality and quantity.

Thirdly, national planning has been much less elaborate, sophisticated and significant in China than in the USSR. Since 1960, all plans have been unpublished. It appears very doubtful whether any recent Chinese plan with the detail and scope normal in Soviet plans has even existed. The number of centrally allocated materials is much smaller in China than in the USSR. According to one estimate (Eckstein 1977 p. 135), in China in 1972 it was only between 100 and 200, whereas in the USSR it was about 2000. It seems that this is a real difference and not merely the result of different classification systems. Five year and long-term plans have had much less significance in China than in the USSR. The First Five Year Plan (1953–57) was only announced in the middle of 1955 and it is not clear to what extent it was operational in the period 1953 to mid 1955. Preliminary targets for the Second Five Year Plan (1958–62) were announced by Chou En-lai at the Eighth Party Congress (1956). The plan itself, however, if it ever existed, was rendered irrelevant by the Great Leap Forward (1958) and the crisis which followed it. A draft Twelve Year Programme for Agricultural Development for 1956–67 was published in 1956 and adopted in 1960,[8] and a Third Five Year Plan was promulgated for 1966–70. The Cultural Revolution began in 1966, however, and created a situation in which planning was virtually impossible. There are press references to a Fourth Five Year Plan, but its articulation and significance are not clear. In 1976 it appears that the Fifth Five Year Plan was either non-existent or non-operational, as a result of the political turmoil of that year. In 1978 it was replaced by the 1976–85 Ten Year Plan.

The methods used to compile the plans have been much less

[8] Grain output ten years after the end of this programme was still well below the figure envisaged for 1967.

sophisticated in China than in the USSR. Although Chinese planners have made use both of input–output and of linear programming, there has been nothing in China to compare with the huge volume of Soviet work in these fields. (For the use of linear programming in the CMEA countries to compile optimal industry investment plans see chapter 5 below.) Nor is there anything in China to compare with the OGAS (see chapter 3 below). In planning technology as in military technology, China appears to be about fifteen years behind the USSR. Furthermore, in China a vast number of small enterprises exist outside the national planning framework, securing their inputs through the market. If by a 'planned economy' is meant one which operates in accordance with a detailed, scientifically based, all-embracing Five Year Plan, broken down by years, calculated and implemented by the centre, China is not, and never has been, a planned economy. (Nor, for most of its history, has the USSR been one.) As the Chinese economist who briefed an American delegation in 1975 honestly explained ('American' 1977 p. 278), 'China is a large and complicated country, and thus precise planning is out of the question. What we try to do is correct the imbalances once they arise.' The reasons for this failure to meet the traditional conception of 'central planning' are, the abandonment of the Soviet model, the prolonged political struggle, the partial ignorance of the central authorities, the inadequate techniques for data processing and the desire to encourage local initiative. Some of these questions are considered further in chapter 3 below.

Fourthly, extensive use is made of indirect centralisation via the political process (party, army and media). The question of centralisation and decentralisation has been much discussed both inside and outside the state socialist countries. Three ideal types can be distinguished, perfect centralisation, perfect decentralisation and perfect indirect centralisation. By perfect centralisation is meant an economy where all decisions are made at the centre. By perfect decentralisation is meant an economy where all decisions are made by individuals, local authorities and firms whose decisions are entirely independent of the wishes of the central authorities. By perfect indirect centralisation is meant an economy in which all decisions are made by individuals, local authorities or firms, but those decisions are exactly those that would have been made if the central authorities had made them. This can come about because the centre has determined the criteria (e.g. profit maximisation or the best possible use of local resources) and the parameters (prices and the rate of interest or newspaper articles and party and army policy) which enterprises or local authorities use. These ideal types are of interest not because they have ever existed or will ever be feasible, but because these concepts enable us to discuss real economic systems. Clearly the traditional Soviet system was a combination of centralisation and decentralisation. Many decisions were taken by central planners, but equally, many decisions were taken by others, such as collective farmers and factory managers, independent of, and contrary to, the wishes of the planners. For example, a well-known problem of the traditional system was the fact that factory managers often fulfilled their plans for gross output by violating their assortment plan. This was not something that the planners instructed them to do but a decentralised decision. What many of the Soviet and East European reformers of the 1960s wanted was to make a transition from the old system, a combination of centralisation and decentralisation, where many of the decentralised decisions were contrary to the wishes of the planners, to a new system which combined centralisation with indirect centralisation and decentralisation and where none of the non-centrally taken decisions would be contrary to the wishes of the planners.

Using these concepts, it is clear that China evolved in 1955–76 from a traditional Soviet-type administrative system which combines centralisation with decentralisation, to a system which combined centralisation with indirect centralisation (to local authorities) and decentralisation (e.g. private plots).[9] The Chinese type of indirect centralisation differed from the East European one in three important respects. First, the criterion and parameters are different. The Maoists used the political process rather than the price mechanism. Instead of profit maximisation and prices and the rate of interest, they used the best possible use of local resources and party and army policy. Secondly, the Maoists criticised the East European practice of devolving decision making to enterprises and instead devolved it to local authorities. Thirdly, the pressure for the changes adopted came

[9] Private plots play an important role in Chinese agriculture. In the GLF they appear to have been generally abolished, with adverse effects on pig, poultry and vegetable production, together with a decline in the supply of manure and other organic soil nutrients. Within a couple of years they were generally reintroduced. They were encouraged once more after the death of Mao.

not from intellectuals, academics and other specialists, but from the party leadership. The way in which the Maoist system of indirect centralisation via the political process to local authorities, works in one specific case, that of small-scale industries, is considered in chapters 4 and 5 below. After the fall of the 'gang of four' in 1976 it looked as if there would be an increase in direct centralisation.

Fifthly, since 1956 the USSR has had a free labour market for urban labour, and intends during the late 1970s to introduce one also for rural labour. In China, on the other hand, at least since the Cultural Revolution, there is no free labour market and all labour is allocated administratively. This system (which has certain resemblances to the Japanese system of life-long employment, to the direction of labour in the UK in the Second World War and to the system prevailing in the USSR in 1940–56) has important consequences. It means that material incentives are less important for the efficient allocation of labour. The Chinese labour force is allocated to its place of work and the allocation is enforced by the rationing of consumer goods. Furthermore, periodically, large numbers of people (e.g. school leavers) for whom there are no urban jobs, are directed to the countryside. These questions are considered further in chapter 6 below. The Chinese system of labour organization has been described (Howe 1978 p. 185) 'as a socialist version of the Japanese system of labour organization, in which the key to a comfortable life is attachment to a large influential corporation'. Prevailing political doctrines in China about material incentives have fluctuated sharply over time. Prevailing practice has also fluctuated, but less sharply.

Sixthly, the Soviet system of one-man management (known in China as the 'one-boss system') was officially abandoned in China at the Eighth Party Congress in 1956. The decision to replace it by a system combining the collective leadership of the party with individual responsibility, was outlined in the speech by Li Hsueh-feng, Director of the department of Industrial and Communication work of the CC. Under one-man management he argued,

> Bureaucracy and commandism became rife, bourgeois ideas of management throve accordingly, arrogant and self-complacent feelings and arbitrary behaviour were common. And among the leading personnel themselves, between the cadres and the masses, and between the various enterprises, instances of bickering, misunderstanding and

disunity increased. In such conditions, the work of these enterprises naturally suffered.

Subsequently, Chinese practice has fluctuated, as China has sought a management model suited to its conditions (Donnithorne 1967 pp. 192–204, Richman 1969 pp. 249–61). During the Great Leap Forward the party committees largely took over the management functions. During the Cultural Revolution workers were encouraged to criticise managers and do away with them and the discipline they enforced. At other times, the importance of qualified managers has been stressed. Richman was struck when visiting China by two features of the Chinese management scene in the 1960s, the big role played by interpersonal and informal organisation, and the collective nature of responsibility (as in Japan). Three important Maoist innovations in industrial management were, the obligation of all managerial personnel to perform manual labour, the elected revolutionary committees which were responsible for executive management in Chinese factories, and the possibility of criticising officials. Their significance is considered in chapter 10 below.

Seventhly, it is well known that the Soviet system of planning is unable to ensure the consistency of the plans, and, hence, generates substantial waste. In an attempt to overcome this the USSR has both improved the planning techniques and made some cautious and limited steps along the road from the allocation of supplies to wholesale trade. China too, has made some moves in the latter direction (e.g. commodity exhibitions and commodity banks) analogous to those in the USSR. It has also, however, developed the supply and sales order conferences, also known as materials-allocation conferences.

At supply and sales order conferences, detailed production, supply and sales relationships, specifications, delivery dates and other contractual details are worked out between the producing and consuming enterprises. These conferences are usually organised along commodity or branch lines. For centrally allocated commodities of major strategic importance, they are normally jointly sponsored by the state planning organs, the materials-allocation agencies, and the ministry in charge of that industrial branch. All the ministries involved in the production of important producer goods sponsor such conferences at least once or twice a year. Such conferences are also frequently held at provincial level and in large industrial centres such as

Shanghai. The participants typically include not only sponsoring agencies, but also representatives of the ministries that are the principal purchasers of the commodity to be produced and the principal suppliers of its material inputs. Lower-level provincial and municipal organs from the same types of bodies are also represented, particularly from areas in which major producers are located. Leading managerial personnel from all the more important producing and consuming enterprises participate in these meetings.

At these various conferences, the authorities with jurisdiction over a particular industry, factory or type of economic activity are concerned with problems of consistency and balance between supply and demand, with the formalisation of inter-enterprise contracts, and the issue of allocation certificates.

The supply and sales order conferences replace normal bureaucratic procedures by face to face contacts between producers, consumers and planners. They are a method of ensuring plan consistency that is neither administrative nor market, as these terms are generally understood. They are an original, and apparently quite effective, way of overcoming the fact that traditional Soviet planning always generates plans that are inconsistent and this leads to substantial waste of resources (Ellman 1973 chapter 1). Chinese reliance on face to face contacts is also shown in the national plan conciliation conferences held in December or January of each year to conclude the process of planning and counterplanning by which Chinese plans, like Soviet ones, are drawn up.

Eighthly, the basic unit of rural administration in China is the commune. Both the number of communes, and the relative importance within them of the household, team, brigade and commune as a whole, appear to have fluctuated over the years in accordance with changes in official policy. The long-term effect of the commune movement has been to create a new and strengthened administrative and governmental unit below the county level. This unit performs some very important economic functions, such as tax collection, supervision of the compulsory farm sales quotas, innovation, experimentation, diffusion of new cropping systems, and the management of some rural small-scale industries. It also plays a major role in the improvement of human resources in the rural areas through the provision of greatly expanded health and education services. At the same time it supervises the supply and marketing cooperatives. It has played no direct role in farm production, however, since 1961. The Chinese model of the role of agriculture in socialist economic development, and its relationship to the Soviet model, is considered further in chapter 4 below.

Ninthly, the role of the provinces is a distinguishing feature of Chinese planning. It is substantially greater than that of Soviet republics. China has 21 provinces, and three autonomous cities (Peking, Shanghai and Tientsin) and five autonomous regions (Sinkiang, Inner Mongolia, Ninghsia, Kwangsi and Tibet) of equivalent status. These provinces cities and regions are administrative bodies intermediate between the centre and the localities and are often more populous than most of the countries of the world. They have considerable powers in the fields of economic planning and administration. The importance of provincial and other local horizontal coordination, as opposed to vertical coordination of the industrial ministry type, was especially stressed in 1966–76.[10] An example of the horizontal coordination stressed at that time is the rural small-scale industrial sector developed to serve agriculture (see chapter 4). Nevertheless, central planning continued to play an important role in the Chinese economy, even in 1966–76. This is shown by such things as the inter-provincial fiscal and real transfers, the central part of 'dual leadership'[11] and the important role of the nation-wide People's Bank. After the downfall of the 'gang of four' in 1976 it seemed likely that the centre would try to strengthen its position in relation to the provinces.

Tenthly, great efforts have always been made in the USSR to ensure that the plans are 'taut', that is, that they provide for the maximum possible output. Taut plans are intended to mobilise fully all available resources and stimulate all participants in the economy to the maximum possible exertions. The fact that in practice the plans are often 'slack', i.e. provide for less output than is possible or more inputs than are necessary, has always

[10] Similarly, in the USSR in the 1930s there was considerable stress on regional self-sufficiency in agriculture. In his speech to the 17th Party Congress (1934), Stalin announced that every region should produce an assortment of agricultural products and not be dependent on other regions for basic agricultural products. This Soviet stress on regional self-sufficiency (and possibly also the Chinese one) resulted from the transport crisis. The availability of transport was too limited for the USSR at that time to take full advantage of the gains from specialisation.

[11] 'Dual leadership' is a widespread system under which an enterprise is managed jointly by a central government ministry and the relevant local authority such as a province or municipality. It corresponds to the traditional Soviet system of dual subordination.

been considered a defect. In China, it appears that the plans are often slack as a matter of deliberate policy (Eckstein 1977 pp. 95–6, Robinson 1976 p. 22). This appears to result from the realisation that the Soviet system of aiming at taut plans generates substantial waste (Ellman 1973 pp. 32–5 and 41–4). It amounts to an acceptance of Bukharin's famous thesis about the difficulty of constructing buildings with bricks that have not yet been produced, and the need for reserves; and a rejection of the Stalinist thesis about the need to plan to 'widen' a bottleneck and not 'on' the bottleneck. In his Report to the Eighth Party Congress (1956) on the Proposals for the Second Five Year Plan, Chou En-lai said that in the First Five Year Plan over-investment had led to shortages and disruption in the economy. Accordingly, he argued that,

> in drawing up the long-term plan, we should set the targets realistically in accordance with the basic requirements of socialist industrialisation and with the possibilities of the material and financial resources and manpower of the country. At the same time, a certain amount of reserves should be built up so that the plan can be put on a sounder basis.

This is a repetition of what Bukharin had said 27 years earlier, and an anticipation of developments in Soviet planning 13 years later.

Eleventhly, basic consumer goods are rationed in China, and have been since the early days of the People's Republic. This facilitates both egalitarian distribution and control over population movement (this is discussed in chapter 8).

CONCLUSION

The USSR has a complex planning system. It is based on Marxist–Leninist ideas, has a rich organisational structure and consists of a large number of stages. There are long-term, five year, annual and shorter period plans. There are special agencies not only to compile plans, but also to check upon their fulfilment. Economic planning in China initially copied the Soviet model but then reacted sharply against it. It soon differed from the Soviet model in a large number of respects. These included, the existence of communes, the failure to find a stable industrial planning system, the administrative allocation of labour and rationing of consumer goods, and the supply and sales order conferences. Other differences are, the slack plans and the role of the provinces, the use of indirect centralisation through the political process and local authorities, the obligation of administrative personnel to perform manual labour and a non-bureaucratic approach (such as living and working in villages and holding CC meetings outside the capital) to data collection and policy formation.

Because of the existence of numerous state socialist countries, with substantially different planning systems, there is no longer a unique model of socialist planning. A wide range of policies and institutions are possible for socialist planned economies. This is a big difference from the days when there was only one state socialist economy and its institutions were generally regarded as *the* model of socialist planning. What is common to planning in all the state socialist countries is the use of state ownership of the means of production, national economic planning, and political dictatorship, in the attempt to mobilise all the resources available to society and use them in the interests of national economic objectives. These normally include, rapid economic growth and in particular rapid industrialisation, an egalitarian income distribution, and the development of the armed forces.

SUGGESTIONS FOR FURTHER READING

Planning in CMEA countries

R. W. Davies, 'Economic planning in the USSR', M. Bornstein & D. Fusfeld (eds.) *The Soviet economy: a book of readings* (4th edn Homewood, Illinois 1974) pp. 17–42.

A. Nove, *The Soviet economic system* (London 1977) chapters 2 & 3.

M. Ellman, *Planning problems in the USSR* (Cambridge 1973) chapter 1.

V. Treml & J. P. Hardt, *Soviet economic statistics* (Durham, North Carolina 1972).

M. Kalecki, 'Outline of a method of constructing a perspective plan', pp. 213–22 of A. Nove & D. M. Nuti (eds.) *Socialist economics* (London 1972).

I. Friss, 'On long term national economic planning', I. Friss, *Economic laws, policy, planning* (Budapest 1971) pp. 112–39.

Planning in China

Studies in Chinese Economic Planning (I), *Chinese Economic Studies* vol. x no. 3 (Spring 1977).

Studies in Chinese Economic Planning (II), *Chinese Economic Studies* vol. x no. 4 (Summer 1977).

National programme for agricultural development 1956–1967 (Peking 1960).

Yuan-li Wu, 'Planning, management and economic development in Communist China', *An economic profile of Mainland China* (Joint Economic Committee US Congress, Washington DC 1967) pp. 97–119.

T. G. Rawski, 'China's industrial system', *China: a reassessment of the economy* (JEC Washington DC 1975) pp. 175–98.

N. R. Lardy, 'Economic planning in the People's Republic of China', *China: a reassessment of the economy* (JEC Washington DC 1975) pp. 94–115.

M. Bastid, 'Levels of economic decision-making', S. Schram (ed.) *Authority, participation and cultural change in China* (Cambridge 1973).

Joan Robinson, *Economic management in China* (London 1976) chapter 3.

A. Eckstein, *China's economic revolution* (Cambridge 1977) chapters 2, 3 & 4.

C. Howe & K. R. Walker, 'The economist', D. Wilson (ed.) *Mao Tse-tung in the scales of history* (Cambridge 1977).

Nai-Ruenn Chen, *Chinese economic statistics* (Chicago 1967).

C. Howe, *China's economy* (London 1978) chapter 2.

M. Oksenberg, 'Communications within the Chinese bureaucracy', *China in the seventies* (Wiesbaden 1975) pp. 87–129.

Hu Chiao-mu, 'Observe economic laws, speed up the four modernizations', *Peking Review* (1978) Nos. 45, 46 & 47.

3

PLAN IMPLEMENTATION: SOME PROBLEMS

A choice is not effective without *implementation*, which may be far from simple, and often imperfectly accomplished. It is dangerous to assume, either that what has been decided will be achieved, or that what happens is what was intended.

B. J. Loasby (1976 p. 89)

INTRODUCTION

The traditional Marxist–Leninist view, as expressed in such works as *State and Revolution* and *The ABC of Communism*, is that the management of an entire national economy like one gigantic factory will be comparatively simple. The technical specialists (e.g. engineers, agronomists) will carry on as before and social rationality will be ensured by eliminating parasitical groups, establishing working-class control, nationalising the means of production and calculating a national plan. That the establishment of social rationality might be a complex matter, involving social and technical difficulties, is completely ignored. Indeed, it is asserted that the problem scarcely exists, since the necessary planning and administration is extremely simple[1] and everyone will have internalised the need to work in accordance with the national plan.[2] This view simply indicates that when

[1] In *State and Revolution* Lenin wrote that 'Accounting and control – that is *mainly* what is needed for the "smooth working", for the proper functioning, of the *first phase* of communist society. *All* citizens become employees and workers of a *single* country-wide state "syndicate". All that is required is that they should work equally, do their proper share of work, and get equal pay. The accounting and control necessary for this have been *simplified* by capitalism to the utmost and reduced to the extraordinarily simple operations – which any literate person can perform – of supervising and recording, knowledge of the four rules of arithmetic, and issuing appropriate receipts.'

[2] In *The ABC of Communism* Bukharin and Preobrazhensky (1969 edn. p. 118) explained that: 'The main direction will be entrusted to various kinds of book-keeping offices or statistical bureaux. There, from day to day, account will be kept of production and all its needs; there also it will be decided whether workers must be sent, whence they must be taken, and how much there is to

socialism was a utopia, an ideal world that did not yet exist, the implementation of the plan was assumed, by Marxists, to be a non-problem. Utopias have an important role to play in society (Mannheim 1936, Carr 1939), but not as accurate descriptions of post-revolutionary society.

Experience has shown that there are a whole series of counterexamples to the traditional view. Indeed, there is now an extensive literature, with important contributions by Liberman (1950), Berliner (1957), Kornai (1959) and Bergson (1964) describing and explaining these counterexamples. Whereas the traditional view was that plan implementation would be a harmonious process for the attainment of social rationality, experience has shown that plan implementation actually contains important elements of conflict, inefficiency and waste. These include, slack plans, wasteful criteria, instability of the plans, rationing of producer goods, sellers' markets, misallocating prices, personal consumption problems, difficulties with innovation and diffusion of new techniques, very long construction and running-in periods for new plants, and bureaucratisation. These phenomena are described on pp. 43–50 and the policy conclusions which have been drawn from them are outlined on pp. 50–65. On pp. 65–79 an explanation of their cause is presented.

EXAMPLES OF WASTE IN PLAN IMPLEMENTATION

Slack plans

A notorious feature of the administrative economy is the tendency by enterprises to strive for a slack plan, i.e. a plan which provides for the production of less output than possible and/or the use of more inputs than necessary. Socialism is supposed to have eliminated the contradiction between the productive forces and the productive relations which Marxists consider to be the reason for the inevitable downfall of capitalism. The fact is,

be done. And inasmuch as, from childhood onwards, all will have become accustomed to social labour, and since all will understand that this work is necessary and that life goes easier when everything is done according to a prearranged plan and when the social order is like a well oiled machine, all will work in accordance with the indications of these statistical bureaux. There will be no need for special ministers of State, for police and prisons, for laws and decrees – nothing of the sort. Just as in an orchestra all the performers watch the conductor's baton and act accordingly, so here all will consult the statistical reports and will direct their work accordingly.'

however, that, under state socialism too, there is conflict between the socioeconomic system and the development of production. This has long been regarded as undesirable by many Soviet economists, and a major feature of the Kosygin reform of 1966–69 was a new incentive system designed to motivate enterprises to aim at taut plans. The Kosygin reform failed in this respect because of the prevalence of administrative uncertainty, the system of incentives for managerial personnel and the risk-averting behaviour of Soviet managers (Ellman 1977). The incentive system introduced in the Soviet Ninth Five Year Plan (1971–75) also failed to overcome the problem, which up till now has been a permanent feature of the administrative economy.

Wasteful criteria

The national economy is a complex hierarchical system whose objective is to maximise national economic welfare. At each level of the hierarchy it is necessary to adopt an appropriate criterion to guide decision makers to optimal solutions. Because maximisation of national economic welfare is too vague a criterion some more precise criterion must be adopted as a proxy for it (Hitch & McKean 1960 pp. 158–81, Nove 1958). The criteria used in the state socialist countries often stimulate waste. The central planners, concerned with maximising output, often ignore the cost of output and its usefulness. Although the Soviet Union has caught up with the United States in the production of a number of intermediate products, they are often produced less efficiently, and the volume of final products derived from them is often lower, than in the United States. In some of the experiments which preceded the Kosygin reform it was found (Khanin 1967) that instructing clothing factories to produce according to the requirements of shops led to a fall in the growth rate. This did not signify that the experiments were a failure. It simply resulted from the fact that when given a choice, the shops ordered a wider assortment of clothes than the planners would have ordered. As a result production runs were shorter and there was less 'output' (measured in constant prices rather than in units measuring consumer satisfaction).

The Ministries are primarily concerned with plan fulfilment and hence sometimes ignore proposals which would raise national economic efficiency but might jeopardise a Ministry's plan, such as the construction of specialised enterprises to provide low-cost components for enterprises belonging to several ministries (Selyunin 1968). The enterprises are primarily concerned with securing a low plan for the production of goods with which they are familiar. They have little incentive to pay attention to the needs of customers, to innovate or to make the most efficient use of the resources which they have. The enterprise plan specifies the value of a large number of target variables. This may well be a source of waste. If there are targets for the use of inputs this may well encourage their wasteful use. If gross output is a target variable then costs may be unnecessarily high or the assortment pattern undesirable.[3] A Chinese textile enterprise, for which quality, defined as the absence of imperfections, was an important target, achieved this very efficiently by cutting out all imperfections so that every length of cloth was dotted with holes (Donnithorne 1967 p. 160)!

Instability of the plans

A characteristic feature of enterprise plans which has a severe adverse effect on the work of enterprises, is their instability (Smekhov 1968). The operational (quarterly and annual) plans of enterprises are often altered repeatedly during the course of the 'planned' period, sometimes even retrospectively. The instability of the plans is a permanent feature of the 'planned' economies.

Rationing of producer goods

The waste which results from the rationing of producer goods was already familiar to observers of War Communism. Kritsman (1924 pp. 102–3) argued that both capitalism and the administrative economy are inefficient, but that their inefficiency takes different forms. Whereas under capitalism there are difficulties with sales and the accumulation of stocks with producers, under the administrative economy there are difficulties with supply and the accumulation of stocks with users.

No surpluses can accumulate with the producers, since the product is not superflous in an absolute sense; as a matter of fact, if such a surplus

[3] A striking recent example (Dorofeyev 1976) of the criterion problem in the USSR was provided by the many restaurants, cafes and snack bars which preferred selling vodka and wine to soft drinks and other commodities, because the sale of alcoholic drinks is such an easy way of fulfilling the sales plan! This facilitates the drunkenness which is such a feature of the USSR.

is formed, it will be immediately allocated when the first demand for it is announced. The multitude of independent allocating organisations, however, unavoidably causes situations in which, for example, an organ demanding paraffin lamps gets all the necessary lamp-chimneys (100 per cent) from one economic organisation, but only 60% of the holders from another, 50% of the wicks from a third one, and only 20% of the burners from a fourth. In this case 4/5 of the lamp chimneys, 2/3 of the holders and 3/5 of the wicks will prove to be superfluous and lie wasted. A month later, the burners, so much needed by the first user, will lie unused with another organ needing paraffin lamps. Similar cases are unavoidable with fuels, raw materials, and various complementary materials.

Fifty-one years after the publication of Kritsman's book, it was still necessary for a Soviet journal (*Ekonomika* 1975 p. 134) to point out that 'The preservation of the system of strict rationing leads to the irrational utilisation of material resources and gives rise to phenomena alien to our society, such as barter, the activities of supply agents and "protectionism".' According to one estimate (*Khozyaistvennaya* 1968 p. 36), 25% of all working time in the USSR is lost through difficulties with the supply system.

Sellers' markets

The state socialist countries normally ration the most important producer goods. In addition, they often ration some consumer goods. Furthermore, in their history, sellers' markets for all or some non-rationed goods have been common. Hence it can be seen that the market situation in them is often one of a sellers' market. Sellers' markets have an adverse effect on the adaptation of production to requirements, on technical progress and on consumer satisfaction. This question is considered further in chapter 8 below.

Misallocating prices

The price system which prevails in the administrative economy is not conducive to the efficient allocation of resources and stimulating technical progress. There is an extensive literature giving examples of this and analysing their causes (Nove 1968 chapters 4 and 8, Bergson 1964 chapters 4 and 8, Zielinski 1967, Berliner 1976 Part II).

A graphic example (Belyaev 1968) of the difficulties which this causes for the economy is provided by an enterprise in Tambov which was making obsolete, though adequate, machines for vulcanising tyres. This gave it a 1968 sales plan of 8.6 million roubles. It was proposed that in 1969 it should switch over to a new automatic line which vulcanises at much greater speed and with considerable economy of labour. Prices, however, are such that sales in 1969 would be only 5 million roubles if the new machines were produced.

Isn't national economic efficiency taken into account in determining the prices of new products?
The price of new chemical equipment depends primarily on its weight.

Hence it is not in the interest of the plant to produce the new machinery. This would reduce its sales and thus its incentive funds. This difficulty in adapting output to requirements results from the combination of the existing price system, the absence of competition, the permanent sellers' market, and the fact that enterprises are judged not by the extent to which they satisfy demand but by the extent to which they fulfil the plan.

Personal consumption problems

An important negative aspect of the administrative economy is inattention to personal consumption. Aspects of this in the USSR are as follows. The assortment of consumer goods and services available is restricted, which shows itself in such phenomena as the inadequate arrangements for maintenance of the housing stock, and the fact that it is customary for persons going abroad and subsequently returning to the USSR to be asked to bring back commodities unavailable in the USSR. In provincial towns and villages the supply of consumer goods is much worse than in the chief cities. (Similarly in China special provision is made for supplying foodstuffs to the key cities of Peking, Shanghai and Tientsin, and also to the province of Liaoning with its great industrial centries.) The supply of consumer goods is frequently intermittent, so that it often happens that basic goods such as eggs are simply unavailable for several days. Similarly, in the USSR (and China) meat is often available in provincial towns only to those who can queue early in the day. Many of the goods that are available are of poor quality.

Queues and shortages are characteristic features of the administrative economy. It often happens that a particular commodity is unavailable in a particular place, or can only be

Table 3.1. *Alterations in the production plan of the Beloomutski clothing factory (Moscow Region) in 2nd half of 1965*

Article	Production (thousands of articles)		Output according to new plan as % of output according to old plan
	According to plan drawn up in the traditional way	According to plan drawn up on the basis of direct contacts	
Winter coats for school children	66.6	116.8	175.4
Half-length winter coats for school children	20.0	13.2	66.0
Spring coats for school children	53.3	98.9	185.5
Children's raincoats	61.7	20.9	33.9
Coats for nursery school children	18.6	4.4	23.7
Winter coats for pre-school children	41.3	15.5	37.5

Source: Lyovin (1967) p. 74.

obtained by queueing, because the commodity has been priced below the equilibrium price, and the activities of the trade and production organs are determined not by consumer demand as expressed in the market but by administrative considerations. This gives rise to irritation among frustrated purchasers and those who have to stand in queues, and to black marketeering.

One of the objectives of the Kosygin reform was to bring the production of consumer goods more into line with requirements. In many cases the transition from production for plan to production for use led to major changes in the assortment pattern. An example is set out in table 3.1.

The striking divergence between the assortment pattern based on instructions from the planners, and that based on orders from the retail trade corroborates the observation of two Poles (Kuron & Modzelewski 1968): 'The adaption of production to needs can be made only by the market buyer – ultimately by the consumer – but never by the central planner who fixes the prices of goods by himself and without references to the market and who judges an enterprise by its execution of central directive indices.'

Difficulties with innovation

It is well known that the state socialist countries have experienced rapid technical progress over long periods of time. They have shown rates of increases of labour productivity and changes in assortment that compare very well with those of the leading industrial country of the nineteenth century (the UK) and of the twentieth century (the USA). On the other hand, this has required very high rates of investment (by international standards) and has not been unique in the post Second World War world. In addition they have tended to copy, rather than originate, new technology, and in the 1960s and 1970s had great trouble in modernising the product-mix of existing plants, and more generally, in reducing the technology gap between themselves and the leading industrial countries. According to a recent careful study (Amann 1977), despite the great emphasis placed in Soviet planning on technical progress, the technological gap between the USSR and the leading capitalist countries is substantial and has not diminished in the past 15–20 years.

Factors hindering innovation have included, the hostility of the authorities to unrestricted intercourse with the capitalist world and especially to the free movement of people, the state monopoly of foreign trade, the risk-averting behaviour generated by the system, the centralisation of initiatives, the emphasis on economies of scale even where this conflicts with rapid changes in assortment, the separation of research from development, the stress on cutting costs of the producers of equipment rather than on service to customers, and the emphasis at all levels of the economic hierarchy on quantitative plan fulfilment (Berliner 1976).

Long construction and running-in periods

It is well known that the construction and running-in periods of new plants in the state socialist countries tend to be excessive both relative to planned periods and relative to international experience. An example is set out in table 3.2. Another example is given in chapter 5.

These lengthy construction periods, which up till now have been typical of the state socialist countries, appear to result from the large number of projects started, the adverse effect of the

Table 3.2. *Time taken to construct thermal electricity stations completed in the USSR in 1959–62*

Period of construction (years)	No. of thermal stations
5–7	8
8–10	8
11–13	8
14–15	2

Source: Krasovsky (1967) p. 52.

rationing of producer goods, and the use of volume criteria to assess the work of construction enterprises.

Bureaucratisation

Both empirical and theoretical analysis emphasises the role of bureaucratisation under socialism. On the basis of the experiences of War Communism, Kritsman (1924 p. 143) argued that '*The basic distortion* of the internal relations of the proletarian–natural economic system *was* its *bureaucratism*.' Similarly, in the course of his well-known theoretical analysis (Lange 1937) of the economics of socialism, Lange stated that 'the real danger of socialism is that of a bureaucratisation of economic life, and not the impossibility of coping with the problem of allocation of resources'. The experience of the Soviet Union and other state socialist countries supports the argument that the bureaucratisation of economic life is a serious danger under state socialism. A major reason for the transition from the administrative economy in Yugoslavia and Hungary, the abortive transition in Czechoslovakia, the discussion of economic reform in the USSR and the Cultural Revolution in China, has been the attempt to reduce the bureaucratic elements in economic life.

POLICY CONCLUSIONS ABOUT WASTE IN PLAN IMPLEMENTATION

The existence and importance of waste during plan implementation has been known for many years. Five well known, and very different, schools of thought as to the policy conclusions which should be drawn from the accumulated experience of more than sixty years are, the Schumpeterian, the neoclassical, the reformist, the technocratic and the Maoist. Consider each in turn.

The Schumpeterian view

The Schumpeterian view is that the state socialist countries have failed to find an efficient substitute for the capitalist entrepreneur. The evidence which is cited to support this point of view includes the difficulties of the state socialist countries with innovation and diffusion of new techniques and products, their dependence on technological imports and on cooperation with the multinationals, their limited success in catching up with the leading capitalist countries, and their virtual complete lack of success in overtaking the leading capitalist countries.

In a very detailed study, based on massive careful research, Sutton (1968, 1971, 1973) argued that Soviet economic development has been based almost entirely on imported Western technology. The conclusion reached by Sutton is that central planning has virtually no capacity for self-generated indigenous innovation. Sutton noticed some exceptions to this rule. In 1930–45, for example, Soviet innovations included SKB synthetic rubber, the Ramzin once-through boiler, the turbodrill, and a few aircraft and machine gun designs. In 1945–65 Soviet innovations included the electro-drill, some aircraft, Sputnik, medical sutures, electro-slag welding, and some examples of 'scaling-up'. Nevertheless, in general (Sutton 1973 p. 423), 'Soviet central planning is the Soviet Achilles' heel'. Soviet central planning has not fostered an engineering capacity to develop modern technologies from scratch, nor has it generated inputs (educational, motivational and material) to achieve this objective. Hence, Soviet economic development in the past has depended overwhelmingly on imports from the West (the concession of the 1920s, the building of entire plants by Western firms in the First Five Year Plan, the continued import of entire plants in the 1960s and 1970s). This dependence will continue as long as the USSR retains central planning, an inefficient economic system which does not provide adequate scope for the entrepreneurial function.

Similarly, Kornai (1971) and Perakh (1977) have argued that rapid innovation is incompatible with the administrative economy, with its emphasis on plan fulfilment. Unlike a market economy, where firms innovate to survive, as part of the competitive process, in an administrative economy everybody is interested only in risk avoidance and securing the necessary papers. The policy conclusions suggested by the Schumpeterian analysis are threefold. First, for the state socialist countries, it is necessary to change the economic mechanism from the administrative economy to one with a substantial role for the market mechanism, competition and the world market. This was done, to a certain extent, in Hungary in 1968. Secondly, for the advanced capitalist countries, they should realise the advantages of their economic system and seek to make the most of them. Instead of listening to anti-capitalist intellectuals, they should create the conditions in which capitalism can flourish so as to enjoy the benefits of technical progress and dynamic efficiency. Thirdly, for the developing countries, they should realise the benefits of capitalism, as demonstrated by the contrasting experience of the capitalist and state socialist countries, embark on the capitalist road, and repeat the successes of Japan, South Korea, Taiwan, Brazil, Singapore, Hong Kong, Kenya and other dynamic economies.

To what extent is the Schumpeterian view correct? It is clear that a number of important qualifications must be made.

First, exclusive stress on Soviet *imports* of technology ignores Soviet *exports* of technology. Not only did the USSR export technology to China in the 1950s, and not only does it export technology within CMEA, but it also exports technology to the leading capitalist countries. Some data on Soviet technology exports to the USA are set out in table 3.3.

Secondly, while it is no doubt ideologically pleasing for Westerners to focus attention on Soviet inadequacies, this both ignores Soviet successes and may in the future give rise to rude shocks, such as Sputnik. After all, the Third Reich too believed in the technical incompetence of the USSR. It turned out to be an expensive belief.

Thirdly, dependence on imported technology is not just a feature of Soviet economic development but is a feature of all countries other than the technological leader (first Britain, then Germany and then the USA). Hence, it may be argued, there is nothing special about Soviet dependence, which is only similar to that of Japan, and reflects not the inefficiency of socialist planning but the lower level of Soviet economic development. This argument is quantified and considered further in chapter 10.

Table 3.3. *Publicly known Soviet technologies in use or in development for commercial application by US companies in 1976*

Area	Technology	Company
Energy	Underground coal gasification	Texas Utility Services
Medicine	Surgical stapling device	US Surgical
	Pharmaceutical technology	American Home Products and Dupont
	Titanium hip prosthesis	US Surgical
Metallurgy	Tube mills to produce thin-wall tubing from hard-to-work metals such as stainless steel and titanium	Carpenter Technology and Universal Oil Products
	Cored wire manufacturing process for electric welding	Chemtron
	Magnetic impulse welding for nuclear fuel elements	Maxwell Laboratories
	Electromagnetic aluminium casting technique	Reynolds and Kaiser Aluminum
	Electro-slag remelting system to produce hollow steel ingots	Cabot
	Technology for the descaling of steel	Fenn Manufacturing
	Evaporation cooling process for blast furnaces	Andco
Mining	Hydraulic mining technology	Kaiser Resources
	Magnesium extraction technology using diaphragmless electrolysers	American Magnesium
	Method for leaching aluminium from ore	Southwire
	Rockbreaking machine	Joy Manufacturing
Miscellaneous	Pneumatic drifter drill (hole hog) for laying underground cables without digging open trenches	Allied Steel & Tractor
	Particle accelerator	Energy Sciences

Source: Kiser (1976) p. 148.

The neoclassical view

The neoclassical view was first formulated by writers such as N. G. Pierson (Netherlands), G. Halm (Germany) and E. Barone (Italy) prior to the existence of any actual socialist economies. It received its classical formulation in von Mises (1920), a work partly based on the actual experience of a socialist economy, namely War Communism in Soviet Russia. According to the neoclassical view one would expect to find (Hayek 1935 p. 204) that output where the use of the available resources was determined by some central authority, would be lower than if the price mechanism of a market operated freely under otherwise similar circumstances. This would be due to the excessive development of some lines of production at the expense of others, and the use of methods which are inappropriate under the circumstances.

Neoclassicals believe that the experience of the state socialist countries, from 1917 to the present time, corroborates this expectation, and hence that socialism is an irrational form of economic organisation, markedly less efficient than capitalism.

The neoclassical analysis raises two issues, one theoretical and one empirical. On the theoretical level, neoclassical comparisons of economic systems tend to compare actual socialism, with its well-known and self-admitted (most of the examples are taken from published sources) problems, with an imaginary capitalism, where resources are allocated with perfect efficiency. This is an example of what Nove has referred to as comparing 'muddle with model' and is clearly a mere debating trick. If the comparison were with actual capitalism, with its class differences; tough work discipline; organisation of work; insecurity; inability of the poor to obtain adequate housing, medical care and education; racial and sexual discrimination; income, wealth and power inequalities; unemployment; idle capacity and inflation; then perhaps the conclusion would not be so simple to reach. On the empirical level there is the careful collection and utilisation of data to throw light on the relative efficiency of the two systems. This is considered in chapter 10 below.

The reformist view

The reformist view, which has been developed by a large number of East European economists, notably Kornai (Hungary), Horvat (Yugoslavia) and Brus (Poland), is that the experience of the administrative economy shows the need to combine centralised state decision making with a market mechanism. In this way it is hoped to combine the advantages of socialism (abolition of exploitation, socialisation of the major economic decisions, full employment, absence of inflation, social security, rapid economic growth) with the advantages of the market (abolition of shortages and queues, efficient use of intermediate products, innovation and rapid technical progress, attention to personal consumption). Reforms along these lines were introduced in Yugoslavia from 1950 onwards and in Hungary in 1968 (although the resulting institutions are very different), were attempted in Czechoslovakia in 1968 and were discussed in the USSR in the 1960s.

In view of its problems neither Yugoslavia nor Hungary is likely to return to the administrative economy (nor would Czechoslovakia have done so had not external factors intervened). Nevertheless, experience has shown that the reformed systems may also suffer from serious problems, such as unemployment and rapid inflation (as in Yugoslavia) and/or a shift in the distribution of income from manual workers in state industry to the white collar intelligentsia, farmers and the self-employed. Furthermore, the revised system remains unsatisfactory from a Marxist perspective (because it does not reduce the differences between scientist and process worker), a liberal perspective (because it does not establish full civil liberties), a democratic perspective (because the state is still not under the control of society) and a labourist perspective (inequality and stratification persist and there are no worker organisations to provide protection against the bosses).

The technocratic view

The technocratic view, which underlies the actions of the Soviet authorities in the 1970s, is that the solution to the problems described in the literature is threefold. First, to improve the techniques of central planning by the automation of planning and management. Secondly, to improve the system of industrial management by the creation of socialist corporations. Thirdly, to cooperate with the multinationals. Consider each in turn.

The automation of planning and management. In order to improve the techniques of central planning an immense research programme was launched in the USSR in the 1970s aimed at establishing a 'Nation-wide automated system for the gathering and processing of information for accounting, planning and control of the national economy'.[4] This is intended to be an interconnected system of management information and control systems that will enable the planners to control in an efficient way the entire national economy. It is analogous to the well-known

[4] Known from its Russian initials as OGAS.

work undertaken by S. Beer in Chile under the *Unidad Popular*, and is an application of the scientific–technical revolution in the areas of planning and management.

In the USSR experimental work on the development of ASUs[5] began in the Eighth Five Year Plan (1966–70). In this period 414 ASUs were introduced in various parts of the economy. Many of these systems gave good results. As a deputy chairman of the USSR Gosplan observed (*Avtomatizirovannaya* 1972 p. 10),

> the operation of the group of systems in engineering, coalmining, the chemical and petro-chemicals industries, in transport and in construction showed that the period for recouping the costs of creating an ASU does not exceed 2–2½ years, and in some cases the costs are repaid within a single year. It is possible to give many examples of how the idleness of machinery is lessened, stocks of materials are reduced, and labour productivity increased, as a result of more rational planning.

In the light of the favourable results of this experimental work, the development of ASUs was one of the chief areas for raising efficiency and improving planning in the Ninth Five Year Plan (1971–75). The directives of the 24th Congress (1971) on the 1971–75 five year plan clearly stated the intention:

> To ensure the *wide application of economic–mathematical methods, the use of electronic computers and organizational technology and means of communication* in order to improve the planning and management of the national economy. To improve substantially the system of accounting and control, to improve statistics.
>
> To develop work on the creation and introducing of automated management systems for the planning and control of industries, territorial organisations, associations, and enterprises, with the intention of creating a nation-wide automated system for the collection and processing of information for accounting, planning and management of the national economy on the basis of a state network of computer centres and a unified communications system for the country. To provide from the very beginning for the organisational, methodological and technical unity of this system.

Some data on the introduction of ASUs into the Soviet economy is set out in table 3.4.

At the present time well-known ASUs include the one for the Ministry of Instrument Building, Means of Automation and Management Systems (ASU Pribor), the airline ticket reservation system 'Sirena', the system 'Tsement' for control of the pro-

[5] ASU is an abbreviation for *A*vtomatizirovannaya *s*istema *u*pravleniya. The literal translation is automated management system. The equivalent English language concept is 'management information and control system'.

Table 3.4. *The creation of automated management systems in the USSR*

	1966–70	1971–75	Total for 1966–75
Number of automated management systems	414	2,364	2,778
of which:			
automated management systems for enterprises	151	838	989
automated management systems for technological production processes	170	619	789
automated management system for territorial organisations	61	631	692
automated management system for ministries and departments	19	168	187
automated data processing systems	13	108	121

Source: *Narodnoe khozyaistvo SSSR v 1975 g* (Moscow 1976) p. 172.

duction of cement, the systems 'Barnaul' and 'Lvov' for enterprises in the electronics industry and the system in the Minsk tractor factory.

According to the State Committee on Science and Technology (*Avtomatika* 1975 p. 190), in 1971–74 inclusive, the operation of these ASUs gave an additional profit of more than 1.2 milliard roubles. The most effective ASUs at the moment are those regulating technological processes where the investment is recouped on average in 1–2 years. The widespread introduction of ASUs was also an important feature of the Tenth Five Year Plan (1976–80). A First Vice-Chairman of the State Committee on Science and Technology has noted that (*Ekonomicheskaya* 1974 p. 10)

> needless to say, the switching of planning to the tracks of branch automated management systems and enterprise automated management systems requires considerable time and effort, material outlays, the retraining of cadres and the solution of a number of technical and organisational problems. To accelerate this process the State Committee on Science and Technology, in conjunction with the USSR State Planning Committee, the USSR Academy of Sciences and the ministries and departments, is carrying out a broad range of projects aimed at improving the processes of planning and management and making fuller use of computers.

To accelerate the commissioning of automated management systems, a shift to the designing of standard computer centres and the writing of standardised programmes for them is under way.

The equipping of automated management systems with uniform computers (Minsk 32s and later Ryad-type machines) will make it possible, given the standardisation of planning and management jobs, to use standard algorithms and packages of applied programmes. This will cut the ministries' and departments' expenditure on the independent development of programmes and will accelerate the commissioning and more complete assimilation of automated management systems. The USSR Council of Ministers has adopted the proposal of the State Committee for Science and Technology and the Ministry of Instrument Building, Means of Automation and Management Systems for organising a special association to write programmes for Ryad-type computers on a centralised basis and according to customers' orders, and to provide the personnel of automated management systems with the necessary assistance in putting these programmes into effect.

The introduction of an ASU at any level is not just a matter of computerising the existing system of planning and management but may require its substantial modification. A deputy head of a department of the Soviet State Planning Committee has argued (*Use* 1975 p. 171) that

An important corollary of the introduction of the Automated System of Plan Calculations [this is one of the sub-systems that constitute the OGAS] is the conclusion that if the calculations made in the State Planning Commission of the USSR and the Ministries are to be properly coordinated, the product list must be greatly expanded – roughly by two orders of magnitude. This, in turn, entails greater centralisation of planning activities.

If the argument presented on pp. 65–79 is accepted, this research programme, although it will improve the management of particular plants and sectors, nevertheless, taken as a whole, is doomed to be a costly failure. It will be costly because of the number of manhours involved, the complex machinery utilised and the information wasted. It will be a failure since partial ignorance, imperfect techniques of data processing and complexity cannot be eliminated.

Socialist corporations. Another technocratic development in the USSR (and also in some other East European countries) in the 1970s was the reorganisation of the economy into associations.

Soviet associations are of two types, industrial associations and production associations. The industrial associations are a replacement for the former chief administrations of ministries.

Their creation is a reorganisation of an intermediate tier of management. The production association normally groups enterprises in particular areas. It is an economic unit composed of several enterprises, often together with research and design organisations, and corresponds to a firm in a market economy. The grouping of enterprises into associations can be regarded as a process of concentration. In this way it is hoped to create organisations which, study the market; link development with production; take advantage of international trade and technical and production cooperation, and of economies of scale; and respond to economic levers.

Comparing the new management structure with the old, the main differences seem to be that the new has fewer tiers and groups the old enterprises into production associations or big enterprises. The purpose of reducing the number of management tiers is to raise the efficiency, responsiveness and flexibility of the management apparatus, and in particular to bring the management organs closer to production. The grouping of enterprises appears to result from the realisation that the enterprise, traditionally the basic economic unit in the state socialist countries, is not suitable as the basic economic unit in an economic mechanism in which autonomous technological development, horizontal (i.e. market) relations and stable central norms are primary factors.

Experience of the Soviet shoe industry (Gorlin 1974) indicates a number of the advantages which the merger of enterprises into production associations brings. They are mainly the result of economies of scale. Particularly important are the gains from specialisation. Another gain is the reduction in management costs. Another is the more efficient use of stocks.

The creation of associations began in 1958 in Poland and subsequently spread throughout Eastern Europe, notably the GDR. After a long, and not altogether successful experience with them (Zielinski 1970), from 1973 there was a further reorganisation of the Polish economy into large economic organisations. The basic idea was to create concerns which would be able to realise economies of scale, make technological innovations, and participate in the international division of labour. It was intended to reduce government control over the details of the production process and endow the large economic organisations with substantial autonomy. The first step towards the realisation of these plans was the experimental constitution in

1973 of 15 pilot entities (enterprises or associations). In 1974 the experiment was enlarged to comprise 65 pilot entities from industry, construction, shipping, foreign trade and domestic trade.

Experience in Eastern Europe has indicated that the merger of enterprises into associations has not only advantages but also problems. One such problem is the danger of monopolistic price fixing, where associations have a say in price determination. This appears to be particularly serious in small countries with a limited home market, such as Hungary and Czechoslovakia. In Hungary monopolistic abuses by trusts were the main reason for their abolition and replacement by voluntary associations (unions). In Romania, when associations were set up in 1969 they were of both the industrial and production type. In 1973 most of the latter were dissolved. By mid 1974 there were only 102 associations, all of which corresponded to the Soviet industrial associations or the pre-1973 Polish associations.

To a considerable extent, the creation of, and reliance on, concerns larger than the traditional enterprise, reflects the admiration for the efficiency and dynamism of the capitalist corporation which is widespread among Soviet and East European officials, business executives and economists.

Cooperation with the multinationals. During the cold war the West waged economic warfare against the state socialist countries (Adler-Karlsson 1968). East–West trade shrank into insignificance. With the relaxation of international political tension in the 1960s, however, it grew quickly. During the 1970s, in the era of detente, East–West economic contacts widened and deepened. The state socialist countries made a major effort to close the technology gap by the import of technology from the capitalist countries. A classic example was Poland in the early 1970s. There an investment boom took place, largely financed by Western credits. This was intended to lead to the creation of a substantial internationally competitive sector of the economy that would earn sufficient foreign exchange to at least repay the credits. A good analysis of the Polish experience is Gomulka (1978). In the 1970s the East European countries moved beyond the import of licenses, machines and entire plants to more intimate collaboration with the multinationals (Wilczynski 1976). This collaboration took a number of forms.

The USSR organised direct R & D cooperation between big capitalist firms and the State Committee on Science and Tech-

Table 3.5. *Main R & D cooperation agreements between Western industrial firms and the USSR at the end of 1973*

Country	Firm	Field
Austria	Plasser und Theurer	Railway equipment
	Schoeller-Bleckmann	Steel alloy
	VÖEST	Iron and steel
Belgium	Picanol	Textile machinery
Belgium/FRG	Agfa-Gevaert	Photochemistry
FRG	AEG Telefunken	Electronics, communication
	BASF	Chemicals
	Daimler-Benz	Cars
	Gildemeister	Machine tools
	Krupp	Iron and steel
	Ruhrkohle	Mining
	Schering	Pharmaceuticals
	Siemens	Propulsion equipment
Italy	ENI	Chemicals
Netherlands	Akzo	Chemicals
Switzerland	Georg Fischer	Engineering
United Kingdom	Beecham	Antibiotics
UK/Italy	Dunlop–Pirelli	Tyres
USA	American Can	Packing and containers
	Brown and Root	Petroleum and gas transportation
	General Electric	Generators
	Hewlett Packard	Electronics
	ITT	Telecommunications, electronics
	Occidental Petroleum	Petroleum, gas, metals, chemicals

Source: *Business Europe* (28 September 1973) p. 306.

nology. It has been estimated that by the end of 1975 about 200 agreements of this type had been arranged. Some information about these agreements is set out in table 3.5.

Another approach to the import of technology is firm-to-firm industrial cooperation. This goes beyond the mere one-off purchase of machines and licenses to long-term technological, production and marketing cooperation. A leading role in firm to firm industrial cooperation has been played by Poland and Hungary. The Economic Commission for Europe estimated that at the beginning of 1973 about 600 industrial cooperation agreements were in force, of which about 200 were with Hungary and 170 with Poland. By the end of 1975 the total had increased to about 1000. A valuable detailed discussion of these agreements is Saunders (1977).

A third approach to technology transfer is the creation, on the territories of the state socialist countries, of joint venture enterprises with investment and management participation by Western firms. This approach has been developed by Yugoslavia and Romania. In mid 1973, six years after the enactment of the appropriate decrees, there were about 80 joint ventures in Yugoslavia, 53 per cent of their capital being in the car industry and 17 per cent in the chemical industry. In Romania, at the end of 1973, within two years of the enactment of equivalent legal regulations, there were four joint ventures: one each in the textile, electronics, car and chemical industries.[6]

How should the collaboration of the state socialist countries with the multinationals be evaluated? According to East European authors it is simply a manifestation of mutually profitable business deals. It is economically beneficial to both sides and stimulates a reduction in international tensions. It is, however, both quantitatively and qualitatively less important than CMEA integration (see chapter 9). According to writers such as Ticktin (1975, 1976b) and Adler-Karlsson (1976) it is a manifestation of a dependency relationship, similar to that between the West and the South. It also shows the enormous economic superiority of capitalism over state socialism. According to writers such as Wilczynski (1976) it is a deeply ironical phenomenon, but mutually beneficial and desirable. According to Perlmutter (1969, 1972) transideological collaboration corroborates the 'emergence' theory. The 'submergence' theory is that one system must be overpowered by the other, the 'divergence' theory that the two systems must become increasingly different and the 'convergence' theory that the two systems must become increasingly similar. The emergence theory, by contrast, emphasises the role of the multinational companies in developing a global system that transcends the boundaries of mere ideologies and social systems.

The author's view is that:

(1) it is a mutally beneficial process, which stimulates technical progress and living standards in the East and increases effective demand in the West.

(2) It demonstrates that a nation state – even the largest – is a sub-optimal unit of economic organisation. Attempts at autarky may well be costly (see also chapter 9 below).

(3) It also demonstrates that, while the West has serious economic problems, the East has worse ones.

[6] Romania has also established a joint venture (a coal mine) in the United States.

(4) It provides additional information about the performance of socialist planning.

The Managing Director of a West German engineering firm which has been involved in East–West industrial cooperation for a decade, has explained that (Saunders 1977 p. 169),

> Especially at the beginning of our agreement we were confronted with a lack of appreciation for some of our requirements (for constant high quality, good appearance, punctuality, availability of spares, accuracy of spares and service literature etc.) which our partners obviously thought had been invented by ourselves – typical grumbling German 125 per centers – until we got them to meet our customers, made them conscious of our competitors, and got them to understand the laws of the market.

This is a very striking tribute to the advantages of a market economy. Another example of the extra knowledge about socialist planning provided by state socialist collaboration with the multinationals can be found in chapter 6.

The Maoist view

According to the Maoist view, which was orthodox in China in 1966–76,

> Socialist society covers a considerably long historical period. Throughout this historical period, there are classes, class contradictions and class struggle, there is the struggle between the socialist road and the capitalist road, there is the danger of capitalist restoration and there is the threat of subversion and aggression by imperialism and social-imperialism. These contradictions can be resolved only by depending on the theory of continued revolution under the dictatorship of the proletariat and on practice under its guidance.[7]

The Maoists argued that the USSR was a bourgeois dictatorship. It had reverted to this position as a result of a long and complex process of class struggle.[8] Hence, the waste and inefficiency of the economy were only to be expected, on the classical grounds explained in chapter 1. In order to prevent similar degeneration in China it was necessary to organise repeated revolutionary upsurges such as the Great Proletarian Cultural Revolution. This would both train worthy successors to the revolutionary cause of the proletariat and, by bombarding

[7] This is an extract from the Preamble to the Chinese Constitution adopted in 1975. Stress on class struggle under socialism was also a feature of Stalinism.

[8] For an analysis along these lines see Bettelheim (1974a).

headquarters, prevent the emergence of a hierarchical bureaucratic society of the Soviet type.

The Maoist analysis presents a number of problems both of diagnosis and of prescription. As far as diagnosis is concerned, the description of the USSR as a country where bourgeois dictatorship has been restored, is manifestly absurd. How can there be a bourgeoisie in a country in which there is no private ownership of the means of production and no inheritance of offical position? Bettelheim mechanically applies to the USSR some Marxist concepts developed for the analysis of capitalism without demonstrating either that the USSR is capitalist or that concepts such as 'bourgeoisie', 'law of value', 'labour as a commodity' etc. illuminate the functioning and development of Soviet society. Clearly the USSR is a dictatorship and is not at the higher stage of socialism envisaged by Marx, but to suppose that the only alternative to 'proletarian dictatorship' is 'bourgeois dictatorship' shows profound conceptual poverty. In addition, the Maoist idea that under Khrushchev the USSR retrogressed is equally absurd. It was under Khrushchev that inequality in the USSR was much reduced (see chapter 7), the coercive model in agriculture and labour largely abandoned (see chapters 4 and 6), and living standards raised very substantially.

As far as prescription is concerned, the idea of the Cultural Revolution and similar movements as spontaneous revolutionary upsurges is obviously a complete illusion. The Cultural Revolution was inspired by Mao, as he himself fully recognised (Mao 1974a p. 271): 'the Great Cultural Revolution wreaked havoc after I approved Nieh Yüan-tzu's big-character poster in Peking University, and wrote a letter to Tsinghua University Middle School, as well as writing a big-character poster of my own entitled "Bombard the Headquarters"... it was I who caused the havoc'. To a considerable extent the Cultural Revolution was simply a manoeuvre by one faction in the leadership (Mao Tse-tung and his supports) against another (Liu Shao-chi and his supporters) in which millions of youths were manipulated in what was both a struggle for power and a confrontation as to which road the Chinese Revolution should follow. Furthermore, when officially organised campaigns (such as the 'Dictatorship of the Proletariat' campaign of 1975) led to genuine mass movements from below (such as the Hangchow strikes of 1975) the authorities reacted not by encouraging the workers and accepting their demands, but by sending in soldiers and persuading the workers to return to work. In addition, since it actually depended on one man at the top, the Maoist prescription left open the possibility that after his death the criticised and humiliated officials together with army officers and others might abandon repeated revolutionary upsurges in favour of a stable bureaucratic society which regarded bombarding headquarters as a hindrance to production and to an orderly hierarchy.

As Vogel (1969 p. 349) has observed, the political revivalism of the GPCR was no more than temporary because it lacked the economic and political base to sustain it. In orthodox Marxist–Leninist terms, it was an abortive and futile attempt to transform the superstructure (the attitudes and behaviour of officials) when the basis was left unchanged. The differences between permanent and temporary workers remained, since the state lacked the resources to provide all the temporary workers with the pay and conditions of permanent workers. Educated youths continued to be sent down since the urban economy continued to provide too few jobs for them. Professors continued (after a gap) to instruct students, since the professors had the knowledge that the students needed. The revolutionary youths could not come to power since the regime depended on the support of the army. The aphorism attributed to Teng Hsiao-ping, that 'Black cat, white cat, what does it matter as long as they can catch mice?' was much criticised during the GPCR.[9] Similarly, Chou En-lai's 'four modernisations' were much criticised in early 1976.[10] Nevertheless, after the 11th Congress both became orthodox once more (the latter de jure and the former de facto), in view of the backwardness of the Chinese economy and the imperative need to catch up. Without the necessary material basis, the aspirations of the Cultural Revolution were bound to remain mere dreams.

AN EXPLANATION OF THE CAUSES OF WASTE IN PLAN IMPLEMENTATION

The fundamental cause of the waste and inefficiencies described on pp. 43–50, in the author's opinion, is a theoretical one, namely

[9] The aphorism means that whether an institution, such as individual material incentives, should be regarded as 'bourgeois' or 'socialist' is of no importance. What is important is whether or not it contributes to production.

[10] The 'four modernisations' were the comprehensive modernisation of agriculture, industry, defence, and science and technology, as outlined in Chou En-lai's report to the Fourth National People's Congress in January 1975.

the inadequate nature of the theory of decision making implicit in the Marxist–Leninist theory of planning. In the USSR, there is a long tradition of publishing critical articles describing particular examples of waste and blaming them on particular bureaucrats. Experience has shown, however, that the publication of critical articles, or the replacement of one bureaucrat by another, are entirely inadequate to eliminate the problems. The difficulty lies deeper. As E. G. Liberman (1970 p. 74) has argued:

> We sometimes wrongly, without the necessary bases, blame gosplans, ministries and supply-marketing organisations for annoying misunderstandings, disproportions, losses in production and the violation of the interests of consumers. When one encounters so many people making mistakes, it is necessary to look for the reason not only in their individual qualities, but in that system, or more precisely in that 'theory', which conceives of planning as the management from the centre of an all-embracing extremely detailed nomenclature of commodites.

The theory of decision making implicit in the Marxist–Leninist theory of planning is inadequate because it ignores the fundamental factors of partial ignorance,[11] inadequate techniques for data processing and complexity. The limitations of Marxist–Leninist theory are different from, but parallel to, those of neoclassical theory. Marxist–Leninist theory concentrates on vertical links and instructions, while neoclassical theory concentrates on horizontal links and prices. Neither theory, by itself, is adequate as a basis for economic policy, although both theories have much to say that it is of interest.

Partial ignorance

If (as in some models) the central authorities had perfect knowledge of the situation throughout the economy (and also adequate techniques for processing it and transmitting the results) then they would be able to calculate efficient plans and issue them to the periphery. In fact, the central authorities are partially ignorant of the situation throughout the economy and this is a major factor explaining the phenomena described on pp. 43–50, which are so unexpected from a Marxist–Leninist point of view.

For example, the problem of slack plans arises from the fact that the necessary information is largely concentrated in the

[11] This term is taken from Loasby (1976). It is preferred to 'uncertainty' because the latter is often used in a restricted, technical, sense in economics.

hands of the periphery, and the data available to the centre is heavily dependent on the data transmitted by the periphery. Since the social situation is not one in which the value of selfless work for the good of the community has been widely internalised, the problem of motivating people on the periphery to submit socially rational plan suggestions arises. (The actual social situation is one in which officials strive to avert risk and avoid responsibility and obedience to instructions from above is highly valued by superiors.) The fact that subordinate members of an administrative hierarchy are more interested in defending their own interests than in the general interest, and the failure of the authorities to reconcile fully the two, is a permanent problem of the administrative economy. It derives its importance from the inability of the central authorities to concentrate in their hands all the information necessary for the calculation of efficient plans and the complexity of the decision-making process (see below).

Similarly, the criterion problem largely results from the fact that the central authorities lack the information necessary to issue all the associations with all-embracing efficient plans and are only able to issue them with certain plan targets and certain criteria.

Similarly, some of the problems of personal consumption are a result of the partial ignorance of the central authorities. For example, the changes in the production plan of the Beloomutski clothing factory (table 3.1 above) resulted, not from any conflict between 'planners' preferences' and 'consumers' preferences', but from the fact that the planners did not know what the consumers preferred. That knowledge was concentrated in the hands of the distribution network.

Similarly, one of the reasons why the rationing of producer goods is a cause of inefficiency is because the organisations that do the rationing are ignorant of where the goods would be of most value to the national economy.

Similarly, with misallocating prices. If the planners had sufficient information and time to make socially rational decisions throughout the economy, and enterprises simply carried out their instructions, then the problem of misallocating prices would not exist.

Partial ignorance about the future is the main reason why the repeated attempts to calculate long-term plans have never led to more than the production of documents that speedily became irrelevant. After a short time it became obvious that the main current problems were not those considered in the plan.

The partial ignorance of the planners is of two types. First, ignorance which is created by the planning process. Secondly, ignorance which is unavoidable. The first type of ignorance has three causes. Subordinates may transmit inaccurate information, the process of transmitting information may destroy some of it, and the addressees of information may not receive it. Consider each in turn.

It is well known that in any bureaucracy (Downs 1967 p. 77), 'Each official tends to distort the information he passes upwards to his superiors in the hierarchy. Specifically all types of officials tend to exaggerate data that reflect favourably on themselves and to minimize those that reveal their own shortcomings.' This explains such phenomena as the exaggeration of agricultural output figures in the USSR, which Khruschev criticised, and in China during the Great Leap Forward. It also explains the exaggeration of input requirements and the underestimation of output possibilities that is a normal part of the process of planning and counterplanning by which plans are drawn up. It is in order to deal with this problem that Soviet incentive systems are devised and altered.

The tendency by officials to distort the information they transmit upwards can be minimised in three ways, by strict supervision, by appropriate incentives, and by avoiding the need for the information. Strict supervision (by the party, a control commission, statistical and financial agencies) is a traditional method used in the state socialist countries to reduce information distortion. It is not without cost. Inappropriate incentive systems (for example for plan fulfilment and overfulfilment) can generate distorted information, and alternative incentive systems can be experimented with. An example of avoiding the need for the information was the gradual, and still partly experimental, replacement of the indent method of determining material requirements by mathematical methods in the Soviet Union in the 1970s.

An example of how the process of transmitting data may destroy some of it is provided by the aggregation problem. During the process of planning there is aggregation by commodities, enterprises and time periods. All three introduce errors (Ellman 1969a). Aggregation errors can be reduced by following suitable aggregation criteria or by enlarging the detail of the plan, but are unlikely ever to be eliminated.

Another example of how socialist planning can create ignorance is provided by what the cognitive theorists of decision making refer to as 'the assumption of a single outcome calculation'. This refers to the fact that the decision making process often 'does not match the uncertain structure of the environment in which events might take a number of alternative courses. Rather, it imposes an image and works to preserve that image.' Hence, 'Pertinent information may enter the decision process or it may be screened out, depending on how it relates to the existing pattern of belief... That information which is threatening to established belief patterns is not expected to be processed in a fashion wholly dominated by the reality principle' (Steinbruner 1974 p. 123).

The classic example, of course, is Stalin's surprise at the German invasion of 1941, despite the advance information transmitted by Sorge and others, resulting from his screening out of information that threatened an established belief pattern. Similarly, Gomulka was surprised at the outcome of his policy of self-sufficiency in grain, despite warnings by economists, such as Kalecki, of its likely adverse effects (Feiwel 1975 chapter 19).

Not only may decision makers screen out accurate information, but they may also suppress its sources. For example, the reaction of the Polish leadership to discussion of the five year plan 1966–70 was not only to ignore the suggestions made (whose correctness was shown by subsequent events) but also to take 'exceptionally violent action' (Brus 1973 p. 107) against the leading discussant. Similarly, one of the causes of the problems of Soviet agricultural policy between the wars was the screening out of accurate information about, for example, the size of harvests and of marketed output, and of the importance of proper crop rotations, and the suppression of the leading specialists in agricultural statistics and agronomy.

An important source of avoidable ignorance in the state socialist countries has been the screening out of information provided by specialists (and sometimes their suppression) because the political leadership distrusted the specialists, regarding them as 'not our people' and politically unreliable.

Once accurate information has been screened out and its purveyors suppressed, reliance may be placed on people who are in fact not competent in the area concerned. As the Hungarian economist Jánossy (1969) has noted, the Stalin era was characterised not only by suspicion of specialists but also by confidence in non-specialists. For example, in working out investment plans, reliance was often placed on engineers not competent in the area concerned, let alone in calculating and evaluating costs. As a result some extraordinarily expensive projects were designed and executed.

Moreover, once accurate information has been screened out, and its sources suppressed, an entirely fanciful picture of reality may play a major role in the perception of decision makers. This is especially easy if there is a strict pre-publication censorship of all publications and only material supporting the illusions of decision makers can be published. For example, it is well known that at the end of Stalin's life his policies were having a very negative effect on agriculture in the USSR and throughout Eastern Europe. One reason for this is that, as Khrushchev pointed out in his report to the 20th Congress of the CPSU 'On the personality cult and its consequences', Stalin's perception of the agricultural situation largely derived from films which portrayed a quite illusory picture of rural prosperity. 'Many films so pictured collective farm life that the tables were bending from the weight of turkeys and geese. Evidently Stalin thought that it was actually so.'

A major feature of developments in the CMEA countries since the death of Stalin has been a reduction in the ignorance of decision makers. The publication of statistical data has been enormously increased. Numerous scientific research institutes have been set up and encouraged to undertake independent work. New, policy-related disciplines such as mathematical economics, sociology and demography have been encouraged. The preparation and publication of orginal policy-related work has been encouraged. Genuine discussions have been held on policy questions (for example, the Soviet discussion of the 1960s about economic reform).

Nevertheless, the partial ignorance of the decision makers, which they themselves have created, may still play a major role in affairs, as Polish events have shown. In Poland in the 1970s attempts to increase the price of food have twice (February 1971 and June 1976) had to be withdrawn, as the authorities reacted to popular feeling. Their ignorance about likely popular reactions resulted from the non-existence of institutions for conveying the views of the workers to the leadership,[12] the unwillingness of subordinates to convey unpalatable facts to their

[12] According to the transmission belt theory, the function of trade unions is just the opposite. A partial substitute is provided by the state security organs.

superiors, the screening out by decision makers of unpalatable information and the suppression of those who provided it.

Some ignorance is just unavoidable. The nature of economic life is such that the economy is continually being affected by events that were not foreseen when the plan was drawn up. This is particularly obvious with respect to harvest outcomes, innovations,[13] either technological or managerial/organisational, international affairs and demographic factors. This ignorance about the future can be reduced, for example, by establishing institutes for research into the international conjunctural situation or demography, but it can never be eliminated. As Keynes (1937 pp. 213–14) observed,

> the expectation of life is only slightly uncertain. The sense in which I am using the term is that in which the prospect of a European war is uncertain, or the price of copper and the rate of interest twenty years hence, or the obsolescence of a new invention, or the position of private wealth holders in the social system in 1970. About these matters there is no scientific basis on which to form any calculable probability whatever. We simply do not know.

Keynes, of course, drew far-reaching conclusions from the importance of ignorance.

Not only are the central decision makers unavoidably partially ignorant, but the attempt to concentrate all relevant information in their hands is costly. It is costly in two ways. First, large numbers of people and considerable specialised equipment are required. Secondly, the erroneous view that social rationality can be attained by calculating a central plan which is then faithfully executed may reduce the responsiveness of the country to new information and hence generate waste. Lerner (1975 p. 214) has argued that

> a distinguishing feature of a system with centralised control is a high degree of *rigidity* of the structure, because adaptation, to both random changes and changes caused by the evolution of the system and the environment, does not take part in the individual parts of the system but only in the central control point. Centralised control permits

[13] An example of the way in which unforeseen technical innovations can prevent socialist planning working smoothly, was given by Chou En-lai in his Report to the Eighth Party Congress (1956). He observed of China's economic plans that, 'Even if they are fairly accurate at the moment when they are drawn up, they may be thrown out of balance by unforeseeable factors. For instance, in 1956, when the utilisation rate of the open-hearth and blast furnaces was raised as a result of the introduction of new technology, the supply of ores and coke failed to catch up.' This type of disruption can be reduced by holding adequate stocks, as was pointed out in chapter 2.

stabilisation of a system over a long period, suppressing both fluctuations and evolutional changes in the individual parts of the system without reconstructing them. However, in the final analysis, this may be damaging to the system because contradictions between the unchanged structure of a system and changes associated with evolution increase to global dimensions and may require such a radical and sharp reconstruction as would be impossible within the framework of the given structure and would lead to its disintegration.

Similarly Beer (1969 p. 398) has noted that 'adaptation is the crux of planning, although it is not its ostensible object. The ostensible object of planning – a realized event – happens from time to time as a fall-out of the planning process which passes it by. The real object of corporate planning is the continuous adaptation of the enterprise towards continuing survival.' Because of partial ignorance, Loasby (1976 pp. 136–7) has argued that

large organisations, if they are to prosper, may have to reject determinism in favour of free will. Delegation may be used, not to programme choice, but to encourage initiative. Amid the uncertainties and chances of war, the initiative, or lack of it, shown by subordinate commanders has often proved decisive. Nelson both demonstrated such initiative as a subordinate and fostered it as a commander; and Slim, rating as 'one of my most helpful generals' the Japanese commander at Kohima who missed a great opportunity by conforming to his orders, praised his own subordinates for their ability to act swiftly to take advantage of sudden information or changing circumstances without reference to their superiors'.

The assumption that all relevant data have already been processed at the centre and that the duty of all subordinates is to carry out the plan may simply result in wasteful and socially irrational responses to the changing situation because subordinates are barred from socially rational responses and the centre lacks the information.[14]

A major weakness of the Marxist–Leninist theory of planning (and of the institutions based on that theory) is that it fails to take

[14] As Crozier (1964 p. 190) has observed, the result of the decision making process which characterises bureaucracies is that the 'People who make the decisions cannot have direct firsthand knowledge of the problems they are called upon to solve. On the other hand, the field officers who know these problems can never have the power necessary to adjust, to experiment and to innovate.' The Maoists were very much concerned with overcoming both these problems. To give the cadres direct firsthand knowledge of the problems, they used cadre participation in manual labour and sending down. To give the field officers the necessary power, they transferred to them considerable authority to implement central policies.

any account of ignorance, despite its fundamental importance. It also fails to take account of stochastic, as opposed to deterministic, processes. It assumes a perfect knowledge, deterministic world, in which unique perfect plans can be drawn up for the present and the future. In fact, we live in a world in which we are partially ignorant about both the present and the future, and in which stochastic processes are important, and our theories, institutions and policies must take account of this. In this respect the Marxist–Leninist theory of planning suffers from the same weakness as neoclassical price theory.[15] This may be ironical, but it is scarcely surprising, since both are nineteenth-century theories which ultimately derive from classical physics, a theory in which ignorance and stochastic processes play no part, and whose success turned it into an extraordinarily influential research programme. The Laplacean demon has long been expelled from physics. It is time to exorcise him from economics too.

Inadequate techniques for data processing

The time has not yet come when the giant computing machines of the Central Planning Board, supplied with all the necessary information by the Central Statistical Office, can take over from where the mechanism of the market system has left off.

W. Leontief (1971 p. 20)

The inadequacy of the techniques used to process such data as are available is the main reason for the instability of the plans and one of the reasons for the long construction periods. The planning techniques currently used (material balances and input–output) are such that the current plans are always inconsistent (Ellman 1973 chapter 1). As the inconsistencies come to light during the planned period, it is necessary to alter the plan so as to allow the economy to function. A typical example of an inconsistency leading to the alteration of a plan is the impossibility of fulfilling a plan because of the lack of a necessary input. When

[15] The reason why according to neoclassical theory 'the Government can in principle always do as well and often better than the market' (Hahn 1974 p. 37), is because the model it analyses, like the Marxist–Leninist one, is a deterministic one which takes no account of the fundamental factors of partial ignorance, inadequate techniques for data processing and complexity. Hence it is unable to discuss the real advantage of markets from an efficiency point of view, dispersal of initiatives and simplicity. (For examples see Ellman 1969b pp. 342–3.) Recent empirical work on the technology gap and innovation in Soviet industry has emphasised the importance of dispersal of initiatives for technical progress.

the production plan affected is that of a construction site then this naturally delays completion of the project.

This problem can be dealt with, to some extent, by improving the planning techniques. For example, a major innovation in investment planning in Eastern Europe in 1960–75 was the calculation of optimal investment plans by means of linear programming and related techniques. This was an improvement in planning techniques because the investment plans drawn up in this way were more likely to be feasible. The plans drawn up by the traditional methods were often not feasible, which is one of the explanations of the chronic long construction periods. This new technique also gave the possibility of doing variant calculations. For example, when the 1976–90 plan was being worked out in the USSR it was decided to compile the optimal plans for the development of each industry in four variants. Two variants differed according to the value used for the norm of investment efficiency, and two according to the volume of consumption assumed. In this way it was possible to study the sensitivity of the optimal location and output decisions to variations in the key parameters. Although this new technique was an improvement on the old ones, its use was far from sufficient to ensure the calculation of efficient plans. Problems with the new technique included, the insufficient availability of the necessary data, the unrealistic nature of some of the assumptions (e.g. constant returns to scale), the need to coordinate the calculation of optimal plans for all the industries with each other and with the macro plan variables, and the fact that the results of the calculations were often not accepted. The improvement of techniques is a continuous process in which further improvements can always be made.

It sometimes happens that major innovations in planning techniques about which high hopes are held, simply fail to achieve the objectives of those who introduce them. For example, during the 1960s, input–output was widely introduced in planning in the European socialist countries. It was the first mathematical technique to be introduced in socialist planning, and high hopes were held by many about the benefits that would flow from using it. It was widely expected that it would eliminate the problem of inconsistent plans because the use of input–output enabled consistent plans to be calculated. In fact, this turned out to be erroneous. Input–output, like material balances, is quite unable to resolve the problem of drawing up consistent plans for all the centrally planned commodities. This did not mean that the new technique was useless. On the contrary it turned out to be very useful for the calculation of pre-plan variants. The problem it had been introduced to solve, however, remained unresolved.

Not only may new techniques fail to solve the problems they were introduced to solve, but experiments with them may simply underline the losses caused by the use of administrative methods. A well-known example was provided by the use of linear programming, in the 1960s, in the USSR to calculate minimum cost transport schemes.[16]

The main reason why China makes extensive use of indirect centralisation, rather than the more orthodox direct centralisation, appears to be that it is such a huge country with an enormous population, most of it engaged in agriculture, and with very limited accounting and statistical personnel. Under these conditions, the partial ignorance of the authorities and the inadequate techniques available for data processing are such that imperfect direct centralisation would be very inefficient.[17]

Complexity

One of the rarely mentioned economic wastes of Soviet-type command systems has been this destruction of élan vital, a production input for which there is no close substitute.

V. Holesovsky (1968 p. 547)

[16] 'This is not a complicated task. Many articles and books have been written and not a few dissertations defended, but almost no freight is shipped by the optimal schemes. Why? Simply because the transport organisations are given plans based on ton kilometres. One can establish computer centres, and conceive superb algorithms, but nothing will come of it as long as the transport organisations reckon plan fulfilment in ton kilometres' (Belkin & Birman 1964).

[17] Even for such a basic statistic as the total population there are simply no reliable figures. It is not that the authorities have accurate data but do not release it. It is simply that the authorities themselves lack the information. In 1971 Vice-Premier Li Hsien-nien stated (Ashbrook 1975 p. 35) that 'Some people estimate the population at 800 million and some at 750 million. Unfortunately there are no accurate statistics in this connection. Nevertheless, the officials at the supply and grain department are saying confidently, "The number is 800 million people." Officials outside the grain department say the population is "750 million only", while the Ministry of Commerce affirms that "the number is 830 million". However, the planning department insists that the number is "less than 750 million". The Ministry of Commerce insists on the bigger number in order to be able to provide goods in large quantities. The planning men reduce the figure in order to strike a balance in the plans of the various state departments.'

Complexity is used here to describe the fact that decision making is dispersed over numerous individuals and organisations. The dispersal of decision making is a normal and necessary reaction to the difficulties of collecting and processing in one spot all the data necessary for rational decision making. It creates, however, numerous problems.

One of the reasons for the inconsistency of the current plans, which in turn is a major cause of their instability, is precisely that the planning of production and supply for the entire national economy is regarded as too complicated for any one organisation, and accordingly is split up among many organisations. This creates numerous coordination problems (Ellman 1973 pp. 24–5).

Similarly, the fact that planning, in the sense of the compilation of plans and checking up on their fulfilment, is split in the USSR between two organisations, Gosplan (the State Planning Committee) and TsSU (the Central Statistical Administration) has traditionally created problems for Soviet planning. For example, the introduction of input–output into Soviet planning in the 1960s was hindered by the fact that the two organisations used different commodity classifications.

The fact that decision making is dispersed ensures that it will be affected by what Downs (1967 p. 216) has termed the Law of Interorganisational Conflict. This states that *Every large organisation is in partial conflict with every other social agent it deals with.*

The Marxist–Leninist theory of planning assumes that all the decision makers in an economy form a 'team', that is, a group of persons working together who have identical goals. In fact the decision makers form a 'coalition', that is, a group of persons working together who have some, but not all, goals in common.[18] An example of the results of this is that, in the USSR, subordinate organisations (ministries, local party committees) often begin the construction of plants the building of which is in their interest (because it makes them less vulnerable to the behaviour of other organisations, or increases the output of 'their' product) even though the initiation of such construction projects may slow down other construction projects and hence have a negative effect on national goals. This is a normal phenomena in the state socialist countries and one of the explanations of the chronic long construction periods.

The fact that decision making is dispersed between organisations which have some, but not all, goals in common, creates

[18] This was extensively discussed in the Czechoslovak literature of the 1960s.

the need for higher level bodies to guide lower level ones to socially rational decisions, i.e. the criterion problem.

It is because decision makers form a coalition and not a team that incentives, both negative and positive, moral and material, play an important motivating role in ensuring the necessary output of work. Of course, there are certain groups of the population that may work well to meet national requirements independently of their own material rewards.

> There can be no doubt that on the highest level of Cuban political leadership and economic management, as well as on other levels, including the lower ones of educational, scientific, medical and artistic activities, true inner dedication to the interests of the community does, in fact, prevail. In most instances, moreover, it is combined with a deeply ingrained 'instinct of workmanship'. The Cuban programs of health, education and social welfare seem major accomplishments, especially in view of the limited resources available for investment in them. [Leontief 1971 p. 22]

Nevertheless, the whole experience of the socialist world indicates that motivating people to work well to achieve the goals laid down in the national plan is a complex and difficult issue which has not so far been solved in an entirely satisfactory manner anywhere. From an analytical point of view the whole problem only arises because, contrary to Marxist–Leninist expectations, many people, even in economies where the means of production are nationalised and there is a national economic plan, are guided not by an internalised need to fulfill the plan, but by other motivations. In other words, they constitute a coalition and not a team. The failure to motivate adequately the labour force was the main cause of the falls in labour productivity in Cuba in the 1960s, in Soviet agriculture in the aftermath of collectivisation and in Chinese agriculture in the aftermath of the Great Leap Forward. In fact, it has been an important source of waste throughout the whole history of state socialism. This question is considered further in chapter 6.

An important criterion for officials in any organisation is risk aversion. Risk aversion is one of the explanations both of bureaucratisation and of the failure of the incentive system introduced in the Soviet economy as part of the Kosygin reform of 1966–69. Why risk aversion is one of the causes of bureaucratisation has been well described by Downs (1967 p. 100). In order to avoid the risk of making a decision that might subsequently be criticised, officials rely mainly or wholly on the established rules and regulations. This may generate 'red tape' and socially irrational decisions, but it is likely to provide the relevant official with a satisfactory answer in any subsequent inquiry.

As for the failure of the Kosygin reform of 1966–69,

> It is easy to see that for risk averting enterprise management, even under the reform, plan underfulfilment and an increase in the plan, are asymmetrical. The loss from each one per cent of underfulfilment (reprimands, inspection by higher bodies, loss of managerial bonuses, reduction in the enterprise incentive funds) is much greater than the gain from each one per cent by which the plan is increased (30% or more of the marginal increments to the enterprise incentive funds and marginal increments to the managerial bonuses). Hence risk aversion is another reason why the new system failed to lead to the universal adoption of taut plans [Ellman 1977 p. 33].

The fact that decision making is dispersed among a coalition, whose members are not allowed, in many cases, to charge for their output, is also one of the causes of bureaucratisation. The reason for this is that it brings into operation what Downs (1967 p. 188) has termed the Law of Non-Money Pricing. This states that *Organisations that cannot charge money for their services must develop non-monetary costs to impose on their clients as a means of rationing their outputs.* Hence, much of the irritating behaviour of bureaucrats often represents a means of rationing their limited resources so that they will be available to those truly anxious to use them. It is precisely because non-market organisations tend to breed bureaucratisation that there is so much stress in the CMEA countries on commercial accounting (*khozraschet*) and, during the 1970s, in the USSR numerous chief administrations of ministries were transformed into industrial associations based on commercial accounting.

Risk aversion and localised criteria are important factors hindering technical progress. Innovation is hindered by a system in which quarterly plan fulfilment is so important and where external effects of the innovation are of little importance to most decision makers.

The importance of the dispersal of decision making in ensuring that even a state owned non-market economy would not necessarily be socially rational, was familiar already to acute observers of War Communism. More than half a century ago Kritsman (1924 p. 116) observed that

If we consider the economy as a whole... we come to the conclusion that in our proletarian–natural economy *exploitation and the market were overcome without overcoming the anarchy of economic life*... As is well known, commodity economy is anarchic economy. It would, however, be incorrect to conclude from this that a non-commodity economy, i.e. a natural economy, is necessarily a non-anarchical, i.e. a planned, economy... For an economy to be anarchic it is necessary and sufficient for there to be a multiplicity of (independent) economic subjects.

With the advantage of half a century's experience we can add to Kritsman's observation the twin points, that the dispersal of decision making is inevitable and permanent (because of partial ignorance and inadequate techniques for processing information), and that an economy with dispersal of decision making may be, but is not necessarily, socially irrational.

CONCLUSION

Experience has shown that the process of plan implementation is not a harmonious socially rational process for the attainment of pre-determined goals. It actually contains substantial elements of waste and inefficiency. Five well-known, but very different, policy conclusions have been drawn from this, Schumpeterian, neoclassical, reformist, technocratic and Maoist. The fundamental reason for the waste and inefficiency of the administrative economy is theoretical, namely the omission from the Marxist–Leninist theory of planning of some essential aspects of reality. They are partial ignorance, inadequate techniques for data processing and complexity.

Chapters 4 to 9 below examine the planning of particular sectors of the economy, from agriculture to foreign trade, in the light of the general arguments developed in chapters 1–3. Chapter 10 evaluates the overall success of socialist planning from the standpoint of the two issues raised in chapter 1, the creation of a higher mode of production and catching up with the leading capitalist countries.

SUGGESTIONS FOR FURTHER READING

A. General

M. Crozier, *The bureaucratic phenomenon* (Chicago 1964).
D. Granick, *Enterprise guidance in Eastern Europe* (Princeton 1976).
J. Kornai, *Overcentralization in economic administration* (London 1959).
R. P. Mack, *Planning on uncertainty* (New York 1971).
M. Rakovski, 'Marxism and Soviet societies', *Capital and Class* no. 1 (Spring 1977).
A. S. Tannenbaum et al., *Hierarchy in organisations* (San Francisco 1974).

B. GDR

G. Leptin & M. Melzer, *Economic reform in East German industry* (Oxford 1977).

C. China

G. Benton, 'China since the Cultural Revolution', *Critique* no. 6.
J. Gray, 'Alternative strategies of social change and economic growth in China', S. Schram (ed.) *Authority, participation and cultural change in China* (Cambridge 1973).
Choh-Ming Li, *The statistical system of Communist China* (Berkeley 1962).

D. USSR

V. Andrle, *Managerial power in the Soviet Union* (London 1976).
A. Katsenelinboigen, 'Coloured markets in the Soviet Union', *Soviet Studies* (January 1977).
R. Miliband, 'Bettelheim and Soviet experience', *New Left Review* 91.
R. Amann, J. M. Cooper & R. W. Davies (eds.) *The technological level of Soviet industry* (New Haven 1977).
H. Ticktin, 'The contradictions of Soviet society and Professor Bettelheim', *Critique* no. 6.

4

PLANNING AGRICULTURE

THE CASE FOR COLLECTIVISM

The case for collective, rather than private, ownership and management of land, is simply one specific aspect of the general socialist argument for socialism rather than capitalism. Comparing socialist with capitalist agriculture, Marxists consider that the socialist form has four important advantages. First, it prevents rural exploitation, that is, the emergence of a rural proletariat side by side with an agrarian capitalist class. Secondly, it allows the rational use of the available resources. Thirdly, it ensures a rapid growth of the marketed output of agriculture. Fourthly, it provides a large source of resources for accumulation.[1] Consider each argument in turn.

Writers such as John Stuart Mill (1891), Doreen Warriner (1969) and Michael Lipton (1974) advocate organising agriculture on the basis of peasants or smallholders operating efficient, family-sized farms. On the basis of theoretical and empirical analysis Marxist researchers argue that this 'solution' to the agrarian problem is illusory. As Engels explained in his famous essay *The peasant question in France and Germany* (1894), 'we foresee the inevitable ruin of the small peasant'. The reasons for this are both social and technical. The former were clearly explained by Lenin in *The development of capitalism in Russia* (1956 edn p. 172), his classic study of Russian rural society in the 1890s. He found that in the Russian countryside,

> all those contradictions are present which are inherent in every commodity economy and every order of capitalism: competition, the

[1] The third and fourth arguments are often conflated. This is a serious source of confusion. It is entirely possible for the marketed output of agriculture to grow rapidly but for agriculture not to provide resources for industrialisation (for example if the marketed output is used to feed a repressive apparatus or is exported in exchange for armaments). Conversely, it is entirely possible for rapid industrialisation to be accompanied by a decrease in the net transfer of resources from agriculture (for example if the increase in industrial inputs in agriculture exceeds the increase in the marketed output of agriculture).

> struggle for economic independence, the snatching up of land (purchasable and rentable), the concentration of production in the hands of a minority, the forcing of the majority into the ranks of the proletariat, their exploitation by a minority through the medium of merchant capital and the hiring of farmworkers. There is not a single economic phenomenon among the peasantry that does not bear this contradictory form, one specifically peculiar to the capitalist system, i.e. that does not express a struggle and an antagonism, that does not imply advantage for some and disadvantage for others. It is the case with the renting of land, the purchase of land, and with 'industries' in their diametrically opposite types; it is also the case with technical progress in farming.

In addition, the Marxist–Leninist tradition lays considerable emphasis on the economies of scale which exist in agriculture as in industry. It also stresses the importance of technical progress, and the need for large units to take full advantage of it. The efficient use of tractors and other machinery requires land holdings larger and more consolidated than typical peasant holdings. All these factors ensure that the peasant, like the artisan, forms part of a mode of production which is destined to be wiped out by the higher labour productivity of large-scale production. Despite their theoretical opposition to it, the Bolsheviks did in fact implement a distributivist land reform in 1917–18, in order to gain political support at a crucial moment. Bolsheviks saw in the outcome the results that Marxist theory would lead one to expect, the emergence of a stratified society in which rich peasants employing wage labour coexisted with an increasing number of poverty stricken labourers.[2] Abdel-Fadil's (1976) sees in the aftermath of the distributivist Egyptian land reform of the 1950s a similar outcome.

The capitalist organisation of agriculture often coexists with substantial rural unemployment and underemployment. Why is this? There are three standard explanations, neoclassical, Keynesian and Marxist.

The neoclassical explanation concerns the marginal product of labour. This is illustrated in figure 4.1. DD' is the demand curve for labour. It is determined by the marginal product of labour. The supply curve of labour is given by SS'. In an economy where labour is scarce relative to land and other means of production the supply curve is $S_{LS}S'_{LS}$ and the equilibrium wage is w_{LS}. In an economy where labour is abundant relative

[2] This view of Soviet rural society in the 1920s was strongly challenged both at the time and subsequently. According to Shanin (1972 p. 199) the Bolshevik understanding was 'a misleading conception of rural society'.

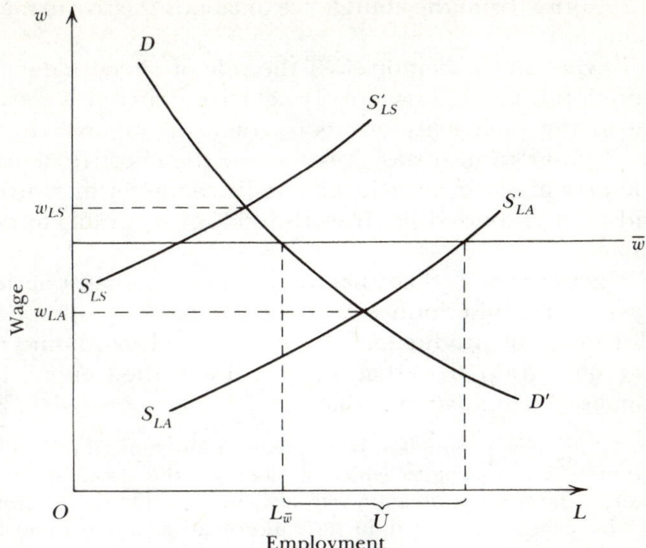

Figure 4.1 The cause of unemployment: the neoclassical view.

to the means of production the supply curve is $S_{LA}S'_{LA}$. The equilibrium wage is w_{LA}. Suppose the actual wage is $\overline{w}$ (e.g. because of custom, subsistence needs or the law). Then employment will be $L\overline{w}$ and unemployment will be *U*. The cause of the unemployment is the excessively high level of wages. Wage labour is an inefficient mode of labour organisation when the marginal product of part of the labour force that wishes to work at the prevailing wage rate is less than that wage. It is for this reason that narodniks argue that peasant farming is more efficient than wage labour in labour surplus economies. Whereas under wage labour, labour will only be employed till the marginal product of labour equals the wage rate and the remainder of the labourers will be unemployed, under peasant farming labour will be performed until the marginal product of labour is zero. As a result, in conditions of labour abundance, under peasant agriculture output will be higher (because more work is performed) and unemployment much lower (both because greater work is performed and because it is spread among family members) than under capitalist agriculture. If underemployment exists in peasant agriculture, the neoclassical view is that it must be caused by the zero marginal product of labour resulting from the abundance of labour relative to means of production.

The Keynesian view emphasises the role of effective demand in determining unemployment. If effective demand is too low relative to the availability of labour, then unemployment will result. The way to deal with it is to raise the effective demand for food products, e.g. by an income redistribution which diverts demand from imported luxuries to food, or by grants to poor consumers.

The Marxist view is that unemployment in capitalist agriculture (as in capitalist industry) is an inevitable result of the capitalist mode of production. Marx explained in volume 1 of *Capital* (1961 edn p. 642) that, in agriculture, the General Law of Capitalist Accumulation is that

> As soon as capitalist production takes possession of agriculture, and in proportion to the extent to which it does so, the demand for an agricultural labouring population falls absolutely, while the accumulation of the capital employed in agriculture advances, without this repulsion being, as in non-agricultural industries, compensated by a greater attraction. Part of the agricultural population is therefore constantly on the point of passing over into an urban or manufacturing proletariat, and on the look out for circumstances favourable to this transformation . . . But the constant flow towards the towns presupposes, in the country itself, a constant latent surplus-population, the extent of which becomes evident only when its channels of outlet open to exceptional width. The agricultural labourer is therefore reduced to the minimum of wages, and always stands with one foot already in the swamp of pauperism.

The function of the unemployed under capitalism is to depress wages[3] and ensure labour discipline.[4] The Marxist view is that under socialism, on the other hand, there is no social requirement for not using labour, and an obvious social need to employ all the available people.

Besides irrational use of labour, capitalist and pre-capitalist agriculture is often marked by the irrational use of land and other inputs. The causes of this can be analysed analogously.

During the process of economic development the growing urban population requires an expanding supply of agricultural

[3] The reserve army of unemployed ensures that (ibid. p. 620) 'The rise of wages [during the boom] . . . is confined within limits that not only leave intact the foundations of the capitalistic system, but also secures its reproduction on a progressive scale.'

[4] The reserve army of unemployed ensures that the employed workers (ibid. p. 636) 'submit to over-work and to subjugation under the dictates of capital'.

products. If the marketed output of agriculture does not grow then the supply of labour to industry is likely to be adversely affected. Socialists consider that the capitalist organisation of agriculture is likely to be less efficient in mobilising agricultural output for industry than the socialist organisation of agriculture.

Marxists also consider that collectivist agriculture can supply a major share of the resources required for rapid accumulation. In a speech at the July 1928 Plenum of the Communist Party's Central Committee, Stalin analysed the question of the origin of the resources required for Soviet industrialisation. He began by considering capitalist industrialisation.

In the capitalist countries industrialisation was usually effected, in the main, by robbing other countries, by robbing colonies or defeated countries, or with the help of substantial and more or less enslaving loans from abroad.

You know that for hundreds of years Britain collected capital from all her colonies and from all parts of the world, and was able in this way to make additional investments in her industry. This, incidentally, explains why Britain at one time became the 'workshop of the world'.

You also know that Germany developed her industry with the help, among other things, of the 5,000 million francs she levied as an indemnity of France after the Franco-Prussian war.

One respect in which our country differs from the capitalist countries is that it cannot and must not engage in colonial robbery, or the plundering of other countries in general. That way, therefore, is closed to us.

What then remains? Only one thing, and that is to develop industry, to industrialise the country with the help of *internal* accumulations...

But what are the chief sources of these accumulations? As I have said, there are only two such sources: firstly, the working class, which creates values and advances our industry; and secondly the peasantry.

The way matters stand with respect to the peasantry in this respect is as follows: it not only pays the state the usual taxes, direct and indirect; it also *overpays* in the relatively high prices for manufactured goods – that is in the first place, and it is more or less *underpaid* in the prices for agricultural produce – that is in the second place.

This is an additional tax levied on the peasantry for the sake of promoting industry, which caters for the whole country, the peasantry included. It is something in the nature of a 'tribute', of a supertax, which we are compelled to levy for the time being in order to preserve and accelerate our present rate of industrial development, in order to ensure an industry for the whole country...

It is an unpalatable business, there is no denying. But we should not be Bolsheviks if we slurred over it and closed our eyes to the fact that, unfortunately our industry and our country cannot *at present* dispense with this additional tax on the peasantry.

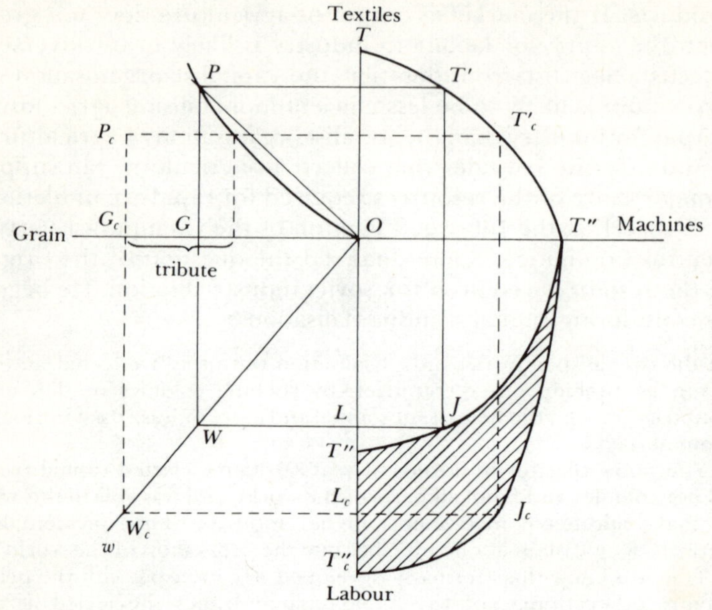

Figure 4.2 The tribute model.

Stalin's idea of the terms on which the marketed output of agriculture can be obtained, as a constraint on the rate of industrialisation, and of a tribute levied on agriculture as a source of resources for industrialisation, is illustrated in figure 4.2.

Figure 4.2 illustrates an economy with two sectors: industry and agriculture. Industry produces two goods, machines and textiles. It does this using machinery and workers. Workers are paid in grain which can only be obtained from the peasants who work in the agricultural sector. They exchange grain for textiles. The amount of grain supplied depends on the peasants' offer curve of grain for textiles. The amount of grain so obtained, and the wage rate in industry, simultaneously determine the labour force in industry in the subsequent period. Time is discrete.

The north-east quadrant shows the production possibility curve in industry. It is technically determined. At time (1), with initial stocks of machines and grain, the planners must choose a point on it – an output mix of machines and textiles. To produce at *T* would ensure that the peasants were well dressed, but entail zero production of machines, i.e. zero investment in industry. To produce at T'' would provide the maximum possible addition to the capital stock in industry, but would lead to the dissolution of the industrial labour force, and zero production in industry at time (2). The planners have to balance these considerations when choosing. Whatever point is chosen (say T') determines investment in industry and the stock of textiles available for sale to the peasantry.

These textiles are sold to the peasants and realise a quantity of grain (say OG) determined by the peasants' offer curve. (The slope of the vector from the origin to P gives the price ratio of the two goods.) The quantity of grain realised determines the point reached on the Ow line. The slope of the Ow line in the south-west quadrant is the grain wage of labour in industry, which is socially determined. The quantity of grain obtained from the peasants determines the point reached on the Ow line (say W) and hence the size of the labour force (OL) in time (2). The south-east quadrant shows the relationship between the labour force and the increment to the capital stock available for production in the industrial sector at time (2) for different choices of output mix at time (1). Given T' (and thus P, G, W, L and J) the production possibility curve TT'' for subsequent periods can be determined.

The model shows the initial capital stock, technology, the terms on which the peasants will sell grain and the real wage rate, simultaneously constraining growth. Assume that the rate of growth so determined is below that desired by the party. Then one way of raising the rate of growth is by the use of coercion to levy a tribute on the peasantry, i.e. to force them off their offer curve to point P_c. This is shown by that part of the figure in dashes. The transition from peasant agriculture to collectivist agriculture is assumed to raise grain procurements to OG_c. This enables more workers to be employed in industry, than with peasant farming, while simultaneously production of textiles is lower and investment higher. This enables the desired higher growth rate to be attained. In the figure, the additional combinations of labour and investment available in period (2) as a result of collectivisation is shown by the shaded area in the south-east quadrant.

Summary

Marxists consider that peasant farming is not a viable way of organising agriculture. Comparing capitalist agriculture with socialist agriculture, Marxists consider that the latter has four important advantages. First, it prevents rural exploitation. Secondly, it allows the rational use of the available labour and other resources. Thirdly, it ensures a rapid growth of the marketed output of agriculture. Fourthly, it provides a large source of resources for accumulation.

PROBLEMS OF COLLECTIVISM

In this section five problems of collectivist agriculture will be considered, economies of scale, labour incentives, the use of collective farms for taxation, inequality, and the use of administrative methods.

Economies of scale play an important role in Marxist–Leninist arguments about why peasant farming is not a viable way of organising agriculture. Experience, however, has shown that agriculture is fundamentally different from industry in that organising workers in large productive units does not in general raise productivity. As Joan Robinson (1964 p. 1) has explained,

> For the deployment of labour, a rather small scale is required. Workers are spread out over space so that discipline is hard to enforce; an incentive wage system is not easy to arrange or administer; there has to be a great diffusion of managerial responsibility; every field is different, every day is different and quick decisions have to be taken. For getting work out of the workers a peasant family is hard to beat. Discipline and responsibility are imposed by the pressing incentive to secure the family livelihood.

This is the main explanation of the abundant evidence (Dorner 1972 p. 120) that 'output per unit of land is inversely related to farm size'. As Lipton (1974 p. 289) has noted,

> Part of this relationship is spurious (because holding size is usually smaller on good soil), but much of it survives even in micro studies where the soil quality can be held constant. Small family farms can saturate the land with plenty of labour per acre, as there is little else for the labour to do (except perhaps at seasonal peaks). Large commercial farms must supervise labour and pay it the full market price, which is likely to rise if they buy too much of it. Another and more surprising fact is that, as Colin Clark has often emphasised, all the careful micro-work shows that *capital* per acre also increases as farm size declines...

Where labour is abundant relative to land, the efficient utilisation of scarce resources requires small, not large, units, a finding paradoxical from a Marxist–Leninist standpoint. Where there is a high labour–land ratio, the main production problem of agricultural development is to raise land productivity and not labour productivity. Hence the lesser gains in labour-abundant farming from organising labour in large units than in industry, where factories raise labour productivity by the division of labour. (The gains from the division of labour in agriculture are also limited by the sequential nature of much agricultural work.) Raising land productivity is largely a matter of the application of modern inputs such as artificial fertilisers.

In addition, there are also managerial diseconomies of scale in agriculture. The efficient large-scale organisation of labour requires efficient planning, administration and bookkeeping work which is unnecessary under peasant farming where each peasant organises his own work himself. The extent of this managerial diseconomy of scale depends on two factors. First, the size of the organisation. The bigger it is, the more serious the problem. Secondly, the educational level of the farmers. An important cause of the adverse effects of organising Chinese agriculture into communes in 1958 was the large size of the workforce per commune, in a society in which the majority of farmers were completely illiterate. They were incapable of handling even the simplest bookkeeping.

Although, in the area of the efficient deployment of agricultural labour, the Marxist–Leninist thesis of the advantages of large-scale organisation is invalid where labour is abundant relative to land, there are important areas in which the Marxist–Leninist thesis of the importance of economies of scale is correct. For example, transport and marketing. Furthermore, when land is scarce, the efficient use of land of different qualities requires specialisation, which is incompatible with peasant farming in the strict sense of the term. But specialisation is compatible with small holder farming – small-scale farming whose output is destined for the market – and with large-scale capitalist farming. Also, the division of land into fragmented plots, and the use of land for boundary lines, are common sources of waste in agriculture when there is private ownership of land. Obviously investment in irrigation, water control and land reclamation may require very large-scale organisations, as in the irrigated areas of Soviet Central Asia or the river valleys of China or the United States.

To establish effective labour incentives for collectivist agriculture is a difficult but very important task. In the USSR, where collectivist agriculture was first established, it was organised on what was virtually a feudal pattern. Work on the communal fields was enforced by coercion and paid almost nothing. The livelihood of the farmers was gained from their private plots, the right to which depended on their performance of labour for the collective farm. This system did produce an increased supply of basic wage goods for the towns, but only at the cost of a low level of labour productivity and very high costs of production in agriculture. In addition, half a century after the transition to collective farming the Soviet Government is still unable to provide the poulation with a continuous supply of high quality foods – fresh fruit and vegetables and meat. The absence of adequate labour incentives was a serious problem in Chilean agriculture under the *Unidad Popular*. The Chilean Socialist Party assumed that the consciousness of the villagers had been so transformed that material incentives could be neglected. As Lehmann (1974 p. 95) has observed, for this to have worked,

> there would have to be a high level of morally based co-operation among the *asentados*, in the absence of an effective material incentive. In practice, however, it was common to hear the argument that there is no point in a man working hard if another spends his time drinking. My interviews with workers and *asentados* in 1969, show a very clear concern for a fair return to physical effort expended in work. Thus, where there is a lack of trust among co-operators they prefer to turn their energies to the family economy where such a return is more secure.

In China, the need for material incentives has generally been recognised, and much of Maoist agricultural policy was directed to devising and implementing collective material incentives.

A serious threat to the success of collectivist agriculture (from the standpoint of the welfare of the villagers and the levels of productivity and output) is its treatment by the Government primarily as a source of taxation. A major purpose of Soviet collectivisation was precisely to raise rural taxation, or as Stalin put it in the passage already quoted, to levy a 'tribute' on the peasantry (see also Stalin 1955a pp. 52–9). This policy did provide the state with an increased supply of basic wage goods (bread, potatoes and cabbage). It also, however, contributed to a high-cost agriculture and chronic urban shortages of quality foods. Some observers consider that Soviet experience shows that although collectivisation is a *necessary* condition for the rational organisation of agriculture, it is not a *sufficient* condition. As Mao (1974a edn p. 64) expressed the lessons which the Chinese have drawn from the Soviet experience:

the experience of some socialist countries proves that even where agriculture is collectivised, where collectivisation is mismanaged it is still not possible to increase production. The root of the failure to increase agricultural production in some countries is that the state's policy towards the peasants is questionable. The peasants' burden of taxation is too high while the price of agricultural products is very low, and that of industrial goods very high. While developing industry, especially heavy industry, we must at the same time give agriculture a certain status by adopting correct policies for agricultural taxation, and for pricing industrial and agricultural products...[5] The collective needs accumulation, but we must be careful not to make too great demands on the peasants. We should not give them too hard a time. Except when we meet with unavoidable natural disasters, we should enable the peasants' income to increase year by year on the basis of increased agricultural production. [ibid. p. 70]

This sound analysis has been ignored in China during periods of Left enthusiasm, with corresponding adverse effects. The transition from collective to private farming in Yugoslavia in 1950 and to some extent in Poland in 1956 was not a sign of a widespread desire for the hard work, long hours and insecurity of peasant farming. It was a sign of the failure of a collectivist agriculture primarily concerned with the taxation of the peasants, and their control by the state, to satisfy the needs of the rural population.

From a socialist perspective, a major problem of collectivist agriculture is that its introduction and maintenance may be based on crude coercion and be incompatible with the transition to a society which is egalitarian and under social control. Collectivisation in the USSR was largely a matter of the application of state power to crush peasant farming, and was necessarily accompanied by widespread deportations. It created a hierarchical society, employing an unparalleled apparatus of repression and with a concentration of power akin to that of the Roman Empire. In China the Great Leap Forward led to an enormous increase in work done, most of which was wasted, and a dramatic fall in output. The inequality between those who had to do the extra

[5] This passage is not in the official text published in Mao Tse-tung (1977a). The latter, however, does include an equivalent passage on pp. 10–11. Similarly, although the exact words of the immediately following quotation do not appear in the official text, the same thought is expressed in very similar words on p. 12.

work and those who inspired the Leap, and the lack of social control over the decisions taken, were extreme.

A major negative aspect of collectivist agriculture in the CMEA countries, which has been copied elsewhere, is the use of administrative methods, such as instructions from above, rather than economic methods, such as price and tax policy, where the latter would be more efficient. The consequent growth of bureaucracy and decline of local initiative has been simply a dead loss to society.

Summary

There are five main problems of collectivist agriculture. First, the absence of some of the economies of scale postulated by Marxism–Leninism. Secondly, the need to design an effective system of labour incentives. Thirdly, the use of collective farms by the state primarily as instruments of taxation and control of the rural population. Fourthly, the extreme inequalities and lack of social control over decisions taken, to which it can lead. Fifthly, the use of administrative methods where economic methods are more efficient.

THE COERCIVE MODEL

The model

In *The Wealth of Nations* Adam Smith analysed 'previous accumulation', i.e. the accumulation the existence of which is a pre-condition for self-sustaining capitalist growth. Taking this notion as his starting point, Marx in Part VIII of *Capital* vol. I analysed 'the so-called original[6] accumulation'. He stressed two factors, the creation of new relations of production (the employment of propertyless labourers by capitalists) and the use of force. ('In actual history', wrote Marx in *Capital* vol. I chapter 26, 'it is notorious that conquest, enslavement, robbery, murder, briefly force, play the great part...The history of the [original accumulation]...is written in the annals of mankind in letters of blood and fire'.) During the Russian Civil War some Bolsheviks adapted Marx's concept to Soviet conditions and analysed 'original socialist accumulation'.

[6] Marx used the phrase 'ursprüngliche Akkumulation'. In the Moore–Aveling translation of *Capital* this is rendered as 'primitive accumulation'. Some writers, such as Gerschenkron and Sweezy, refer to 'original' or 'primary' accumulation, and this, as Pollitt (1971) has noted, is the better translation.

As interpreted, for example, in Bukharin's famous work *The economics of the transition period* (1920 pp. 101–2) original *socialist* accumulation has in common with original *capitalist* accumulation primarily the use of coercion to create a labour force. As such the concept provided a convenient rationalisation of party economic policy during the Civil War, for example the militarisation of labour and the use of force to obtain agricultural products. During NEP the concept was used by Preobrazhensky in the course of his well-known analysis of Soviet economic growth. As Szamuely (1974 p. 106) has noted, with special reference to a paper of 1921, Preobrazhensky's analysis of socialist construction

> builds its strategy on sharpening class struggle. We must notice, however, that in the author's eyes this is not the objective, but the unavoidable road to development...The precipitating cause with Preobrazhensky is not the defence of some ideal of economic organisation, but the requirement of economic growth. In other words, Preobrazhensky interprets the question 'who beats whom' of the transitional period as the question of the disposal of the surplus product, and not in terms of the fight for state power or economic competition between the capitalist and the socialist sectors; and this is why with him economic growth unavoidably leads to some political conflict which is resolved by armed contest. In his opinion this conflict will come the sooner, the faster is economic development. By this economic development he understands mainly industrialization, that is, the development of mechanical large-scale industry, at the expense of the surplus product of the 'petty-bourgeois environment' – that is, the peasantry. Faster industrialization is served by the concentration of resources for accumulation in the hands of the State, which again concentrates them in the chosen field of key importance. It is quite obvious, although Preobrazhensky never says so, that a fast development of this nature involves a neglect of large productive sectors – above all of agriculture – sharp breaks in the existing economic structure and the upsetting of economic equilibrium for a long time. To this extent, also his prophecies relating to political shocks and conflicts have their basis.

In the mid 1920s the idea of 'original socialist accumulation', i.e. of socialist construction by means of coercion against the peasantry, was decisively rejected by the party. In a well-known paper of 1925 (*Bol'shevik* No. 8) Bukharin argued that it was unnecessary and even harmful to the economy to carry on class warfare by administrative methods. If a 'St. Bartholomew's massacre' were organised for the village bourgeoisie, the socialist state would lose large resources for economic growth, which could otherwise be exploited for its purposes through channels of taxation and the banking system. In the late 1920s, however,

Table 4.1. *Marketed output of basic wage goods, USSR 1928–32*[a] *(millions of long tons)*

	1928	1929	1930	1931	1932
Grain	8.3	10.2	17.9	18.8	13.7
Potatoes	4.1	5.5	8.8	9.1	8.4
Vegetables	1.1	1.5	2.5	3.2	2.3

[a] Mass collectivisation in the USSR began in the autumn of 1929.
Source: Ellman (1975).

under the influence of the increasing difficulties with grain procurements and the criticism of party policy by the Left, views within the party changed.

In his speech in July 1928, quoted above, Stalin announced his acceptance of the need to levy a 'tribute' on the peasantry to provide resources for investment. At the end of 1929 he launched the policies of dekulakisation, collectivisation and taking grain.[7] These policies required the use of coercion on a large scale, over many years. The logic of Stalin's policy was analysed above.

The outcome

The collectivisation of agriculture in the USSR did lead to a sharp increase in the marketed output of basic wage goods (bread, potatoes and cabbage). This is shown in table 4.1. This increase in marketed output was not a result of increased production, but of the state taking products which would otherwise have been eaten by livestock or the rural population. Hence there was a catastrophic drop in livestock numbers in 1929–32 and a famine in 1932–3.

The collectivisation of agriculture in the USSR also provided a substantial increase in the urban labour force. The mass deportations from the villages, together with the sharp drop in animal products and grain supplies per capita, severely depressed rural living standards and drove millions of villagers to the towns.

Although the State did obtain an increased supply of wage goods as a result of collectivisation, it had to provide substantial

[7] For a description of the latter see Lewin (1974).

Table 4.2. *Unequal exchange between agriculture and industry in the USSR at selected dates (millions of labour adjusted roubles[a])*

	1913	1923/4	1928	1929	1930	1931	1932	1937	1938
Marketed output of agriculture[b]	5539	1956	3710	4581	4815	4882	3781	3458	3530
Consumer and producer goods obtained by agriculture from industry	1717	606	1836	2060	2358	2107	1950	2144	2152
Unequal exchange (row 1 – row 2)	3822	1350	1874	2521	2457	2776	1831	1314	1377
Coefficient of equivalentness (row 1 ÷ row 2)	3.22	3.22	2.02	2.22	2.04	2.31	1.94	1.61	1.64
Unequal exchange as a proportion of agricultural output, in %	36.30	17.00	18.80	27.70	27.50	31.10	21.70	15.70	16.70

[a] This is the unit in which Barsov measures (Marxian) values. 1 labour adjusted rouble is the average amount of labour time embodied in 1 rouble's worth of commodities in 1928. It may seem odd that the figures in row 1 for 1937 and 1938 compared with 1932, and in row 2 for 1937 and 1938 compared with 1930, should show declines. The reason for this is that the figures are in labour time, not units of output.

There is no reason to suppose that there would be a fundamental qualitative alteration in the situation depicted in the table if the unit of measurement were prices or quantities.

[b] 'Marketed output of agriculture' means products produced by agriculture and sold to the non-rural population or abroad. It excludes output sold by one farmer to another or to rural non-agriculture.

Source: Barsov (1974) p. 96. Barsov himself states that the precise figures should only be considered as approximations. Nevertheless, his work is based on detailed analysis of a wealth of published and unpublished statistics, some of high quality, and has to be taken seriously. The statistical sources used by Barsov for the compilation of the table are: for 1913 the calculations of Strumilin, Vainshtein and Dichter; for 1923/4 the official balances for that year published in 1926; for 1928–30 the unpublished official material product balances compiled in 1932; for 1931 & 1932 archival material; for 1937 & 1938 the unpublished official material product balances compiled in 1939. The 1928–30 balances are much in advance of the national income accounts available for other countries for this period, and form a landmark in the international history of social accounting. An English translation of them is forthcoming.

resources for agriculture. A significant share of Soviet investment since 1929 has always been devoted to agriculture. Much of this investment has been wasted. Collectivisation itself meant that much of the investment in tractors was simply required in order to offset the disinvestment in animal traction power caused by the state taking the grain which was needed to keep the animals alive. In addition, the very sharp increase in food prices on the free market meant that much of the squeeze on living standards was transferred to the working class. According to a Soviet researcher, the amount of unequal exchange was higher in 1913 than in any year of Soviet power, and higher in 1928 (i.e. prior to collectivisation) than in the late 1930s (i.e. after collectivisation). His results are set out in table 4.2.

The significance of table 4.2 is that it suggests that collectivisation did *not* lead to an increased net transfer of commodities from agriculture. Hence Stalin's 1928 implicit argument for collectivisation, based on the idea that it would lead to an increased net transfer of commodities to industry, turns out to have been wrong, at any rate in the Soviet case.

The actual process of accumulation which took place in the USSR during the first three five year plans differed in three important respects from that analysed in Preobrazhensky's book *The new economics.* First, there was no increase in unequal exchange between agriculture and industry. Secondly, the fall in urban real wages (what Trotsky had earlier termed 'the self-exploitation of the working class'), played an important role in financing the increase in accumulation. At the end of the First Five Year Plan, real wages per worker were only about half of what they had been at the beginning of it. The decline in working class living standards, however, was much less than the decline in real wages, because of the big increase in the urban participation rate (e.g. the abolition of urban unemployment during the First Five Year Plan). By the end of the Second Five Year Plan, urban per capita consumption was above that at the beginning of the First Five Year Plan. Thirdly, the whole process was based on coercion rather than use of the price mechanism.

After Stalin's death, the coercive model was gradually abandoned in the USSR and Eastern Europe. The reason for this was the adverse effect of the model on output and on the availability of quality foods in the towns. According to US specialists (Millar 1977), in 1951–75 total Soviet agricultural output grew at not less than 3.4% p.a. The population in this period grew at only 1.4% p.a., so that per capita output grew at c. 2% p.a. This was a very satisfactory performance, and one much better than in many other countries. Besides this quantitative improvement, there was also a qualitative improvement with a significant increase in the output of high quality products. Considered historically, the most important achievement of post-Stalin agricultural policy has been to eliminate famines in the USSR. Famines were endemic in Tsarist Russia. The USSR has experienced four famines, in 1921–22, 1932–34, 1941–43 and 1946–47. In addition, throughout the period 1931–52 Soviet people were dying of starvation or food deficiency diseases. (In the 1930s the USSR experienced a major malaria epidemic largely arising from food shortages.) As a result of the progress of the Soviet economy since the end of the Great Patriotic War, it seems entirely likely, however, that the famine of 1946–47 will be the last famine ever in Russia/USSR (save only in the wake of nuclear war). This is an achievement of fundamental importance in a country traditionally prone to famines.

The reasons for this impressive performance appear to be, a huge increase in modern inputs (e.g. chemical fertilisers and machinery), an improvement in the economic position of the farmers (whose real incomes have increased enormously in this period), an increase in the sown area and a more consumer-oriented economic policy. The latter is manifested by the fact that since the late 1960s the USSR has been investing in agriculture on an enormous scale, and that since the early 1960s it has been prepared to buy grain in large quantities from abroad, as is done by West European countries. The more consumer-oriented economic policy has only been possible because of the success of Soviet industrialisation.

Nevertheless, Soviet agriculture in the third quarter of the twentieth century suffered from four problems. First, its low initial level (largely resulting from the policies pursued in the previous quarter century). Secondly, the fact that it was a high-cost agriculture, requiring massive inputs of land, investment and labour. Thirdly, output, especially of grain, fluctuated sharply from year to year due to weather conditions. Fourthly, the investment, labour and price policies pursued in the distribution sector (see chapter 8) were not favourable to the general availability of good quality food.

Hungary under the NEM (which was a major break with the coercive model) is another example of successful collectivist agriculture. There has been a satisfactory rate of growth of output, labour productivity, food consumption and exports.

Nevertheless, from a Marxist–Leninist point of view, this is not entirely satisfactory as an example of successful socialist agriculture, for three reasons. First, the private sector still accounts for about a third of output and is particularly important in the production of pork, fruit, wine and vegetables. Secondly, the relatively high incomes earned by some farmers caused some dissatisfaction in a country that is supposed to be run in the interests of the working class. Thirdly, production cooperation agreements with capitalist firms (e.g. for the production of tractors and the development of intensive poultry and egg production) played some role in this progress.

Summary

In the coercive model, which was applied in the USSR under Stalin, the resources for rapid industrialisation are obtained from agriculture by coercion. The application of this model did enable the state to increase sharply its inflow of basic wage goods and its stock of labour. It also was, and is, an important explanation of the high costs and low productivity of Soviet agriculture. From the standpoint of intersectoral flows, the increase in marketed output of basic wage goods was offset by the decline in the marketed output of livestock products and the increased flow of industrial goods (e.g. investment goods) to agriculture. The increase in investment in the USSR after 1928 required both labour and commodities. The increase in the labour force came mainly from agriculture and was fed on food obtained from agriculture. The increase in commodities came largely from industry and construction themselves.

In a speech of 1928 Stalin considered two sources of Soviet accumulation, the working class and the peasantry. The purpose of Soviet collectivisation was to finance industrialisation by levying a tribute on the peasantry. In the outcome a large share of the burden *did* fall on the peasantry. Agricultural output fell but marketed output of basic wage goods rose, so that many peasants starved. Simultaneously, however, real wages fell (largely because of the scarcity of food) and employment enormously increased so that the major part of the contribution to the increase in investment came from the working class.

The coercive model was gradually abandoned in the USSR and the other CMEA countries after Stalin's death, because of its adverse effect on output.

THE MAOIST MODEL

The model

The Maoist model of agricultural development differs from the coercive in three main respects. First, whereas Soviet collectivisation was primarily aimed at collecting tribute, Chinese collectivisation was primarily aimed at increasing output. Secondly, in the Maoist model a major role in rural social transformation is played by the rural party organisations. Thirdly, in the Maoist model great efforts are made to utilise fully all the available resources.

Because China embarked on collectivisation long after the USSR, it was able to learn from the experience of the USSR. In *On the ten major relationships* (1956) Mao referred to 'the prolonged failure of the Soviet Union to reach the highest pre-October level in grain output'. The conclusion he drew, as can be seen from the passage quoted on p. 91 above, is that the Soviet stress on collecting tribute had hindered production. A successful collective agriculture, with rising production, required that the real income of the peasantry should grow steadily. In accordance with this line of analysis, in China the marketed output of grain *fell*, both absolutely and relatively, after collectivisation, in marked contrast with the situation in the USSR. This is shown in table 4.3.

Because it came to power after a long civil war in which its strength lay in rural areas, the Chinese Communist Party had very large numbers of rural cadres and a considerable knowledge of rural social conditions when it achieved power. This was a complete contrast with the situation in the USSR and had many important policy consequences. For example, whereas land reform in the USSR was a mainly spontaneous process, in China it was organised and directed by the party. Similarly, collectivisation in China did not have to be primarily extractive because the strength of the rural party organisations enabled the Government to obtain quite a high rate of marketed output even with private ownership, as can be seen from table 4.3. In addition, whereas Soviet collectivisation relied heavily upon direct coercion, the Chinese cadres generally succeeded in organising collectivisation without employing direct coercion.

In traditional rural China there existed substantial surplus labour during the farming off-season (November–February),

Table 4.3. *Collectivisation and grain extraction USSR and China (millions of tons[a])*

	(1) Output	(2) Net marketed output	(3) (2) as % of (1)
		USSR[b]	
1928	73.1	8.3	11.4
1929	71.7	10.2	14.2
1930	77.2	17.9	23.2
1931	69.5	18.8	27.0
1932	69.6	13.7	19.7
		China[c]	
1953–54	142.5	24.4	17.1
1954–55	145.4	22.0	15.1
1955–56	158.4	24.8	15.7
1956–57	165.9	18.7	11.3

[a] The absolute magnitudes of the output figures for the USSR and China are not comparable because:

(1) The figures for the USSR are in long tons and for China in metric tons.

(2) The figures for the USSR were compiled by a conventional procedure which should have given figures which are comparable with each other. There is no reason to suppose, however, that it gave figures comparable with those for other countries.

(3) The figures for Chinese grain output in the table are for rice (husked), wheat, coarse grains, potatoes (measured in grain equivalent) and soya beans. (They differ from the most frequently quoted grain output series mainly because rice is measured husked not unhusked. In addition the series in the table includes soya beans and is for agricultural years not calendar years.) The Soviet figures are for rye, wheat, barley, oats, buckwheat, millet, maize (i.e. corn) and other grains.

[b] Collectivisation in the USSR began at the end of 1929 and embraced the majority of peasant households by the end of 1932.

There is some uncertainty about the Soviet grain output statistics for 1928–32. In particular, it is possible that output was less in 1932 than in 1931.

[c] Collectivisation in China took place mainly in 1955–56.

Sources: Ellman (1975) p. 847, Nolan (1976) p. 199.

unutilised natural resources (e.g. limestone, coal, rivers suitable for the generation of hydro-electricity) and an acute shortage of modern inputs (e.g. chemical fertilisers, farm machinery and electricity) for agriculture. A major aspect of the Maoist model was an attempt to use fully the available resources to the greatest extent possible in the interests of agriculture. This took a number of forms.

First, the use of off-season farm labour for labour-intensive rural infrastructure activities. These included the construction of water control and irrigation systems, land terracing, afforestation, road building, the construction of schools, hospitals, other public buildings and housing. Since the labourers on these projects were usually paid in work points[8] issued by their normal production teams, and construction machinery was conspicuous by its absence, the cost to the state was zero or very little. The advantage of this system is that extra output is produced at zero or very small state opportunity cost. The disadvantages are that arduous work is performed during time which may well have considerable private opportunity costs for the labourers (e.g. in terms of leisure or household activities), that it may have an adverse effect on agricultural output (if some of the labour is not really surplus or if the resulting reduction in food and cash payments per work point has disincentive effects), and that the output may be useless (like the Pyramids of Ancient Egypt) or harmful (e.g. badly planned irrigation projects).

Secondly, the development of rural small-scale industries. By rural small-scale industries is meant industrial enterprises administratively subordinated to counties, communes or brigades, and not to higher level bodies. Being subordinate to a county usually implies obtaining the bulk of inputs, and distributing the bulk of outputs, within the county. Rural small-scale industry is not necessarily rural (some of it is located in county towns) and is not always so small (some plants employ more than 500 people). Its essential characteristics are that it largely functions outside the state planning and administrative system, that output per plant and per person is much lower than in the state sector, that it often makes more use of indigenous technology than the state industrial sector with its large plants often using imported machinery, that it is mainly concerned with serving agriculture, that it mainly uses local resources and that average employment per plant is less than in the state industrial sector. It is a sector which has evolved substantially over time and been heavily influenced by the course of political events. It began during the Great Leap Forward, was generally closed down in 1961 and 1962, and was revived again during and after the Great Proletarian Cultural Revolution. The main rural small-scale industries are energy (e.g. hydro-electricity and coal mining), iron and steel, chemical fertilisers, cement and farm machinery.

Many of the rural small-scale industries set up at the time of

[8] The 'work point' system is explained in chapter 7.

the Great Leap Forward were very inefficient, producing poor quality products at high cost. During and after the Cultural Revolution they seem to have been more rational, using local resources to produce goods useful for agriculture. Small nitrogen fertiliser plants, for example, seem to have played a useful role in a country where food output, foreign exchange and engineering capability for large process plants are all serious constraints slowing down development. Nevertheless, from 1976, as the large imported modern plants come on stream, the share of output contributed by the rural small-scale sector is expected to decline. Similarly, in the cement industry there was a rapid expansion of the number and output of cement plants in the rural areas in the late 1960s and early 1970s. This seems to have been rational in view of the high transport costs and usefulness of the output. Indeed, the cement industry is regarded by Sigurdson (1977) as the most successful of the rural small-scale industries. An American engineer who inspected some of these plants has suggested, however ('American' 1977 chapter 7), that they had been a useful expedient, but because of their low productivity and the not very high quality of their output, only a temporary one. The rural small-scale iron and steel industry seems to have been the least successful in view of its high costs and the poor quality of much of the output. The spread of rural electrification (mainly for productive purposes) is, of course, a radical and very progressive development for a huge and overwhelmingly agricultural country.

The main advantage of the rural small-scale sector is that it can use resources which have a zero state opportunity cost to produce goods useful for agriculture. It can also play a useful role in adapting labour to industry. The main disadvantages seem to be that productivity is low and quality often low also. On the whole it seems to be a justified but temporary expedient under conditions of extreme scarcity of resources, which facilitates a more efficient allocation of resources than would otherwise have taken place.

The Maoist attempt to use all the resources available in rural areas in the interests of agriculture in striking contrast to the coercive model. A feature of the Soviet manpower scene in the Stalin period, and to a lesser extent also in the 1950s and 1960s, was the existence and persistence of rural underemployment. The main cause of this was political. The Bolsheviks viewed the countryside as a source of tribute and possible political enemies and neglected the welfare of the rural population. In China on the other hand, rural infrastructure projects, rural small-scale industries, farm subsidiary enterprises and handicrafts have been encouraged. (Private rural enterprise has, of course, been severely restricted, to an extent which has fluctuated over time.) The Chinese Communist Party has viewed the abundance of rural labour as a great resource and striven to make the best use of it. Households, teams, brigades and communes (like a peasant family) have an incentive to use labour till its marginal product is zero. Unlike private ownership, however, their existence does not lead to a stratification of rural society into owners and labourers. It also enables large-scale projects to be tackled. Similarly, in Hungary a feature of the reaction against the coercive model was the encouragement given to the subsidiary activities of the collective farms in the early years of the NEM.

The outcome

During the 1950s, there was a rapid transformation of rural social relations in China. A large-scale land reform in 1950–52 (mostly in 1950 and 1951) was followed by the organisation of mutual aid teams, cooperatives (first elementary and then advanced) and finally communes (1958). The transition from peasant agriculture to fully socialist cooperatives (i.e. collectivisation) mainly took place in 1955–56. Collectivisation in China was much more successful than in the USSR in a number of important respects. First, there was no decline in grain output. Secondly, there was no dramatic decline in livestock numbers. For example, in the two years 1928–30, the number of pigs in the USSR fell by 47% and by 1932 had fallen still further. In China, on the other hand, the number of pigs fell by only 17% in 1954–56, and then increased in 1956–58. Thirdly, it required far fewer deaths as a proportion of the rural population. Fourthly, it was not accompanied by the death or deportation of the best farmers.[9] This greater success resulted from the non-extractive nature of the

[9] To some extent this comparison is too favourable to China. As far as the triumph of voluntarism is concerned, the Chinese analogy with the year of the breakthrough (1929) was not 1955–56 but the Great Leap Forward (1958). This, like its Soviet counterpart, did lead to a significant decline in output of crops and livestock numbers and deaths from starvation. As far as political violence in the countryside is concerned, the peak period in China appears to have been not collectivisation (1955–56) but land reform. According to one source (Bandyopadhyaya 1976 p. 45) during land reform approximately 11 million households of landlords and rich peasants (about 50 million person) were subjected to severe struggle, of whom about 20 million persons were sentenced to execution, imprisonment or banishment.

collectivisation, the greater strength of the party in the countryside and the possibility which China had (but which the USSR as the pioneer did not have) of learning from the experience of other countries. An important aspect of the latter point was that collectivisation was better prepared and planned in China than in the USSR, where basic issues such as the private plot were only worked out during and after the collectivisation process. Nevertheless, this gain relative to the Soviet experience was thrown away by the Great Leap Forward, which led to a sharp fall in crop output and livestock numbers. The revolutionary euphoria of 1958–59 in certain party circles in China, like that of 1929–30 in the USSR (and also like that during the Civil War in the USSR and in the 1960s in Cuba) had a severe negative effect on output.

The main achievements of the 1950s were an immense increase in labour inputs (e.g. into irrigation works) and a substantial change in the distribution of income. An important aspect of the latter was a substantial reduction in rural income inequality (see chapter 7 below). Another important aspect was the increase in the share of the national income going to accumulation as a result of redirecting what was formerly property income derived from agriculture (Lippit 1975). Much of the increased labour input (e.g. into backyard steel furnaces and poorly planned irrigation projects) was wasted. The increase in agricultural output was modest. The combination of these factors ensured a sharp fall in real income per unit of labour input and this, together with the 1958–59 attempt to move towards distribution according to need, led to a decline in labour incentives. This, together with the managerial diseconomies of scale in agriculture, was an important cause of the three bad harvests 1959–61.[10] During the following years output has risen, largely as a result of the application of modern inputs (e.g. chemical fertilisers). The increase in labour inputs made possible by collectivisation has played an indispensable role in the development of the labour-intensive rural infrastructure activities and the rural small-scale industries, described above.

The exaggeration in Maoist theory of the extent to which it is possible efficiently to change relations of production prior to

[10] Other causes were a reduction in the sown area and poor weather (which was stressed in published official documents). In the present state of ignorance it appears impossible to assess precisely the relative importance of these causes. According to a Red Guard publication of 1967, Liu Shao-chi, then Head of State, charged that the crisis of 1959–61 was 70% man-made and only 30% attributable to natural calamities.

changes in the forces of production, explains the resurgence of the family as the basic unit of consumption and of a considerable part of production in the wake of the economic crisis of 1959–61. Precisely because the forces of production were unchanged, the advantages of the family for the deployment of labour (see p. 88 above) remained. As Donnithorne (1967 p. 91) noted a few years after the Great Leap Forward,

> The resurgence of the rural family as the basic unit of consumption and of a considerable part of production, has been the most striking feature in China's countryside. Its efficiency as an economic unit is due to the immediacy of the incentives to hard work and thrift and to the convenient way in which its multifarious aspects dovetail into each other. Domestic swill feeds livestock; manure nourishes land; farm and handicraft products can be taken together to market; the surveillance of children, of livestock and of cooking can be carried on simultaneously with the production of handicrafts or care of vegetables and fruit trees near the house. Thus, odds and ends of materials and of the time of young and old are used to better advantage than when these varied activities are carried on in specialized fashion by different people. Greater differentiation of roles must await changes in productive methods.

The main problem of Chinese agriculture is the low level of output, rate of growth of output and productivity (Padoul 1975). Although there is considerable uncertainty about both population and output data, it seems likely that in the twenty five years 1952–77 there was no significant increase in Chinese per capita grain production. Indeed, according to some estimates, grain output per head throughout the existence of the People's Republic has been below that of the 1930s. According to one estimate (Howe 1978 p. 171), average per capita consumption of grain in China in the 1970s is only 25 per cent above that in notoriously poverty stricken Bangladesh.

An Indian economist (Bandyopadhyaya 1976 chapter 5) has argued that in 1952–73 the rate of growth of grain output in China was only $^2/_3$ of that in India. This is rather a striking finding. Is it true, and if so what are its implications?

In assessing this result and its implications, the following should be borne in mind. Calculation of the rate of growth of grain output in China is very sensitive both to the base date chosen and the production figures used for the base period. For example, using official production data, the average annual rate of growth of grain output up to 1974 is the very respectable rate of 3.6% if 1949 is taken as a base, but only the less satisfactory 2.4% if 1952 is taken as a base. Similarly, if official data are used for 1952, the 1952–73 growth rate is 2.4%, whereas if the higher figure for 1952 estimated by outside observers is used, the rate comes down to 2.1%. In view of the fact that 1949 was a civil war year and 1952 a relatively normal year, it seems sensible to take 1952 as a base. On the other hand, which, if either, figure for 1952 grain output is the correct one, is difficult to judge. Indeed, in considering Chinese grain output statistics one has to bear in mind the possibility that grain output, like the size of the population, is one of those extremely important things for which the Peking authorities simply do not have accurate data. In 1956 Chou En-lai stated that (Chao 1970 p. 187) 'We are not yet completely clear as to what the actual amount of food production was in 1954.'

Furthermore, taking 1952 as a base and using the higher 1952 output figure, as Bandyopadhyaya does, one notes that the whole of the Indian superiority arises from the aftermath of the Great Leap Forward. For 1952–58 Bandyopadhyaya estimates the rate of growth of Chinese grain production at 3.3% and for 1963–73 at 3.9%. The average for these two sub-periods taken together is greater than the Indian growth rate. In addition, since Chinese yields per unit of land were higher than those for India throughout the period, one would expect increases in yield to be easier in India than in China. Moreover, the currently available figures suggest that in 1952–73 the rate of growth of population was greater in India than in China. This means that the difference in the rate of growth of grain output per capita, the measure relevant for welfare purposes, was less than that for the rate of growth of output. Indeed, according to a US estimate (CIA 1976) the Chinese population control programme achieved significant successes in the 1970s. This suggests that an important Maoist contribution to improving the Chinese food situation was a successful programme of population control. In addition, it is not clear whether Bandyopadhyaya's 15% deduction from the Chinese output data to allow for the fact that, unlike the Indian output data, they do not refer to barn output, is appropriate after 1960. Furthermore, if instead of taking 1952–53 as a base, one takes 1953–54 as a base, then even on Bandyopadhyaya's own figures (1976 chapter 5 table 5) the Chinese record in grain production per head is (marginally) better than the Indian. Moreover, in China, unlike India, the rate of growth of non-grain food products (i.e. vegetables, fruit, fish and livestock products) seems to have been significantly greater than for grain.

Perhaps the main conclusions to be drawn from this comparison are as follows:

(1) Taking the period 1952–73 as a whole, there is no satisfactory evidence of a higher rate of growth of grain output or grain output per head in China than in India.

(2) The Chinese record was affected very adversely by the Great Leap Forward and its aftermath. In both 1953–58 and 1963–73 the rate of growth of grain output per head in China appears to have exceeded that in India.

(3) In 1952–73 both countries had rates of growth of output and of output per head inadequate to ensure substantially rising real incomes and to feed rapidly growing urban populations.

(4) In both countries, in the 1950s emphasis was placed on social changes (e.g. land reform, cooperatives, communes) as a means of raising land productivity. In the 1960s, however, emphasis switched to technological change (e.g. improved seed and implements, the provision of fertilisers and insecticides).

How adequate is the diet which the Chinese people receive? This is difficult to judge in the absence of data on disease and nutrition. The fragmentary information available suggests that since the establishment of the People's Republic, death rates have fallen sharply, infant mortality has fallen dramatically and life expectancy has increased substantially. It would seem that, on the whole, food supplies in the People's Republic have been adequate for basic needs, excepting 1959–62 when food availability fell below subsistence minimum in some regions and there were deaths from food deficiency diseases. How many deaths is not clear, in the absence of satisfactory population statistics. Orleans' estimates of China's population (*China* 1975 p. 77) imply a figure of roughly 4 million premature deaths in 1959–62. On the other hand, a Soviet estimate (*Ekonomika KNR* 1976 p. 46) using a different time series for China's population, is that the population in 1962 was about 24 million less than it would have been if the population had grown in 1959–62 at the rate at which it was growing in the mid 1950s. (Not all the 24 million represents deaths, of course. Part represents a fall in births.) Which, if either of these estimates is anywhere near the truth, is impossible to say in the present state of ignorance.

The main achievement of Chinese agricultural policy has not been in the field of production but of distribution. It seems that, except in 1959–62, the authorities have normally been able to provide the basic minimum of food, clothing, shelter, education and employment to the entire population. As Sinha (1975 pp. 218–19) has noted,

> with the present state of quantitative information one cannot say whether the [average] levels of food consumption in China today are better or worse than in the mid-1930s. But one can easily say that because of the egalitarian policies the level of food consumption of the poorer people is much better now than it was in the 1930s. For the same reason it can be said that poorer people in China are eating better than in India or that the Chinese can withstand food scarcity better than the Indians. In the commune-type of organisation, where the value of a work-point varies with output, the income and food consumption of each member is linked directly with output. In bad years income and food consumption of everyone goes down. Under Indian conditions of private property and wage employment, the employment of agricultural labour and poor peasants who live partly on wage employment is drastically curtailed in times of drought, thereby reducing their capacity to buy food, especially when food prices are rising. As such, they become easy victims to food scarcity.

Has Chinese collectivisation enabled the net transfer of resources from agriculture to industry to be increased? According to a recent survey of the evidence (Paine 1976 p. 285), 'although data problems preclude any firm conclusion about the absolute magnitude of the intersectoral resource transfer in any particular year, the direction of the transfer [i.e. a steady shift *in favour* of agriculture] during the first half of the 1950s is clear in *relative* terms from both the financial and real standpoints'. As far as the policies pursued since the end of the 1959–61 economic crisis are concerned (ibid. p. 295), 'Whether or not these policies merely reduced the extent of agriculture's net contribution to accumulation in the rest of the economy or turned it into a net deficit sector is not clear.' In other words, Chinese experience, like Soviet experience, indicates that the argument for collectivisation based on its alleged efficacy in increasing net transfers from agriculture to industry, is wrong.

Summary

The main differences between the coercive and Maoist models of the role of agriculture in socialist economic development have been that the latter did not emphasise tribute collection and did emphasise the role of the rural cadres and the need to mobilise fully all the resources available in rural areas in the interest of agriculture. The outcome of Chinese agricultural policy has been rates of growth of output and output/head which have been modest by international standards. The main achievement appears to have been to ensure a basic minimum of food, clothing, shelter, education and employment for virtually all the population.

CONCLUSION

Marxists consider that peasant or smallholder farming is not a viable way of organising agriculture. Comparing capitalist with socialist agriculture, Marxists consider that the latter has four important advantages. First, it prevents rural exploitation. Secondly, it allows the rational use of the available labour and other resources. Thirdly, it facilitates a rapid increase in the marketed output of agriculture. Fourthly, it helps transfer resources for investment from agriculture to industry. The experience of collectivisation in various countries shows that it has a number of problems, e.g. the absence of some of the postulated economies of scale, labour incentives, the use of collective farms for taxation, inequality, and the use of administrative methods. It also shows that the third and fourth arguments for collectivisation are erroneous. In addition, it shows that the first argument ignores the enormous inequalities of power and lack of social control over decisions taken, to which collectivisation normally leads.

The practice of collectivisation in various countries has differed very much, as a result of different conditions, notably the relationship between the revolutionary party and the peasantry. For example, whereas Soviet experience provides a counterexample for the second argument for collectivisation, Chinese experience provides partial corroboration for it. Similarly, whereas Soviet experience is an example for the third argument as far as basic wage goods are concerned, Chinese experience seems to be a counterexample for it (although absence of data makes it impossible to be sure about the rate of growth of marketed output since collectivisation).

In the USSR the coercive model of collectivist agriculture was successful in increasing the marketed output of basic wage goods, and the urban labour force. It also created, however, a quasi-feudal social system and a high-cost low-productivity agriculture. It was abandoned after 1953 because of its adverse effect on output. In China, assessment of the Maoist model is hampered by lack of data. It appears, however, that the Maoist model led to the provision of a basic minimum of food, clothing, shelter, education and employment for virtually all the population. It did not, however, lead to a satisfactory rate of growth of output.

Neither the coercive model, nor the Maoist model, of collectivist agriculture, is suitable for a country aiming at a rapid rate of growth of agricultural output or equality. As far as collectivist agriculture in general is concerned, like private agriculture, it is compatible with a wide range of outcomes, favourable and unfavourable, depending on non-ownership factors.

SUGGESTIONS FOR FURTHER READING

General

A. Bhaduri, 'On the formation of usurious interest rates in backward agriculture', *Cambridge Journal of Economics* vol. 1 no. 4 (December 1977).

M. Ellman, 'On a mistake of Preobrazhensky and Stalin', *Journal of Development Studies* (April 1978).

S. Ishikawa, *Economic development in Asian perspective* (Tokyo 1967).

R. P. Sinha, *Food and poverty* (London 1976).

USSR

E. Strauss, *Soviet agriculture in perspective* (London 1969).

J. R. Millar, 'The prospects for Soviet agriculture', *Problems of Communism* (May–June 1977).

Eastern Europe

East European economies post-Helsinki (Joint Economic Committee US Congress, Washington DC 1977) pp. 289–378.

China

V. D. Lippit, *Land reform and economic development in China* (New York 1975).

P. Schran, *The development of Chinese agriculture 1950–1959* (Illinois 1969).

K. Chao, *Agricultural production in Communist China 1949–1965* (Madison 1970).

R. P. Sinha, 'Chinese agriculture: A quantitative look', *Journal of Development Studies* vol. 11 (April 1975).

T. P. Bernstein, 'Leadership and mass mobilisation in the Soviet and Chinese collectivisation campaigns of 1929–30 and 1955–56: A comparison', *China Quarterly* no. 31 (July–September 1967).

P. Nolan, 'Collectivisation in China – some comparisons with the USSR', *Journal of Peasant Studies* vol. 3 no. 2 (January 1976).

China: A reassessment of the economy (Joint Economic Committee US Congress, Washington DC 1975) pp. 324–435.

J. Sigurdson, *Rural industrialisation in China* (Cambridge, Mass. 1977).

The American rural small-scale industry delegation, *Rural small-scale industry in the People's Republic of China* (Berkeley 1977).

K. Bandyopadhyaya, *Agricultural development in China and India* (New Delhi 1976).

J. E. Nickum, 'Labour accumulation in rural China and its role since the cultural revolution', *Cambridge Journal of Economics* vol. 2 no. 3 (September 1978).

H. J. Groen & J. A. Kilpatrick, 'China's agricultural production', *Chinese economy post-Mao* (Joint Economic Committee US Congress, Washington DC 1978) vol. 1 pp. 607–52.

5

INVESTMENT PLANNING

For many economists investment is a purely technical process, the introduction into production of more and better machines. For a Marxist, however, accumulation has both technical and social aspects. Marx and Engels were, naturally, as fascinated as their contemporaries by the new machinery which the Industrial Revolution had created. They were, also, however, concerned with the origins and development of capitalist society. Marx objected to contemporary explanations of how 'previous' accumulation had come into being. He suggested that for the vulgar economists of his time it played about the same role in economics as original sin in theology. 'In times long gone by,' he wrote in *Capital* vol. 1 chapter 26, 'there were two sorts of people: the diligent, intelligent, and, above all, frugal elite: the other, lazy rascals, spending their substance, and more, in riotous living...Thus it came to pass that the former sort accumulated wealth, and the latter sort had nothing to sell except their own skins.' Marx attacked this notion and argued that the essence of Smith's 'previous' accumulation was actually 'the historical process of divorcing the producer from the means of production' commonly by force, e.g. the English enclosures and the Scottish clearances. The 'epoch-making' moments in the history of original accumulation are those when 'great masses of men are suddenly and forcibly torn from their means of subsistence, and hurled as free and "unattached" proletarians on the labour market'. In the development of the capitalist economy, Marx argued, the 'expropriation of the agricultural producer, of the peasant, from the soil, is the basis of the whole process'. Similarly, in *Capital* vol. 1 part 4 he explained how the concentration of workers into factories and the development of machinery under capitalism was not a purely technical phenomenon but had important social aspects. These included, the authority of the managerial hierarchy, the divisions between managers, foremen, skilled and unskilled workers, the extension of the working day, the intensification of labour, the separation of planning and implementation, the conflict between workers and capitalists, cyclical unemployment and the degradation of the worker.

In this chapter five technical problems of investment planning will be considered. They are, the share of investment in the national income, the allocation of investment between sectors of an economy, industry planning, the technical form of the investment and investment cycles. (Some of these decisions may well be interdependent, as Sen (1968 pp. 9–10) has noted.) The Marxist problem of the development of new relations of production will not be completely neglected, however, but will be considered in chapters 6 and 10.

THE SHARE OF INVESTMENT IN THE NATIONAL INCOME

The problem of deciding what proportion of the national income ought to be invested is of great practical importance and has generated a vast theoretical literature. Three different approaches will be considered here, the utility maximising, descriptive and growth maximising.

The utility maximising approach

In this approach the problem is to maximise a utility function subject to certain constraints. Graphically the situation is as depicted in figure 5.1. If net investment were zero, in the absence of technical progress, the situation would be as shown by consumption path (1), a constant rate of consumption. If a small amount of present consumption is sacrificed, then a consumption path such as (2), which grows steadily over time, is possible. Similarly, if more present consumption is sacrificed, then higher growth rates and ultimately higher levels of consumption, as on paths (3) and (4), are possible. The question is, which path should be chosen?

Either we consider a situation in which there is a finite time horizon, or one in which there is an infinite time horizon. In the first case, the solution is largely determined by the length of the time period and the valuation of the terminal capital stock. In the second case two possibilities have been considered.

The first is to reduce the infinite case to the finite case by

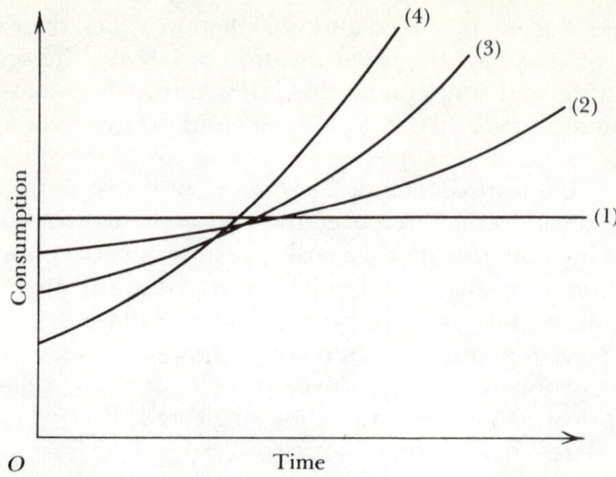

Figure 5.1 Feasible consumption paths.

introducing an horizon, consumption beyond which does not count. This has been done in two ways. One way was Ramsey's concept of 'Bliss', a hypothetical level of consumption which satiates all desires. This assumption may have appealed to a Fellow of King's College, Cambridge, who had everything that man could reasonably want, but its general plausibility is open to question, to say the least. The other way is to introduce a discount rate to make infinite consumption streams comparable. The logic of pure time preference, *for an immortal society*, is doubtful. It is, however, a sound idea to introduce a discount rate on the assumptions that per capita consumption is rising over time and that the marginal social significance of consumption is inversely related to the level of per capita consumption. Its numerical determination, however, raises numerous difficult issues (*Guidelines* 1972 chapter 13).

The second is to introduce a preference ordering of all the feasible consumption streams between now and infinity. The main problem with this approach is how to determine the preference ordering. The chief attraction of those orderings which have been considered in the literature is their mathematical tractability. Furthermore, on the usual assumptions, the 'optimal' share of accumulation in the current national income is excessively high (because future consumption has not been discounted).

The main weakness of the utility maximising approach,

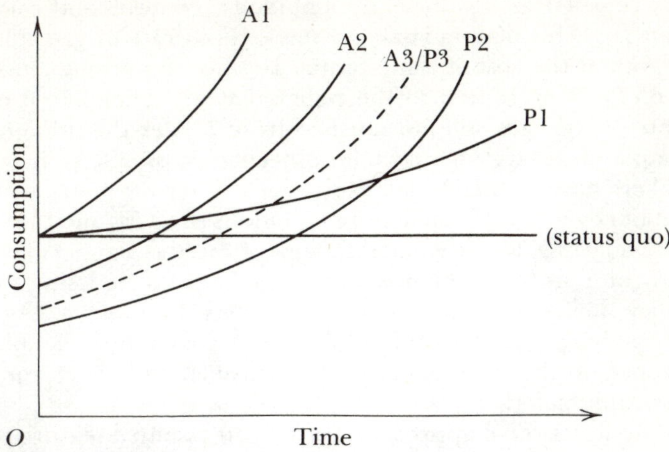

Figure 5.2 The convergence of aspirations and feasibilities.

however, is that the problem that it tackles is not the one which planners face. Economic policy is not decided by people who start off from a well-defined preference ordering of all the feasible consumption streams between now and infinity. This observation is the starting point for the descriptive approach.

The descriptive approach

The descriptive approach has been developed by the distinguished Hungarian economist Kornai in his (1970). It begins from the proposition that the plan formulation process as it actually takes place is primarily a process of interaction between the aspirations of the political authorities and the tentative plans which have been explored by the planners. Diagramatically, this idea can be represented as in Figure 5.2. A plan is necessary because the status quo, in which consumption remains steady over time, is regarded as unsatisfactory by the policy makers. Accordingly they instruct the planners to calculate a plan which ensures rising consumption over time. The planners come up with *P1*, which enables consumption to rise over time without any sacrifice of present consumption. The policy makers were hoping, however, for a plan such as *A1*, which, without any sacrifice in current consumption, would enable consumption to grow at a rapid rate. Hence they reject *P1* as inadequate. The planners, noting that their previous plan was rejected as insufficiently ambitious, go away and calculate plan *P*2. This plan envisages a more rapid rate of growth than *P*1, but at the cost of a substantial sacrifice in present consumption. *P*2 is presented to the policy makers. They like it better than *P*1, but are still not satisfied by it. Under the influence of the planners' arguments about objective possibilities, the policy makers have reduced their aspirations. They now only aspire to *A*2, but even this is much more ambitious than *P*2, and therefore they reject *P*2 as inadequate. In view of this the planners go away and compute a new plan, *P*3. On receiving and analysing *P*3, the policy makers reduce their aspirations further, to *A*3. An acceptable plan has been found (*A*3/*P*3), which the policy makers accept and the planners regard as feasible, and which can now be promulgated.

The descriptive approach captures an essential feature of the socialist planning process, that plans are worked out by a process of interaction between the aspirations of the political leaders and the calculation by technicians of what is feasible. It does not, however, throw any light on the normative question of what the share of investment in the national income ought to be. For an attempt to answer this question we turn to the growth maximising approach.

The growth maximising approach

This argument has been developed by the Yugoslav economist Horvat in his (1958). It is based on three assumptions. First, that the objective of economic policy is to maximise the rate of growth. Secondly, that the marginal productivity of investment is a diminishing function of the share of investment in the national income. Thirdly, that the marginal productivity of investment reaches zero well before the share of investment in the national income reaches 50%, because an economy has a maximum absorptive capacity. 'The easiest way to use this concept is to conceive the economy as a giant productive capacity capable of being expanded at a certain *maximum* rate, also at a lower rate, but *not at a higher* rate. Any additional inputs (investment) would not produce *additions* to but *reductions* of output.' The idea is that, above a certain point, the technical and social problems caused by the reorganisation of production to accommodate the investment, are such that the marginal product of the investment is zero.

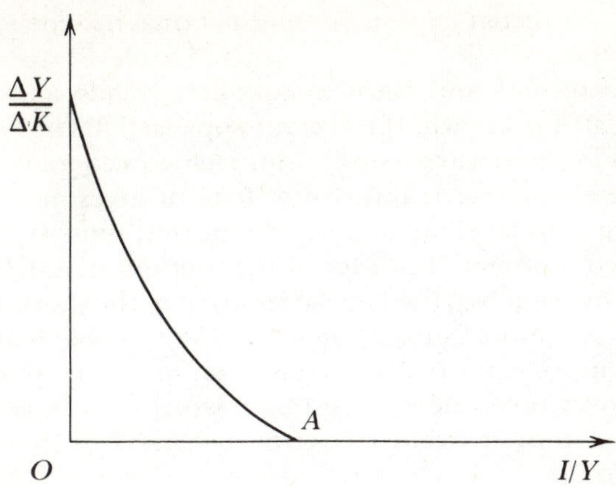

Figure 5.3 Absorptive capacity and the optimal rate of investment. $\Delta Y/\Delta K$ is the incremental output–capital ratio, I/Y is the share of investment in the national income.

Skill and knowledge will always be increasing, but the physiological substratum and social habits impose quite definite limits to the *speed* of the change. The increase of production requires continual readaptation of the whole social structure. This may not be evident in a slowly expanding economy. Yet, suppose that the rate of growth is 10%. Then in a generation of two twelve-year periods output would increase 10 times. Our children would have to manipulate an output 100 times as great, and our grandchildren an output 1,000 times as great. An underdeveloped and poor country of today would after only seventy years manipulate an annual social income of some $100,000 *per head of population* – do not these figures sound startling? Obviously there is a physical limit to the rate of expansion to which society is able to adapt itself.

Given these three assumptions, the problem of planning the optimal share of investment can be illustrated by figure 5.3. The diagram depicts a situation in which, when the share of investment is low, the return on marginal investment is high. As the share rises the return falls. When the absorptive capacity of the economy is reached, the maximum rational share of investment (*A*) is attained.

Accordingly, for any economy, the problem of finding the optimal share of investment resolves itself into the empirical question of finding out what the maximum absorptive capacity of that economy is. According to Horvat (1965 p. 575), his criterion 'produces a share of investment in national income of about 35%...if recent experience and national income statistics may be trusted'.

Given the second and third assumptions made above, and assuming that *A* is known, the Horvat approach fits in well with the 'overtaking and surpassing' approach to economic policy discussed in chapter 1. It gives that share of investment which enables the gap to be eliminated in the shortest time. It can only be considered 'optimal', however, if the 'optimum' is defined as that share which enables the gap to be closed in the shortest time, rather than in a more conventional way.[1] A valuable feature of the Horvat approach is that it directs attention to the possibility of wasteful over-investment (investment which is in excess of *A*). It seems that this situation has often occurred in the CMEA countries.

This section has so far only considered the analytical issue of what the optimal share of investment ought to be, while ignoring the political issue of how to attain the desired level of investment. The latter issue is particularly important and difficult. It was in the First Five Year Plan (1928–32) that the USSR made the transition from the kind of investment ratio characteristic of third-world countries to the much higher investment ratio characteristic of state socialist countries. In 1928–32 there was a gigantic increase in investment in the USSR, with the volume of investment more than quadrupling and rising from 15% of the net material product in 1928 to 44% in 1932. The question of the sources of this enormous increase in investment was examined in Ellman (1975).

From a Keynesian point of view, the sources of the increase in investment in 1928–32 were (a) the utilisation of previously wasted resources (e.g. unemployed labour), (b) the increase in the urban labour force, (c) the increase in the volume of basic wage goods marketed by agriculture, (d) the fall in urban real wages, (e) imports (both of machines and skilled labour), and (f) the increase in the output of industry and construction during the First Five Year Plan. The two key mechanisms for obtaining the additional investment resources were collectivisation (which made possible the increase in the volume of basic wage goods marketed by agriculture and the increase in the urban labour force) and the rapid inflation (which facilitated the fall in urban real wages).

[1] That Horvat's 'optimal' share is not 'optimal' in the conventional welfare economics sense was shown by Sen (1961 pp. 485–6). Horvat's approach can be thought of as a variant of the utility maximisation approach in which a constraint (absorptive capacity) is introduced and the maximand is switched from a subjective one (utility) to an objective one (growth).

From a Marxist point of view, the origin of the huge increase in accumulation during the First Five Year Plan was (a) an increase in absolute surplus value resulting from the increase in the urban labour force (30 %), and (b) an increase in relative surplus value resulting from the fall in real wages (101 %), less (c) a decrease in unequal exchange with agriculture (−31 %). The four key mechanisms for obtaining the additional accumulation were: the transition of the unions from trade unionism to production mindedness, the rapid growth of forced labour, the replacement of a market relationship between agriculture and the industrial sphere by a coercive relationship, and the increased differentiation between the elite and the masses.

Detailed examinations of the sources of the increase in accumulation in China appear to be lacking. Lippit (1975) has drawn attention to the role of land reform in enabling what was formerly property income to be converted into investment resources.

Summary

Three approaches to the choice of an optimal share of investment in the national income were considered, the utility maximising, descriptive and growth maximising. The first has given rise to a huge literature. Its weakest point is its basic assumption, that planning is concerned with maximising utility. The second provides a good description of the planning process, but offers no prescription. The third is a useful way of thinking about the problem for an economy aiming to maximise the rate of growth. Both theory and practice suggest that actually attaining a desired level of investment involves changes in the relations of production.

THE SECTORAL ALLOCATION OF INVESTMENT

An important feature of the early stage of socialist industrialisation has been the allocation of investment resources primarily to producer goods industries rather than consumer goods industries. In the USSR, where socialist planning has existed longest, the share of consumer goods in total industrial output fell almost continually from 1928 to 1966, but since then has been stable. The data are set out in table 5.1.

A similar, but rather slower, transformation seems to have taken place in China, as indicated by the data in table 5.2.

During the period in which the share of producer goods in total

Table 5.1 *Division of Soviet industrial production between consumer and producer goods (in %)*

(1) Year	(2) Producer goods	(3) Consumer goods
(1913	35.1	64.9)
1928	39.5	60.5
1940	61.2	38.8
1946	65.9	34.1
1950	68.8	31.2
1955	70.5	29.5
1960	72.5	27.5
1966	74.4	25.6
1975	74.0	26.0

Note: Column (2) refers to what in Soviet planning and statistical practice is known as group A, and column (3) to group B. This division corresponds neither to the Marxist distinction between Departments 1 and 2, nor to the division between heavy and light industry.
Source: *Narodnoe khozyaistvo SSSR v 1975g* (Moscow 1976) p. 192.

Table 5.2. *Division of Chinese industrial production between consumer and producer goods (in %)*

(1) Year	(2) Producer goods	(3) Consumer goods
1952	35	65
1957	48	52
1965	53	47
1970	55	45
1974	62	38

Source: Eckstein (1977) p. 215.

industrial production was rising in the USSR it was customary for Soviet economists to assert (*Political Economy* 1957 p. 721) that 'the law of priority growth of the production of the means of production...is a necessary condition for ensuring the uninterrupted advance of socialist production'. This formulation is actually a paraphrase of the view expressed by Stalin in *Economic problems of socialism in the USSR* (1952) that, 'the national economy cannot be continuously expanded without giving primacy to the production of means of production'. As policy

Table 5.3. *Share of consumer goods in industrial output in selected countries (in %)*

	1871	1901		1924			1946	
Great Britain	52	41		40			31	
France	65[a]	44[b]		35[c]			34[d]	
Germany	n.a.	45[e]		37[f]	25[g]		—	23[h]
USA	44[i]	34[j]		32[k]			30[l]	
Switzerland	62[m]	45[n]		38[o]			34[p]	
Italy	n.a.	72[q]		53[r]	37[s]		—	
Japan	n.a.	n.a.		59[t]			40[u]	
USSR	—	—	67[v]	—	61[w]	39[x]	—	29[y]

[a]1861–65, [b]1896, [c]1921, [d]1952, [e]1895, [f]1925, [g]1936, [h]1951, [i]1880, [j]1900, [k]1927, [l]1947, [m]1882, [n]1895, [o]1923, [p]1945, [q]1896, [r]1913, [s]1938, [t]1925, [u]1950, [v]1913, [w]1928, [x]1940, [y]1955.
Source: Patel (1961).

changed this position was abandoned, and replaced by the view (Dovgan' 1965) that the sharp increase in the share of producer goods output in total industrial output had been necessary during the early stages of socialist industrialisation, but that it is *not* a necessary condition of steady economic growth that the share of producer goods output in total industrial output rises indefinitely. The traditional Soviet orthodoxy was abandoned in China before it was abandoned in the USSR. Already in *On the ten major relationships* (1956) Mao criticised the excessive emphasis on heavy industry at the expense of light industry and agriculture in the USSR and Eastern Europe. He suggested that China should learn from this experience and develop light industry and agriculture proportionately.

Is there any economic justification for the proposition that the share of group A in total industrial production ought to rise during the early stages of socialist industrialisation, and if so, what is it? One line of argument is that the increase in the share of producer goods in total industrial output is a normal feature of economic growth regardless of the mode of production. Some figures which have been selected to support this view are set out in table 5.3.

Assuming that it is a fact that there is a general tendency for the share of producer goods in total industrial output to rise over time,[2] it is easy to explain it in terms of the nature of technical progress.

[2] For a denial of the validity of this 'fact' see Wiles (1962 pp. 286–8).

Economic development largely consists of the replacement of the production of commodities primarily with labour, with the assistance of a small quantity of intermediate goods and a very limited capital stock, by the production of commodities primarily by capital goods with the assistance of long chains of intermediate goods and limited labour. Comparing eighteenth-century cotton textile production with twentieth-century synthetic fibre production, the latter requires, in addition to the requirements of the former, construction of the factory, electricity to power, light and heat it, a heavy engineering industry to produce the capital equipment needed, and a chemical industry to produce the synthetic fibre. If, as a result of technical progress, an increasing proportion of the gross output of consumer goods industries is accounted for by inputs of intermediate products, and a decreasing proportion of the gross output of consumer goods industries is accounted for by value added in the consumer goods industries, as in the above example, then over time the share of consumer goods output in total industrial output will fall. A similar result will occur if an increasing proportion of consumer demand is for products a low proportion of whose gross output consists of value added by consumer goods industries.

The first economist to focus attention on the relationship between the consumer goods and producer goods industries in a plan for rapid economic growth was the Soviet economist Feldman.[3] He derived two important results, one about the ratios of the capital stocks in the two sectors, the other about the allocation of investment to the two sectors. The first result was that a high rate of growth requires that a high proportion of the capital stock be in the producer goods sector. This is illustrated in Figure 5.4. Feldman's second theorem was that, along a steady growth path, investment should be allocated between the sectors in the same proportion as the capital stock. For example, suppose that a 20% rate of growth of income requires a K_c/K_p of 3.7. Then to maintain growth at 20% p.a. requires that 3.7/4.7 of annual investment go to the consumer goods industries, and 1.0/4.7 of annual investment go to the producer goods industries.

The interrelationship of the two theorems is shown in table 5.4, in which Feldman explained how any desired growth rate, given

[3] Feldman's model was published in the USSR in 1928. For an English translation see Feldman (1964). For an analysis of the model by one of the founders of Western growth theory see Domar (1957).

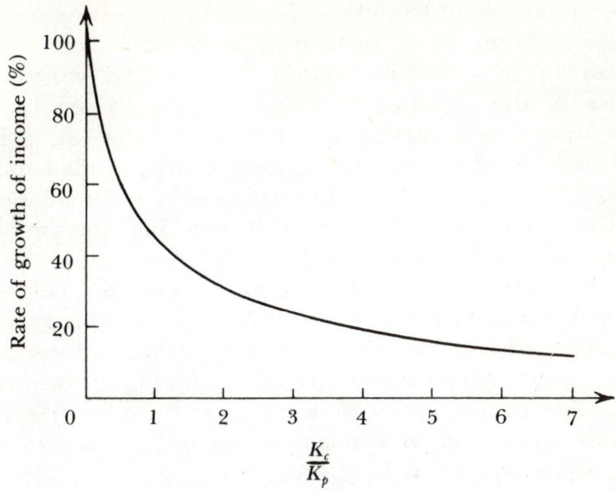

Figure 5.4 Feldman's first theorem.
K_c is the capital stock in the consumer goods industry, K_p is the capital stock in the producer goods industry.

Table 5.4. *Feldman's two theorems*

$\frac{K_p}{K_c}$	$\frac{dY}{dt}$ (in % p.a.) $\left(\text{when } \frac{K}{Y} = 2.1\right)$	$\frac{\Delta K_p}{\Delta K_c + \Delta K_p}$
0.106	4.6	0.096
0.2	8.1	0.167
0.5	16.2	0.333
1.0	24.3	0.500

the capital–output ratio, determined both the necessary sectoral composition of the capital stock and the sectoral allocation of investment.

Given the capital–output ratio, the higher the K_p/K_c ratio, i.e. the greater the proportion of the capital stock in the producer goods sector, and correspondingly the higher the $\Delta K_p/(\Delta K_c+\Delta K_p)$ ratio, i.e. the greater the proportion of new investment in the producer goods sector, the higher the rate of growth. With a capital–output ratio of 2.1, to raise the growth rate from 16.2 % to 24.3 % requires raising the proportion of the capital stock in the producer goods sector from 1/3 to 1/2, and the share of investment in the producer goods sector from 1/3 to 1/2.

The conclusion Feldman drew from his model was that the main task of the planning organisations was to regulate the capital–output ratios in the two sectors and the ratio of the capital stock in the producer goods sector to that in the consumer goods sector. For the former task, Feldman recommended rationalisation and multi-shift working, for the latter, investment in the producer goods sector.

Both at the time, and for some decades thereafter, Feldman's conclusion, that to begin a process of rapid economic growth it is necessary to expand rapidly the capacity of the producer goods industries, seemed paradoxical. It was contrary to the traditional view that the 'proper' path of development was 'textiles first'. As Shanin, a prominent Russian economist, argued in 1925 (Spulber 1964 pp. 209–10):

We must:

(1) Develop more intensively, and in the first instance, those branches of agriculture which produce large masses of goods for export, and those branches of industry with whose development our industrial export capability is linked. Development of consumer goods production and of our economy's export branches is our central object.

(2) Simultaneously, utilizing these export resources for import purposes, we must adopt a course of initially slower and more cautious development of heavy industry. With the proceeds from exports we must systematically import equipment, processed metals, etc., so that substantial outlays on their production do not have to be made at the present time. Funds made available (as a result of having rejected the forced-draft development of heavy industry) we must pour into light industry and the export branches of the economy.

Our economic strategy should involve, first, export of agricultural commodities, and second, investment of capital in the branches which serve that export. Relying on our agricultural basis, we must build grain elevators, refrigeration plants, and bacon factories, the investments required for these undertakings being infinitely small when compared with the expenditures which would be required by the immediate full-scale development of heavy industry.

At the same time we must do our utmost to speed the development of industries processing farm produce. We must strive to develop the sugar industry so that we can export sugar. The textile industry must, in its advance, reach the point where it can make its appearance on the Near East market. We must speed the development of other industries producing manufactured goods for export.

Table 5.5. *Consumption paths on various investment strategies*

	Initial investment in the consumer goods sector (strategy *S*)			Initial investment in the producer goods sector (strategy *F*)		
Year	Consumption	K_c	K_p	Consumption	K_c	K_p
1	500	1000	0	500	1000	0
2	550	1100	0	525	1050	100
3	550	1100	0	550	1100	100
4	550	1100	0	575	1150	100
5	550	1100	0	600	1200	100
6	550	1100	0	625	1250	100

This certainly contrasts very sharply with the conclusion (Spulber 1964 p. 194) which Feldman derived from his first theorem that 'an increase in the rate of growth of income demands industrialization, heavy industry, machine building, electrification...' What was Feldman's proof, and is it valid?

Feldman's own argument was rather laborious, but the essence of the matter is very simple and can be explained by means of an arithmetical example. Consider a two sector (consumer goods and producer goods) economy with a capital–output ratio of 2 in each sector which has available 100 units of investment resources which can be invested either in the consumer goods sector or in the producer goods sector. The choice is represented in table 5.5.

If the initial investment is made in the consumer goods sector then there will be a once and for all consumption increment of 50. Consumption will rise from a level of 500 in year 1 to a level of 550 in year 2, and thereafter remain on a plateau. If, on the other hand, the initial investment is made in the producer goods sector, then there will be an annual increment of 50 to the capital stock in the consumer goods sector, which will ensure an annual consumption increment of 25. Consumption will rise by only 25 in year 2, but it will also rise by 25 in each subsequent year. When the initial investment is made in the producer goods sector there is an initial loss of possible consumption, but by year 3 consumption is equal on the two paths, and from year 4 onwards annual consumption is greater on strategy *F* than on strategy *S*, and the absolute difference increases annually. Given a long enough time horizon, strategy *F* is clearly superior.

The reason why investing in producer goods is advantageous in models of an economy divided into horizontal sectors, is very simple. An investment in the producer goods sector enables the capital equipment of the consumer goods sector to expand. This is not a flash in the pan. After each period of production in the producer goods sector, the capital stock in the consumer goods sector rises. This enables the output of consumer goods to rise. There is a steady rise in the output of consumer goods, the annual increment being the capital stock in the producer goods sector divided by the product of the two capital–output ratios. In the example, the capital stock in the producer goods sector is (from period 2 onwards) the initial investment of 100 units.

An investment in the consumer goods sector, on the other hand, merely results in a once and for all expansion of the productive capacity of that sector, and consequently a zero growth rate in the output of consumption goods (after the initial increase).

From this point of view, the crucial difference between an investment in the producer goods sector and in the consumer goods sector is as follows. The former produces a steady stream of capital goods for use in the consumer goods sector, each of which in turn produces a steady stream of consumption goods. The latter, however, merely produces a steady stream of consumption goods, the absolute level of this stream thereafter remaining unchanged.

The argument depends crucially on the assumptions that construction periods are the same in both sectors, machines are immortal and the sectoral capital–output ratios the same. If these assumptions are dropped, it is possible to assign values to the construction periods, lives of the capital goods and the sectoral capital output ratios, that reverse the result. The argument also assumes a long enough time horizon and a closed economy.[4] Feldman's argument was developed in terms of a two sector model, but applies equally to a model of a closed economy divided into m ($m > 2$) horizontal sectors, provided the time

[4] Unlike Feldman, Shanin assumed both an open economy and that the allocation of investment and the supply of investment resources were interdependent. He also refused to confine himself to the long run, but considered also short-run implications of different investment allocations. Given his assumptions, a powerful case can be made for his conclusions.

horizon is long enough and appropriate assumptions are made about the construction periods, lives of the capital goods and sectoral capital–output ratios.

The main lesson to be learned from the Feldman model is that the capacity of the capital goods industry is one of the constraints limiting the rate of growth of an economy. There may well be other constraints, such as foreign exchange, urban real wages or marketed output of agriculture. Indeed, it is possible that one or more of these is/are the binding constraint/s and that the limited capacity of the producer goods sector is a non-binding constraint. Economic planning is largely concerned with the removal of constraints to rapid economic growth. Accordingly, in its early stages a prominent role is often played by the rapid development of the producer goods sector. This was recognised by the Indian economist Mahalanobis (1953) at the start of Indian planning, and has been recognised as necessary for Britain if her economic decline is to be halted and reversed (*Reshaping* 1974 pp. 72–4).

Feldman's division of an economy into two sectors is crude and scarcely operational. A major advance in economic analysis since the publication of his paper has been the development of numerical multi-sectoral models (Leontief 1966). One important use of these models is to study the relationship between the rate of growth of the national economic aggregates and the relative output of the various industries. In the usual input–output notation

$$X = (I - A)^{-1} Y$$

Assuming that A is given, X can be calculated for varying values of Y. Assuming that the variants of Y considered refer to some future year, this enables the changes in the relative output of the different industries in this final year resulting from various hypothetical national income aggregates, to be studied.

Such studies are now an integral part of the planning process in the state socialist countries. An example taken from Soviet experience with the elaboration of the 1966–70 Five Year Plan is set out in table 5.6. The table shows how the technological relationships between industries are such that, the higher the rate of growth of the national economy, the wider the divergence between the rate of growth of an industry such as engineering and an industry such as the food industry.

Table 5.6. *Industrial implications of different macroeconomic growth rates (rates of growth in % p.a.)*

	Variants				
	1	2	3	4	5
Net material product	5.6	6.1	6.6	7.1	7.5
Consumption	6.7	6.8	6.9	7.0	7.0
Investment	2.5	4.1	5.7	7.3	8.7
Engineering and metal working	7.1	8.2	9.3	10.4	11.4
Light industry	6.3	6.6	6.8	7.0	7.2
Food industry	7.1	7.3	7.4	7.5	7.6

Source: Ellman (1973) pp. 70–1.

Summary

The technological structure of a closed economy is such that the higher the rate of national economic growth required, the higher the rate of growth of the output of industries such as engineering and the greater the share of investment that has to be allocated to them. In a closed economy where the capacity of these industries is an operative constraint, a major task of planning for raising the growth rate must be to direct investment resources towards expanding the capacity of these sectors. This proposition was first formulated in a 1928 paper by the Soviet economist Feldman and is now generally accepted.

INDUSTRY PLANNING

In the state socialist countries investment plans are worked out for the country as a whole, and also for industries, ministries, departments, associations, enterprises, republics, economic regions and cities. An important level of investment planning is the industry. Industry investment planning is concerned with such problems as the choice, of products, plants to be expanded, location of new plants, technology to be used, and sources of raw materials. To resolve these questions it is necessary to collect and process the necessary data.

Data collection

For a producer goods industry, part of the demand will be for given products, but there will in general be considerable substitutability between products. It will therefore be necessary to gather data on the relative costs and usefulness of different products. If this is not done properly, and the results acted on, then waste will result. For example, as Abouchar (1971) has pointed out, a major source of waste in the Soviet cement industry prior to the Second World War was the large number of grades produced and the failure to capture the gains from standardisation.

The possibility of expanding existing plants largely depends on the availability of space, labour and raw materials, and the cost of transport of output to customers. Similarly, possible locations of new plants depend largely on the availability of raw materials and labour and on transport costs. An important difficulty at this stage is that in general the prices of producer goods and labour power in the state socialist countries are not equal to their national economic opportunity cost. It may therefore be necessary to mount a special investigation of costs, or use the shadow prices resulting from the investment plan of the appropriate industry. In an economy in which producer goods are rationed, it is not in general true that the prices at which transactions take place (*Guidelines* 1972 p. 62) 'may...provide a good first step in the estimation [of social costs]'.

In a well-known aphorism, Lenin defined communism as 'Soviet power plus electrification', and the introduction into production of advanced technology has always played a major role in socialist planning. The first state socialist country, which under capitalism was notorious for its wooden ploughs, is now well known for its sputniks. In the traditional Soviet type of organisation each industry has a Ministry which is responsible for adopting the latest ideas, incorporating them in its investment plan and imposing a unified technical policy on its industry. Complaints are frequent, however (see for example Bek 1971), that innovation is hindered by the monopoly position of the major R & D organisations. Examples of technical conservatism at the R & D stage in the USSR include the fact that alternatives to the home-grown SKB process for the manufacture of synthetic rubber were almost ignored, and that processes for the manufacture of alloy and quality steel other than electric-slag remelting received inadequate attention (Amann 1977).

The possibilities for obtaining raw materials depend on known reserves, geological prospecting and foreign trade possibilities. The state socialist countries have devoted extensive efforts to geological prospecting, in which field they have a good record.

Data processing

The main method used at the present time in the CMEA countries for processing the data relating to possible investment plans into actual investment plans is mathematical programming. The use of mathematical programming for calculating optimal investment plans is an example of the possibilities for efficient control of national economies which the scientific–technical revolution in the field of management and control of large systems is bringing about.

In order to illustrate the method, an example will be given which is taken from the Hungarian experience of the late 1950s in working out an investment plan for the cotton weaving industry for the 1961–65 Five Year Plan (Kornai 1967 chapter 5). The method of working out the plan can be presented schematically by looking at the decision problems, the constraints, the objective function and the results.

The decision problems to be resolved were:

(a) How should the output of fabrics be increased, by modernising the existing weaving mills or by building new ones?

(b) For part of the existing machinery, there were three possibilities. It could be operated in its existing form, modernised by way of alterations or supplementary investments, or else scrapped. Which should be chosen?

(c) For the other part of the existing machinery, either it could be retained or scrapped. What should be done?

(d) If new machines are purchased, a choice has to be made between many types. Which types should be chosen, and how many of a particular type should be purchased?

The constraints consisted of the output plan for cloth, the investment fund, the hard currency quota, the building quota and the material balances for various kinds of yarn. The objective function was to meet the given plan at minimum cost.

The results provided answers to all the decision problems. An important feature of the results was the conclusion that it was much cheaper to increase production by modernising and expanding existing mills than by building new ones.

It would clearly be unsatisfactory to optimise the investment plan of each industry taken in isolation. If the calculations show that it is possible to reduce the inputs into a particular industry below those originally envisaged, then it is desirable to reduce planned outputs in other industries, or increase the planned output of the industry in question, or adopt some combination of these strategies. Accordingly, the experiments in working out optimal industry investment plans, begun in Hungary in the late 1950s, led to the construction of multi-level plans linking the optimal plans of the separate industries to each other and to the macroeconomic plan variables. Multi-level planning of this type was first developed in Hungary, but has since spread to the other CMEA countries.

Problems of industry planning

The three chief problems of industry planning appear to be, the lack of the necessary data, technical conservatism, and departmentalism. Consider each in turn.

Soviet experience has shown (Ellman 1973 pp. 77 & 86–7) that the biggest obstacle to the compilation of useful optimal industry plans is the lack of the necessary data. In the section on the use of mathematical models in a book on improving planning written by some officials of the Soviet Gosplan it is stated that (Drogichinsky 1971 p. 184):

> the information required for models, optimising the utilisation of resources, is not readily available, and it is necessary to gather it separately. It is this work which occupies at the present time not less than 80% of all the work involved in solving such problems, and for complicated problems – 90%.
>
> At first sight this situation may arouse surprise, because for the working out of plans, it would seem, all the necessary information is available. For the efficient utilisation of models, however, for example for planning production, the nomenclature must be substantially wider than that confirmed in the plan. This results from the necessity to exclude the influence of possible assortment changes on the decision taken. The following examples may clarify this. In the national economic plan there are two figures for the production of leather shoes and children's shoes. The calculations underlying the plan are based on 7 aggregated groups of shoes and 4 small groups. For the problem which enables the maximum production of shoes subject to the structure of demand and the given resources to be calculated, shoes are divided into

257 types, and the full nomenclature of shoes and related items runs to about 36,000 items. The types are chosen in such a way that an alteration in the assortment inside each of them would have a much smaller influence on the plan than changes in the assortment between types.

The data required are not purely physical, but have to be made comparable by means of prices and a rate of interest. The prices and recoupment period used in many of the calculations were unsatisfactory in a number of respects. It was even necessary to devote extensive research to calculate the 'proper' figures to use for transport costs, the actual freight tariffs being of little significance from an efficiency point of view! All these difficulties are a result of the partial ignorance of the planners.

The technical conservatism of the major R & D organisations is often a serious problem. Some examples were given above. Its seriousness for the economy arises from the policy of concentration of initiatives.

Departmentalism refers to the fact that planning organisations often give greater weight to the interests of their own organisation than to the national economy as a whole. For example, Val'tukh (1977) and Bufetova & Golland (1977) estimate that at the present time in the USSR investment in the production of better *quality* steel would generally produce bigger returns to the national economy than the investment of the same resources in producing a greater *quantity* of steel. The ministry, however, ignores this possibility, since it is evaluated by quantity of output and the gains from greater quality accrue to the users. This is an example of the problems for the national economy created by the fact that decision makers form a coalition and not a team. The central planners, who are supposed to check the proposals of the branch ministries, often do not have enough knowledge of the problems of the users, interest in responding to them, or authority over the branch ministries, to do other than rubber stamp the suggestions of the producers.

Summary

A major type of investment planning is industry planning, carried out by the branch ministries. The main method used for this at the present time in the CMEA countries is mathematical programming. Considerable difficulties exist in the drawing up of rational industry plans, largely resulting from the partial ignorance of the planners and the fact that the decision makers form a coalition and not a team.

THE CHOICE OF TECHNIQUE

A feature of traditional Soviet planning is the emphasis on large modern plants, embodying the latest international technology, and often imported or scaled-up versions of foreign plants. Well-known early examples were the Stalingrad tractor plant and the Magnitogorsk iron and steel plant. Such plants can take full advantage of economies of scale. In addition, it is thought that their construction will be a quick way of reducing the technology gap and catching up with the most advanced countries. They also have the political advantage of creating proletarian islands in a peasant sea. As constructed in the USSR, these plants have often been labour-intensive variants of capital-intensive techniques. This means that for the auxiliary operations (such as materials handling), unlike the basic operations, labour-intensive methods have often been used in order to save scarce investment resources. This is discussed further in chapter 6.

The adoption of this type of technology was not the result of precise calculations by economists as to the relative merit of this or that type of technology. Indeed, during the Stalin era (1929–53), the orthodox view in the USSR was that the function of economists was to provide ex-post rationalisations of government economic policy. In *Economic problems of socialism in the USSR* (1952) Stalin decisively rejected the view that the function of political economy

> is to elaborate and develop a scientific theory of the productive forces in social production, a theory of the planning of economic development...The rational organisation of the productive forces, economic planning etc. are not problems of political economy but problems of the economic policy of the directing bodies. These are two different provinces, which must not be confused...Political economy investigates the laws of development of men's relations of production. Economic policy draws practical conclusions from this, gives them concrete shape, and builds its day to day work on them. To foist upon political economy problems of economic policy is to kill it as a science.

As Yaroshenko, one of the participants in the discussion of the draft textbook of political economy to which Stalin was reacting, put it, in a passage quoted by Stalin: 'healthy discussion of the rational organisation of the productive forces in social produc-

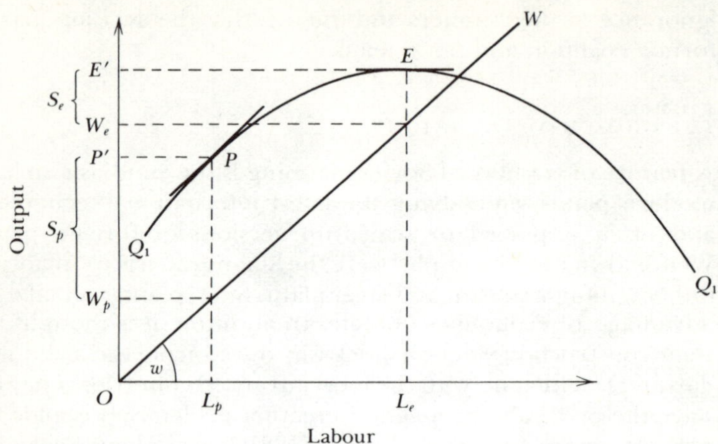

Figure 5.5 The choice of technique.

tion, scientific demonstration of the validity of such organisation' was replaced by 'scholastic disputes as to the role of particular categories of socialist political economy – value, commodity, money, credit etc.'

Many years after the traditional Soviet policy was first implemented, it was rationalised by Dobb (1960 chapter 3) and Sen (1968). They argued that in an economy where the share of investment is sub-optimal and all profits are reinvested and wages consumed, investment ought to take the form of capital-intensive projects (i.e. projects with a high capital–labour ratio) and *not* labour-intensive ones. The logic of this argument can be seen by looking at figure 5.5, which is taken from Sen.

Consider an economy with a given quantity of investment resources which can be combined with varying quantities of labour to produce output. Labour is assumed to have a zero social opportunity cost (because it is assumed that the country is characterized by large open or disguised unemployment). The production function is given by the curve Q_1Q_1. The wage rate is given by tan w and the wage bill by OW. Consider the choice between two techniques of production, P and E. P is the more capital-intensive technique and E the more labour-intensive technique. At P the marginal product of labour equals the wage rate and the surplus is maximised. At E the marginal product of labour equals zero and output is maximised. The criterion of maximum output and employment per unit of investment would indicate that E is the preferred technique. Consider, however, technique P. It has a lower output and employment than E, but the surplus of output over consumption (i.e. $S_p \equiv OP' - OW_p$) is greater than the surplus generated by E (i.e. $S_e \equiv OE' - OW_e$). If the share of investment in the national income is sub-optimal, then the additional surplus $(S_p - S_e)$ resulting from the adoption of technique P may be more valuable to the economy, because it permits an increase in the share of investment and the rate of growth, than the loss of consumption $(W_e - W_p)$ and employment $(L_e - L_p)$ that adopting technique P will cause. Hence technique P, and not E, is the desirable one. In general, developing countries should use 'conveyor belts' rather than 'wheelbarrows'.

Considered as a rationalisation of traditional Soviet policy, the Dobb–Sen argument is entirely irrelevant, since there is no reason to suppose that under traditional Soviet planning the share of investment has been sub-optimal or that the surplus generated by the construction of modern plants was a significant source of investment finance. Indeed, it seems likely that the share of investment has often been in excess of the absorptive capacity of the economy, and the new plants, with their long construction and running-in periods, production of producer goods and foreign exchange requirements, a significant source of inflationary pressure. The argument, ironically, has most relevance under capitalism as a defence of the social utility of the traditional family-controlled business, that has no access to outside finance, squeezes real wages and reinvests all profits.

An important disadvantage of the traditional Soviet strategy is that it can lead to a substantial waste of resources and hence to lower living standards than are necessitated by the level of accumulation chosen. The waste arises from the fact that there may be material and human resources which have a zero opportunity cost from the standpoint of the national industrialisation programme but which could be used to provide useful goods and services. For example, a collective farm may be able to establish a workshop to produce toys out of local timber during the farming offseason. Such local initiatives, which were illegal in the USSR during the Stalin period, cost society nothing and benefit the members of the collective farm. Accordingly, a feature of the reaction against the Stalinist model, both in Eastern Europe and China, has been a stress on the usefulness of capital-saving techniques and small enterprises. Indeed, in

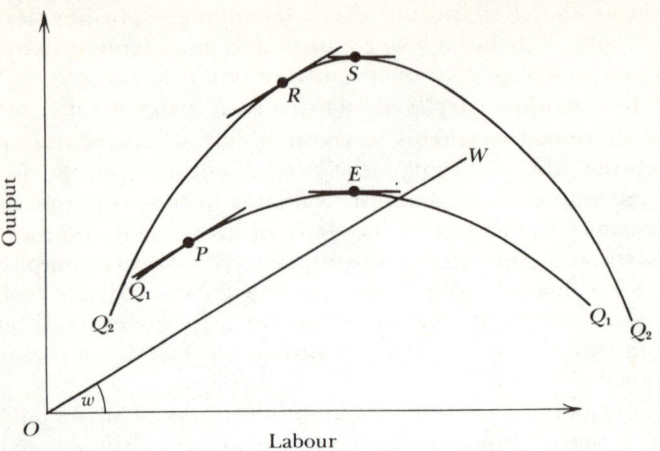

Figure 5.6 Technical progress and the Dobb–Sen criterion.

some countries, where there are no significant economies of scale and private persons are able to obtain resources (e.g. their own labour or that of their families, or their own home) otherwise unavailable for social production, small-scale private enterprise is permitted (e.g. in running shops, restaurants, motor car repairs and housing repairs). Although this can be (and often is) criticised from the standpoint of utopian socialism, with its emphasis on moral factors rather than material ones, from a Marxist perspective it makes excellent sense. It contributes to the efficient utilisation of resources and hence to the attainment of a high level of labour productivity.

A well-known theoretical challenge to the traditional Soviet policy was delivered by the Polish economist Kalecki (1972 chapter 10). He emphasised that in the short run the adoption of the Dobb–Sen strategy would lead to a loss of employment and ouput. He objected to a policy that would delay the transition to full employment and waste potential output. He also suggested that in the long run technical progress considerably reduces the practical significance of the Dobb–Sen argument. The reason for this is that with technical progress the marginal product of labour corresponding to each level of the capital–output ratio will, in general, grow. This means that the optimum technique, on the surplus maximisation criterion, has a capital–labour ratio which falls over time. Hence, although there is a static case for the Dobb–Sen position, once dynamic factors are introduced, even on their choice criterion the policy implications are at variance with the traditional Soviet policy. This second argument is illustrated in figure 5.6.

The production function in period 1 is Q_1Q_1, and in period 2, as a result of technical progress, Q_2Q_2. Consider the choice between techniques *E* and *P*. *P* maximises the surplus, but provides less employment and output than technique *E*. In period 2 the same is true for *R* and *S*, but the difference in capital intensity is smaller and *R* is less capital intensive than *P*. Hence the Dobb–Sen argument loses much of its practical significance when dynamic factors are introduced.

Kalecki's first argument is true and important, but avoids the question of weighting the loss of output and employment against the gain to investment. Kalecki's second argument does not eliminate (although it does reduce) the advantages of the more capital-intensive technique at any moment in time. In addition, the trend in the capital–labour ratio suggested depends on an assumption about the nature of technical progress which is not the only possible one.

Another challenge to the traditional Soviet policy has come from China. There a policy has been adopted, generally known as 'walking on two legs', which stresses the need to adopt both investment-intensive techniques and also investment-saving techniques. This is discussed by Bagchi (1978) and Robinson (1977). According to Robinson (1977 p. 164)

> The way to generate the maximum possible surplus is to organise employment of all available workers, provide them with an acceptable minimum standard of life and to direct all who are not required to provide the ingredients of the minimum into investment industries. The surplus does not have to be first saved and then invested. Devoting resources to building up the stock of means of production is saving and investing at once.
>
> The acceleration of accumulation depends, as was shown in the famous Feldman model, on the extent to which the output of machine-building industries is ploughed back into enlarging their own productive capacity. The criterion for the choice of technique, so long as investible resources are scarce relatively to the availability of labour to be drawn into industry, ought surely to be to maximise product per unit of investment, not to maximise surplus.

The last point is a repetition of Kalecki's first argument.

The Chinese policy of using, where possible, capital-saving techniques has led to the widespread development of both urban and rural small-scale industry. (The latter was discussed in chapter 4.) Experience has shown that, despite the widespread existence of very important economies of scale, small-scale industry can have several important advantages. First and most important, it can produce goods that otherwise would not have been produced. This may have an important positive effect on output, labour morale and labour productivity. Secondly, it can produce output quickly, unlike large modern plants which may have long construction and running-in periods. Thirdly, the diseconomies of small enterprises may be compensated by the use of otherwise unutilised resources. Fourthly, it can provide employment. Fifthly, the training received by those working in small-scale industries may be a significant contribution to training the labour force required by a national industrialisation programme. Sixthly, the existence of small enterprises may allow the large ones to specialise fully, and hence enable the full advantages of the division of labour to be reaped. Whereas in the USSR specialisation is hindered by the Ministerial system of administration and the wasteful supply system, in Japan it is encouraged by a multitude of sub-contractors. This is one of the reasons why labour productivity in Japanese industry is higher than in Soviet industry. The sixth advantage does not, in fact, seem to have been significant in China. Chinese factories, like Soviet ones, are considerably more vertically integrated (i.e. less specialised or more 'self-reliant') than US ones.

Experience has also shown that a big disadvantage of a policy of encouraging capital-saving techniques is that it may lead to the use of inferior techniques. This has happened both in China and in India.

A large-scale programme for the development of small-scale industries requires a very different style of economic management from that implicit in the traditional Soviet model. In the latter model, the job of medium- and low-level economic management is to carry out instructions from above. The use of local initiative to improve the allocation of resources can be a criminal offence. In the former it is necessary to give local officials wide autonomy. This was recognised by Mao in *On the ten major relationships.*

At present scores of hands are reaching out to the localities, making things difficult for them. Once a ministry is set up, it wants to have a revolution and so it issues orders. Since the various ministries don't think it proper to issue them to the Party committees and people's councils at the provincial level, they establish direct contact with the relevant departments and bureaux in the provinces and municipalities and give them orders every day. These orders are all supposed to come from the central authorities, even though neither the Central Committee of the Party nor the State Council knows anything about them, and they put a great strain on the local authorities. There is such a flood of statistical forms that they become a scourge. This state of affairs must be changed.

This does seem to have happened. Ishikawa (1972 pp. 73–4) has noted that in contemporary China

> The party leadership plays a crucial role in the establishment of the industrial enterprises under the direct control of the county governments. This leadership is exercised at present mainly to initiate local industries within the means of the local governments and by mobilising the co-operation of other local enterprises...This type of leadership seems to be different from the behaviour that is often observed in a highly centralised system of government where an official's behaviour is influenced by individualistic considerations of performance criteria or by the profit–loss calculation...This kind of party leadership...is a special [investment inducement] mechanism, which could not exist in the context of a Soviet-type bureaucratic system and it is also an indispensable ingredient of the present system of organisation of county industry.

It is also an example of the use of indirect centralisation via the political process to local authorities.

In the USSR, Stalin's theoretical legacy was criticised at the Twentieth Congress of the Soviet Communist Party (1956) and the way left open for Soviet economists to contribute to raising efficiency. The first area in which they achieved significant results was in the field of project evaluation. In 1960 an official Method of project evaluation was published, which combined the practice of Soviet planning with the theoretical generalisations of Soviet economists.

This Method tackles the following sub-optimisation problem. Assume that the plan fixes an output target for a particular sector. More than one technically-feasible method of producing this output exists. Which should be chosen? If one project has both a lower initial capital cost and a lower annual running cost than the others, then clearly it should be chosen. It may be, however, that one project has a higher capital cost but a lower annual running cost than the others. In this case, the rule propounded in the Method was that, the more capital-absorbing project is chosen only if the additional investment cost can be recouped by savings on current costs within a period equal to or smaller than, the normative recoupment period officially established for that sector.

The two projects case can be analysed as follows. Let I_1 be the capital outlay on the project with the larger initial cost, and I_2 the capital outlay on the project with the lower initial cost, and c_1 and c_2 be the respective annual operating costs of the projects, then

$$\frac{I_1 - I_2}{c_2 - c_1} \equiv T$$

where T is the recoupment period.

If $$T \leqslant T_n$$

where T_n is the normative recoupment period for the sector, then project 1 is chosen.

If $$T > T_n$$

then project 2 is chosen.

The comparison is normally undertaken using not T, but its reciprocal, e, 'the coefficient of comparative economic efficiency'.

Suppose that there are more than two technically feasible projects.

$$\frac{c_2 - c_1}{I_1 - I_2} \leqslant \frac{1}{T_n}$$

is the criterion for choosing 1 in preference to 2. This inequality can be rewritten

$$c_1 + I_1 \frac{1}{T_n} \leqslant c_2 + I_2 \frac{1}{T_n}$$

Generalising to the more than two projects case, choose that variant which minimises

$$c + I \frac{1}{T_n}$$

i.e. choose that project which minimises the sum of operating costs plus capital charge.

The officially promulgated normative coefficients varied between sectors. Some examples are given in table 5.7.

After this Method was promulgated in the USSR very similar criteria were adopted throughout Eastern Europe. In Poland, Czechoslovakia and Hungary a transition was fairly quickly made from the recoupment-period criterion to the present-value criterion. In the USSR, on the other hand, the 1969 second edition of the Method introduced some changes, such as a uniform coefficient of efficiency rather than one differentiated by sectors (subject to certain exceptions) but basically adhered to the recoupment-period approach.

Table 5.7. *Recoupment periods in different industries*

Industry	Recoupment period (years)	Coefficient of efficiency
Metallurgy (ferrous and non-ferrous)	7	0.14
Electric power	7–10	0.14–0.1
Coal	5	0.2
Petroleum and gas	5	0.2
Timber and wood-working	5	0.2
Chemical	3–5	0.33–0.2
Machine building	3–5	0.33–0.2
Light	3–5	0.33–0.2
Construction and construction materials	6	0.17
Transport	10	0.1

Source: *Basic* (1965) p. 101.

Since the promulgation of the first edition of the Soviet Method, official methods for project evaluation have been issued throughout the world, for example in the UK (*Investment* 1965), and by international organisations for developing countries (*Manual* 1968–69, *Guidelines* 1972). An important difference between the NEDC, OECD and UNIDO criteria on the one hand, and the Soviet one on the other, is that the latter compares different methods of producing the same output, whereas the former evaluate individual projects producing anything.

Perhaps the main lesson to be learned from the experience of the European state socialist countries is that the use of a rational criterion for deciding between investment projects is only part of the process of reducing waste in investment. One of the problems common to all these investment criteria is that they are concerned with the choice between given investment variants, and do not consider the generation of the variants between which choice has to be made. Important factors which influence the latter are foreign trade policies and the criteria used for evaluating the work of economic organisations. Poor decisions in these areas may lead to substantial waste despite the use of rational criteria to decide between given projects. For example, as pointed out in the previous section, organisations judged by the quantity of their output are unlikely to be very interested in proposals to increase quality at the expense of quantity, regardless of their national economic efficiency. Often no genuine use of rational criteria to choose between projects takes place at all. What actually happens is that the criteria are used to make an

Table 5.8. *Construction periods and economic institutions (years)*

	Capitalist countries	Poland during the three year plan[a] (1946–49)	Poland during the six year plan[b] (1950–55)
Coal mine of 5,000 ton capacity per day	8–10[c]	—	13–15
Electric thermal power station of 200–300 MW	c. 2[d]	—	4–5
Quality steel mill of medium size	2–3[e]	—	over 7
Canned meat factories, slaughter houses	—	0.75–1.0	3–4

[a] The three year plan was a rehabilitation plan similar to those throughout Europe after the Second World War. On its construction and implementation the Socialist Party had considerable influence.
[b] The six year plan was Poland's first Soviet-style plan.
[c] UK & FRG.
[d] Western Europe.
[e] Western Europe. (A similar mill was built in pre Second World War Poland in two years.)
Source: Zielinski (1973) p. 5.

arbitrary choice look scientific. For example, a favoured project is advocated, and made to look attractive by a comparison, using the criterion, with a purely spurious alternative.

Another way of reducing waste is to cut the construction and running in periods for new plants. Ways of doing this include reducing the share of investment in the national income to the optimal level, improving the criteria for evaluating the work of construction organisations, and improving the supply of materials to construction sites. An example of the waste resulting from excessive construction periods is given in table 5.8.

Summary

The traditional Soviet view is that capital-intensive plants, embodying the latest international technology, and often imported or scaled up versions of foreign plants, should be built. This view was rationalised by Dobb and Sen. They argued that in an economy where the share of investment in the national income is sub-optimal, and profits are reinvested and wages consumed, techniques should be chosen so as to maximise the surplus. This argument is not relevant to the USSR and also probably not relevant to the other state socialist countries.

The traditional Soviet view was criticised in theory by Kalecki and in practice both in Eastern Europe and in China. Kalecki emphasised the loss of employment and output caused by following the traditional Soviet policy, and the diminished practical importance of the Dobb–Sen argument caused by technical progress. The Chinese developed the policy of 'walking on two legs', using both capital-intensive and capital-saving technologies. Emphasis on capital-saving techniques may lead to the adoption of wasteful inferior techniques. Widespread development of small-scale industry requires a different style of economic management from the traditional Soviet type.

In the USSR, efforts to reduce waste in technological choice have been of a technocratic kind, with the development of formal criteria for project evaluation. Their introduction, however, is only a part of the long and difficult struggle to reduce waste in investment planning.

INVESTMENT CYCLES

A characteristic feature of capitalism is its cyclical development. Marxists have traditionally considered this to be one of the inefficiencies of capitalism, one of the examples of the anarchy of production, which would not exist in a socialist economy. In this connection it is interesting to consider whether or not history has corroborated the Marxist view.

Experience has, in fact, shown that economic development under state socialism does not necessarily proceed smoothly. It is entirely possible, as has been shown by events in China, Cuba, Czechoslovakia and Yugoslavia, for output in one year to fall below that of the previous year. For example, according to US estimates (Ashbrook 1975 p. 23), the Chinese GNP fell by 5 % in 1959, 1 % in 1960 and 23 % in 1961. Still more common have been substantial fluctuations in the rate of growth of investment. Some data are set out in fig. 5.7.

The curves in figure 5.7 show three-year moving averages (with equal weights) of annual growth rates of industrial production, of construction and of industrial investment for eight countries for the period 1951–65. They are evidence of substantial investment fluctuations, especially in Czechoslovakia, Hungary and Yugoslavia. What explains these fluctuations? The attempt to answer this question has given rise to an extensive discussion (Olivera 1960, Lange 1961, Goldmann 1964, Goldmann & Flek 1967, Eckstein 1968, Bajt 1971, Soos 1976).

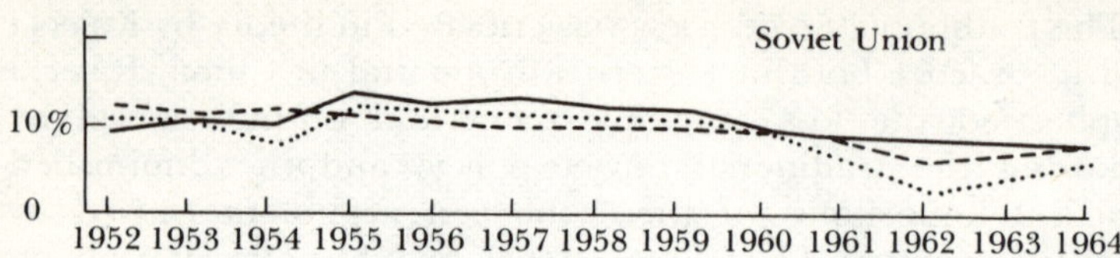

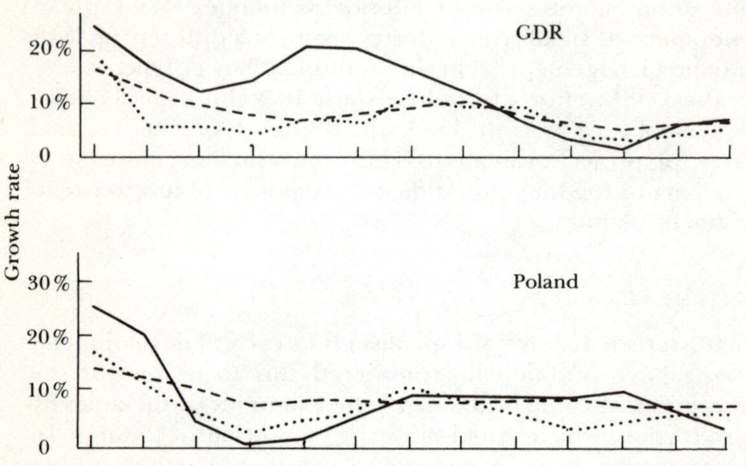

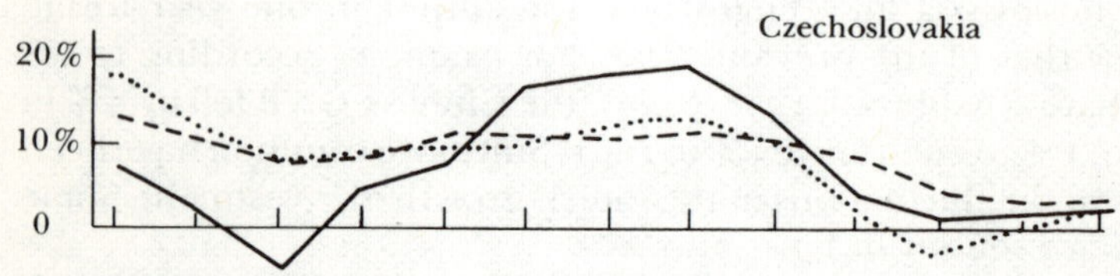

Figure 5.7 Investment cycles in the CMEA countries 1951–65. —, Industrial investment; --, industrial production; ..., construction. Source: Bajt (1971) pp. 58–9.

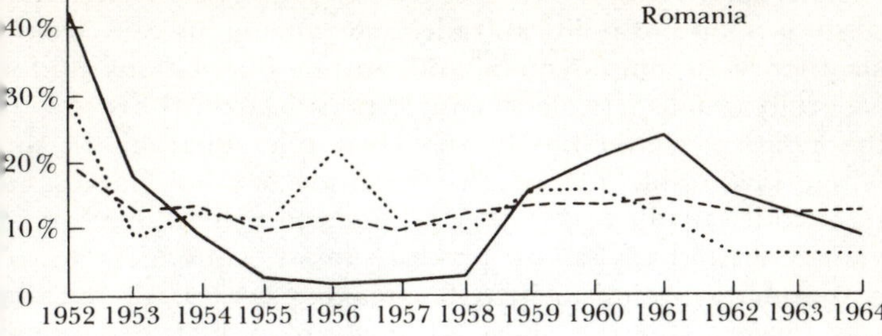
Romania
40 %
30 %
20 %
10 %
0
1952 1953 1954 1955 1956 1957 1958 1959 1960 1961 1962 1963 1964

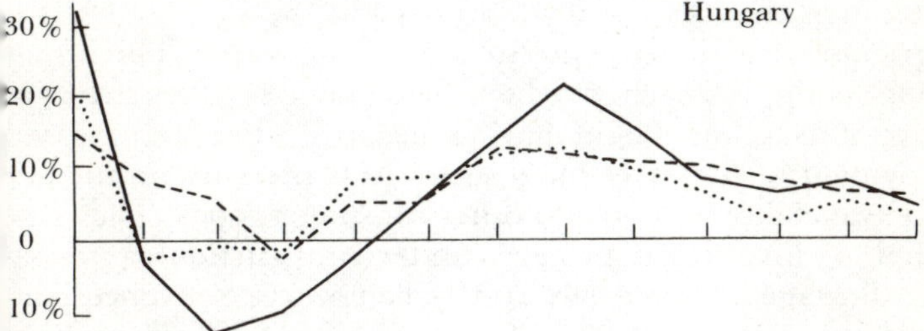
Hungary
30 %
20 %
10 %
0
10 %

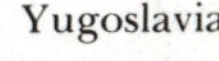
Yugoslavia

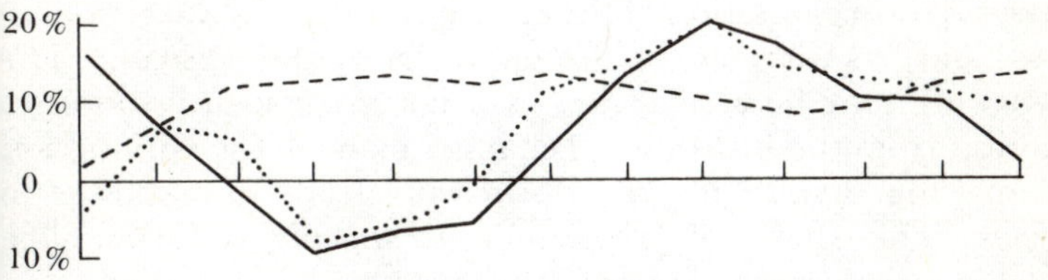
20 %
10 %
0
10 %

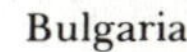
Bulgaria

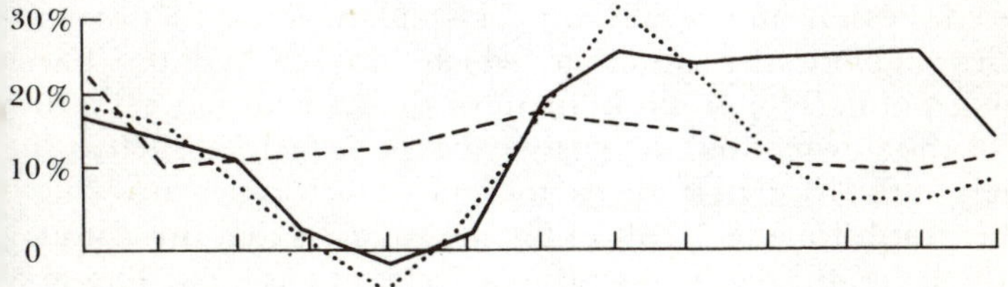
30 %
20 %
10 %
0

It seems that a major cause of investment cycles under state socialism is a kind of political trade cycle, analogous to Kalecki's classic theory of employment and output fluctuations under managerial capitalism (Kalecki 1943). It results from the reactions of the political leadership to the economic situation. In the upswing, favourable factors, for example a good harvest, a foreign trade surplus, plan overfulfilment, or the utilisation of previously wasted resources, produce rapid economic growth. This stimulates optimism in policy-making circles. They raise growth targets and the share of investment in the national income. Numerous grandiose investment projects are begun. Institutional changes are made to expand the socialised sector of agriculture at the expense of the private sector. The upper turning point is reached when these policies cease to have positive effects and begin having negative effects. Increased employment in the investment sector puts pressure on the per capita availability of food and other consumer goods. The large number of investment projects under construction causes an acute shortage of materials and skilled workers. Hence construction periods are drastically extended and the efficiency of investment falls. The downswing comes when labour productivity falls under the influence of declining consumption and the increased disorganisation of the economy caused by the very high growth targets adopted in the euphoria of the upswing. The downswing may be accelerated by a fall in agricultural output resulting from the institutional changes made in the euphoria of the upswing. Eventually the downswing leads to a change in policies. The share of investment is sharply reduced. The available investment resources are concentrated on projects that can be completed in a reasonable time. Changes are made in agricultural policy so as to stimulate output. Growth targets are lowered. Pessimism prevails in policy-making circles. These new policies stabilise the situation, which has reached the lower turning point. The overfulfilment of the easy targets set at the end of the downswing, or partly exogenous factors, such as the harvest or the foreign trade balance, give rise to a new upswing.

The graph for the USSR in fig. 5.7 suggests that this country was the least affected by investment cycles in 1951–65. This may reflect a learning process, the USSR being the country with the longest experience of socialist planning. Alternatively it may simply reflect the fact that for obvious structural reasons the

JSSR was much less affected in this period by partly exogenous actors such as the harvest and the foreign trade balance than ountries such as China and Hungary.

ummary

tate socialism is not a sufficient condition for the elimination of nvestment cycles. The main cause of investment cycles under tate socialism seems to be a kind of political trade cycle nechanism.

ONCLUSION

ive important technical problems of investment planning are, he optimal share of investment in the national income, the llocation of investment between sectors of an economy, industry lanning, the technical form of the investment and investment ycles.

As far as the optimal share of investment is concerned, a useful ay of thinking about the problem, for an economy aiming to naximise the rate of growth, is Horvat's growth-maximising pproach. This fits in well with the 'overtaking and surpassing' pproach to economic policy. A valuable feature of this approach that it draws attention to the possibility of wasteful ver-investment.

For many years in the CMEA countries it was orthodox that he law of the priority growth of the production of the means f production...is a necessary condition for ensuring the ninterrupted advance of socialist production'. A theoretical asis for this view was provided by the Soviet economist eldman in 1928. The key assumptions of his two-sector model re, a long time horizon, a closed economy, the independence f the allocation of investment and the supply of investment esources, equal construction periods in the two sectors, nmortal machines and identical capital–output ratios in the two ectors. The main lesson to be learned from the Feldman model that the capacity of the capital goods industry is one of the onstraints limiting the rate of growth of an economy. In a closed conomy where the capacity of this sector is a binding constraint, major task of planning for raising the growth rate must be to irect investment resources towards expanding the capacity of this sector. The use of input–output enables the high growt industries to be pinpointed more precisely, while preserving th essence of Feldman's insight.

A major type of investment planning is industry planning carried out by the branch ministries. The main method use for this at the present time in the CMEA countries is mathem atical programming. Considerable difficulties exist in the drawin up of rational industry plans, largely resulting from the partia ignorance of the planners and the fact that the decision maker form a coalition and not a team.

The choice of techniques is an interesting and much discusse problem. The traditional Soviet view is that (labour-intensiv variants of) capital-intensive plants, embodying the latest inter national technology, and often imported or scaled-up version of foreign plants, should be built. This view was criticised i theory by Kalecki and in practice both in Eastern Europe an China. The Chinese developed the policy of 'walking on tw legs', using both capital-intensive and capital-saving techno logies. Emphasis on capital-saving techniques may lead to th adoption of wasteful inferior techniques. Widespread develop ment of small-scale industry requires a different style of economi management from the traditional Soviet type. In the USSR, a in other parts of the world, efforts to reduce waste in techno logical choice have been of a technocratic type, with th development of formal criteria for project evaluation. Thei introduction, however, is only a part of the long and difficul struggle to reduce waste in investment planning.

State socialism is not a sufficient condition for the eliminatio of economic cycles. In particular, investment cycles are commo under state socialism. Their main cause seems to be a kind o political trade cycle mechanism.

SUGGESTIONS FOR FURTHER READING

Share of investment

J. Kornai, 'A general descriptive model of planning processes', *Econ omics of Planning* nos. 1–2 (1970).

B. Horvat, 'The optimum rate of investment reconsidered', *Economi Journal* (1965).

Sectoral allocation

R. W. Davies, 'Aspects of Soviet investment policy in the 1920s', C. H. Feinstein (ed.) *Socialism, capitalism and economic growth* (Cambridge 1967).

G. A. Feldman, 'On the theory of growth rates of national income', pp. 174–99 & 304–31 of N. Spulber (ed.) *Foundations of Soviet strategy for economic growth* (Bloomington, Indiana, USA 1964).

E. Domar, 'A Soviet model of growth', E. Domar, *Essays in the theory of economic growth* (New York 1957).

M. H. Dobb, 'The question of "investment priority for heavy industry"', M. H. Dobb *Papers on capitalism, development and planning* (London 1967).

D. Granick, *Soviet metal fabricating and economic development* (Madison, Milwaukee USA and London 1967).

K. N. Raj and A. K. Sen, 'Alternative patterns of growth under conditions of stagnant export earnings', *Oxford Economic Papers* (1961).

K. N. Raj, 'Role of the "machine-tools sector" in economic growth', C. H. Feinstein (ed.) *Socialism, capitalism and economic growth* (Cambridge 1967).

Industry planning

J. Kornai, *Mathematical planning of structural decisions* (1st edn Amsterdam 1967, 2nd edn Amsterdam 1975).

Michael Ellman, *Planning problems in the USSR* (Cambridge 1973) pp. 75–90.

L. M. Goreux & A. S. Manne, *Multi-level planning* (Amsterdam 1973).

Choice of technique

A. K. Sen, *Choice of techniques* (3rd edn Oxford 1968).

A. Chilosi, 'The theory of growth of a socialist economy of M. Kalecki', *Economics of Planning* no. 3 (1971).

Mao Tse-tung, *On the ten major relationships* (Peking 1977).

S. Ishikawa, 'A note on the choice of technology in China', *Journal of Development Studies* vol. 9 (1972).

S. Watanbe, 'Reflections on the current policies for promoting small enterprises and sub-contracting', *International Labour Review* (November 1974).

'The standard method for determining the economic efficiency of investment and new technology in the national economy', *Problems of economics* vol. III no. 6 (1960).

Economic Planning in Europe (UN Geneva 1965) chapter 4, section 6.

A. Bergson, *The economics of Soviet planning* (New Haven & London 1964) chapter 11.

'The standard method for determining the economic efficiency of investment', *Matekon* vol. VIII no. 1 (1970).

A. Abouchar, 'The new Soviet standard methodology for investment allocation', *Soviet Studies* vol. 24.

D. M. Nuti, 'Large corporations and the reform of Polish industry', *Jahrbuch der Wirtschaft Osteuropas* vol. 7 (Munich 1977) section 7 ('The selection of investment projects').

A. K. Bagchi, 'On the political economy of technological choice and development, *Cambridge Journal of Economics* vol. 2 no. 2 (June 1978).

Investment cycles

A. Bajt, 'Investment cycles in European socialist economies: A review article'. *Journal of Economic Literature* (1971).

A. Eckstein, *China's economic development* (Ann Arbor 1975) chapter 11.

K. A. Soos, 'Causes of investment fluctuations in the Hungarian economy', *Eastern European Economics* vol. XIV no. 2 (1976).

6

PLANNING THE LABOUR FORCE

It shall be the duty and honour of every able-bodied citizen of the USSR to work, according to the principle 'he who does not work, neither shall he eat'.

Constitution of the USSR (1936)

Those in urban employment are in a way a privileged elite, into which many a peasant's child would wish to climb. They work and live in more secure and comfortable conditions than the agricultural population and in general receive much higher cash remuneration, as well as labour insurance and medical benefits; this applies more particularly to the regular workers in modern enterprises who are an elite within an elite.

Donnithorne (1967 p. 182)

OBJECTIVES

The main objective of labour planning in the state socialist countries is to facilitate the fulfilment and overfulfilment of the national economic plan by ensuring that the requisite types of labour are available in the right quantities and places and perform the necessary work. This involves, developing the abilities of the labour force, so as to produce the right types of labour, providing full employment so as to avoid waste of resources, ensuring a rational regional distribution of employment and ensuring the efficient utilisation of labour. Each of these objectives will be considered in turn.

Development of the abilities of the labour force

The technical re-education of a society involves not only the implantation of technical knowledge and skill but also a certain mental readjustment. This requires time. Consequently, certain dividends arising from the introduction of new techniques may be realized only after a long period, perhaps as much as the life of a generation. From this point of view the comparatively short time in which the Soviet Union managed to educate its technical cadres is impressive, and an encouraging example for those underdeveloped countries which stand today very much where the Soviet Union did at the end of the 1920s. In this respect the Soviet 'model' of industrialization has proved a success and demands special and careful study.

Swianiewicz (1965 pp. 263–4)

In the Utilitarian tradition, the objective of economic activity is consumption. Productive labour is a disutility which is only engaged in until the diminishing marginal utility of earnings equals the marginal disutility of work. For a Marxist, on the other hand, productive labour is potentially an opportunity to take part in a creative activity. A major aspect of the Marxist critique of capitalism is that it transforms the work process in such a way as to generate meaningless jobs and a stratified society. A classic modern exposition of this view is Braverman (1974). Accordingly a major objective of the Marxist movement is to transform the labour process so as to replace the narrowly specialised worker by an individual who has wide possibilities for creative labour. As Marx put it in *The German Ideology*:

in communist society, where nobody has one exclusive sphere of activity, but each can become accomplished in any branch he wishes, society regulates the general production, and thus makes it possible for me to do one thing today and another tomorrow, to hunt in the morning, fish in the afternoon, rear cattle in the evening, criticise after dinner, just as I have a mind, without ever becoming a hunter, fisherman, shepherd or critic.

It is in accordance with this tradition that the imaginary author of the lectures in Preobrazhensky's book *From NEP to socialism* (1922) is simultaneously a professor of history and a fitter in a railway workshop. Similarly, a study of Tanzania (Rweyemamu 1973) emphasises that a *socialist* industrialisation strategy must include the development of *socialist* relations of production.

Utilitarianism treats man as the possessor of an insatiable appetite, greater satisfaction of which is an 'increase in welfare'. An alternative view is one which sees man not as a consumer of utilities but as a doer, a creator, an enjoyer of his (or her) human attributes. These attributes may be variously listed and assessed. They may be taken to include the capacity for rational understanding, for mastery of the whole of a socially necessary labour process, for moral judgement and action, for aesthetic creation or contemplation, for the emotional activities of friendship and love. Whatever the uniquely human attributes are taken to be, in this view their exertion and development are seen as ends in themselves and not simply as means of consumer satisfaction. This point has been elaborated by Macpherson (1973). Accordingly, a major objective of socialist planning in the field of labour is to develop the abilities of the labour force. This has important implications for policy in such areas as education, participation rates and hours of work.

Labour policies in the state socialist countries have developed under the influence both of the Marxist critique of capitalism and of the real historical problems confronting these societies. Hence they partly diverge from, and partly converge to, the path taken by the capitalist countries.

Since the first Sputnik was launched, considerable attention has been focused by Western writers on Soviet education. The effort devoted to ensuring mass literacy, and the stress on universal primary education, are well known. From our point of view, perhaps the main features of Soviet educational and training policies have been, the emphasis on vocational education and training, the concentrated nature of higher education, overmanning, and the absence of child labour.

Because the initial labour force for the plants opened in the USSR in the late 1920s and early 1930s was largely drawn from peasants and urban youths who had no background or legacy of skills, it was unavoidable that the Soviet Union should develop extensive training facilities. Many of these raw recruits could neither read nor write and had never held a wrench or screwdriver in their hands before. With such raw human material to work with, the plants initially were required not only to train workers to handle their machines and to conform to the factory regime but also to provide the rudiments of an elementary education. As a result, extensive educational and training programmes were established at the factories themselves.

Most of the training was on-the-job in character, but numerous factory and works apprentices' schools were opened at places of work to train apprentices for skilled trades. During the First Five Year Plan these schools trained over 450,000 skilled workers. Every year since, about 100,000 skilled workers have been trained through these schools. In addition, between 1940 and 1959 an annual average of 2.5 million workers and employees were taught new trades and specialisms on-the-job, and an additional 5.0 million were given training to improve their skills each year. Also, many workers learned their 'three Rs' in factory-run evening schools.

Table 6.1. *Number of graduates of higher educational institutions (USSR 1928–59, and USA 1926–58, thousands)*

Field	USSR	USA	USSR as % of USA
Engineers	1,118	620	180
Medical doctors	420	182	231
Agricultural specialists	389	166	234
Natural sciences	430	704	61
Total of above	2,357	1,673	141
Humanities, social sciences, etc.	1,772	5,199	34
Overall total	4,129	6,871	60

Source: Eason (1963) p. 63.

Eason (1963 p. 62) has noted that 'The experience of the Soviet Union lends support to the view that major strides in raising the quality of labour can be made without elaborate and extensive educational facilities.' The advantage of on-the-job training, particularly during the early industrialisation period, is that it conserves scarce resources. The use of scarce investment resources in constructing special educational facilities is minimised. In addition, the educational gestation period is shortened since the full range of subjects of a normal school is not covered. Emphasis on on-the-job training is not a peculiarly Russian phenomenon. It was and remains a characteristic of American industrial training as well.

Formal education, however, has not been neglected in the state socialist countries. A striking feature of it, however, has been that it has been concentrated on areas of importance to the national economy. This is illustrated by the data in table 6.1. The outcome depicted in the table is a result of basing higher education on manpower planning rather than on, say, the Robbins principle of providing places in higher educational institutions on the basis of the preferences of schoolchildren.[1]

A problem of educational planning, Soviet style, is that lower-level teachers and administrators are under considerable pressure to pass all, or virtually all, the students in any year, so as to avoid underfulfilling the plan. This ensures that a

[1] Professor Lord Robbins was the chairman of an official committee which recommended this principle as the basis for higher educational planning in the UK. Hence the term 'Robbins principle'.

proportion of those with diplomas are in fact not qualified for their supposed specialism. A well-known literary example of this is given in *The first circle* (Solzhenitsyn 1970 pp. 38–9).

A feature of Soviet industry has traditionally been a low level of labour productivity compared with the most advanced capitalist countries. It has often happened that entire plants have been imported from the capitalist world but the labour force employed in them has been much larger than analogous plants in the capitalist world. Partly this simply reflects the relative inefficiency of Soviet industry. Partly, however, it reflects deliberate policies. One such policy has been to use labour-intensive methods in auxiliary operations, so as to conserve scarce investment resources. (This policy has been used also in Chinese industry.) Another has been overmanning so as to employ some more of the abundant labour available and adapt it to the rhythm of modern industry. There is an important sense in which the output of Soviet and Chinese industry has been a joint product – industrial output and workers with improved qualifications.

A feature of Soviet labour policy compared with the practice of capitalist countries at comparable stages of development has been the very limited reliance on child labour. As Eason (1963) has observed, of the population between 10 and 15, the proportion in the Soviet labour force fell from 59% in 1926 to 23% in 1939 and 12% in 1959. This decline mainly reflects the spread of schooling.

An important aspect of Soviet labour policy has been urban participation rates much higher than those in capitalist countries at comparable stages of development. This results from the fact that a much higher proportion of Soviet women are employed. This partly reflects the Bolshevik rejection of the bourgeois subjection of women, partly reflects the series of demographic catastrophes (e.g. the Great Patriotic War) experienced by the USSR, and partly reflects the difficulty of keeping a family on one income. In addition to positive features, the Soviet emancipation of women has a number of negative features. For example, Soviet women, by and large, have to work much harder than men. This is partly because they do both paid employment and unpaid domestic labour. Partly it is because they do much of the heavy manual work. Furthermore, women in the USSR primarily hold the lower-level posts. For example, Soviet medicine is primarily a feminine profession but most of the senior positions in it are held by men. In addition, household chores are a heavier burden than in comparable capitalist countries because of the lack of investment and low levels of employment in distribution and services such as laundries. In the hard years of Soviet industrialisation, 1929–50, Soviet women formed a particularly disadvantaged proletarian stratum.

In China, as in the USSR, state socialism has brought a big increase in female participation rates and important changes in the position of women in society.

An important aspect of Soviet labour policy has been hours of work much below those in capitalist countries at a similar level of economic development. The eight hour day, a classic objective of the labour movement, was decreed immediately after the Great October Socialist Revolution. In 1929 and 1930 the work week was reduced further to *c.* 41 hours a week. In 1940 the standard work week was increased to 48 hours (six 8 hour days). Under Krushchev hours of work were again reduced to *c.* 41 hours a week, and have subsequently remained at this level. In addition a decree of 1967 announced a transition to a five-day week, and this was generally achieved by 1970. Furthermore, retirement age in the USSR is below that in many capitalist countries at 60 for men and 55 for women.

Similarly in China, retirement age is normally 60 for men and five years earlier for women. As far as hours of work in China are concerned, workers in the state sector of industry have, since 1956, been supposed normally to work 8 hours a day, 6 days a week. Longer hours are in fact often worked, especially towards the end of plan periods. At many periods workers have in addition been obliged to participate in political activities. In China absenteeism has been sufficient of a problem for some enterprises to institute bonuses for regular attendance. Cotton mills in Shanghai, and presumably elsewhere, experience higher absenteeism in the summer, a common phenomenon in all newly industrialising countries where factory workers still have close ties with the agricultural economy. In the USSR drunkenness is a serious social problem, with effects ranging from absenteeism to poor work, wife beating and murder.

Workers in state socialist countries are far better off from the standpoint of social security (in old age or illness) than workers in capitalist countries at comparable stages of development, or than workers in the socially backward capitalist countries (e.g. the USA). In Eastern Europe this results from the existence of good earnings-related old age pensions and sickness pay, free medical care and the absence of cyclical unemployment. In China it results partly from the same factors and partly from the fact that the rural population is organised in communes which provide basic security for their members.

Inter-system comparisons of industrial diseases, accidents and deaths is not possible because of lack of data for the USSR and China. For the USSR, the absence of data suggests a poor record. A US delegation that visited the Soviet coal-mining industry in 1972 made a special effort to find out about safety. Though unsuccessful in obtaining any data, the delegation deduced from discussions with Soviet officials that in underground mining Soviet fatalities per million tons mined are several times greater than the US figure. They also concluded that mine fires and explosions must be quite frequent. There is much discussion in the USSR of programmes for combating pneumoconiosis, but no information on its frequency. The US delegation could get no statistics on this matter either, but their impressions were that silicosis and black lung were quite prevalent and increasing (Campbell 1976 p. 257). The main reasons for the poor Soviet record in industrial safety are the priority given to production and the absence of independent trade unions.

A well-known feature of the labour process in the USSR compared, for example, with the USA, is its lower intensity, i.e. its slower pace and lower effort. From a capitalist, or consumer, point of view, this is a 'problem' of socialist planning. From a labourist point of view it is an advantage.

An important feature of employment under state socialism is job security. The prospect of losing one's job because of the vagaries of the conjunctural situation, which is a permanent reality and major source of anxiety under capitalism, does not exist under state socialism. By and large, all workers under state socialism enjoy the kind of job security enjoyed by civil servants under capitalism. In the capitalist countries the expansion of state employment has substantially improved conditions of employment (e.g. job security, pensions, promotion prospects etc.). Similarly, the spread of state employment to the whole economy under state socialism has led to the virtual universal spread of these favourable employment conditions. Some economists and administrators in the state socialist countries are concerned about the lack of flexibility and incentives that job security causes, but from a working-class point of view it is a major achievement of state socialism.

Full employment

Marxists consider that unemployment is one of the wasteful and irrational features of capitalism. In addition it is socially unjust, falling disproportionately on manual workers, especially unskilled manual workers. Marxists consider that unemployment is not a peripheral feature of capitalism which can be prevented by Keynesian demand management policies, but an integral part of this mode of production. Marx explained in volume 1 of *Capital* that:

> The greater the social wealth, the functioning capital, the extent and energy of its growth, and, therefore, also the absolute mass of the proletariat and the productiveness of its labour, the greater is the industrial reserve army. The same causes which develop the expansive power of capital, develop also the labour-power at its disposal. The relative mass of the industrial reserve army increases therefore with the potential energy of wealth. But the greater this reserve army in proportion to the active labour-army, the greater is the mass of a consolidated surplus-population, whose misery is in inverse ratio to its torment of labour. The more extensive, finally, the lazarus-layers of the worker class, and the industrial reserve army, the greater is official pauperism. *This is the absolute general law* of capitalist accumulation.

Marxists consider that the maintenance of permanent full employment is incompatible with the capitalist mode of production because full employment under capitalism will hinder accumulation by undermining labour discipline, generating inflation, threatening profits, and hindering the manning of new plants.

The experience of the state socialist countries shows that maintaining permanent full employment is no easy matter, even when there is state ownership of the means of production and national economic planning. The USSR in the 1920s and China in the 1950s both experienced large-scale unemployment. The reason for this, in both cases, was the large-scale influx of peasants into the towns. The rate of the influx was much in excess of the growth of jobs in the towns. Both countries dealt with the problem by the use of administrative measures. In the USSR from 1930 to the late 1970s the Soviet authorities prevented the excess rural population causing urban unemployment by administrative controls over the outflow of labour from the villages (depriving villagers of internal passports).[2] This re-

[2] An internal passport is an identity document. Without one it is illegal to live in a town.

Table 6.2. *Estimated ranges of urban male unemployment in China 1949–60*

	Total unemployed (millions)	As a percentage of the labour force
1949	6.6–13.8	18.2–31.7
1950	5.0–12.5	13.2–27.6
1951	2.7–10.3	6.8–21.8
1952	3.1–11.0	7.5–22.3
1953	3.0–10.9	6.9–21.3
1954	5.7–13.9	12.7–26.2
1955	7.7–16.1	16.8–29.6
1956	7.9–16.5	16.5–29.2
1957	9.6–18.3	19.5–31.6
1958	0.2– 9.3	0.3–14.9
1959	7.2–16.2	12.4–24.2
1960	10.7–20.2	17.3–28.3

Note: The figures are given as ranges rather than precise figures to emphasise that they are rough estimates.
Source: Eckstein (1968b) p. 369.

flected, and enhanced, the position of the rural population as second-class citizens. In China, urban unemployment resulting from the influx of peasants into the towns was a very serious problem in the 1950s. Some data relating to the 1950s is presented in table 6.2. The figures in table 6.2 underline the magnitude of the problem. The main method of dealing with it is by 'sending down' (*hsia-fang*) people from the towns to the countryside. This means that people, generally recent arrivals, are rounded up and sent back to the countryside.[3] This has the great advantage of saving on urban food demands and hence on the marketed output of agriculture. Once the unemployed are back in their villages, the responsibility for feeding them rests primarily on themselves, their families and their production teams. In their villages the former unemployed have both an obligation to work and a right to a share in the output of their private plot and of their team. Sending down was also used, after the victory of state socialism in South Vietnam, Laos and Cambodia, to reduce the unproductive urban populations in those countries. In Cambodia it was used on a particularly large scale. The use of sending down has enabled China and Cambodia

[3] This is analogous to the repatriation of immigrant workers from the industrialised West European countries when the demand for their labour fell.

to avoid the bloated urban agglomerations and shanty towns that are common in third world countries. In China sending down appears to have been successful in reducing the urban unemployment from the high figures of the 1950s. By 1971 the authorities claimed that full employment had been reached. In 1978 the existence and importance of unemployment was again officially recognised. This may have resulted from a lesser reliance on sending down by the post-Mao leadership.

The USSR has experienced continuous urban full employment since 1930. (Rural underemployment in the USSR was discussed in chapter 4.) Urban full employment is also normal in the other state socialist countries. This elimination of urban unemployment results from five phenomena.

First, the 'rational low wage policy' (Howe 1973a p. 56). It is normal in the state socialist countries, especially in the early stages of industrialisation, for the rate of growth of real wages to be kept well below the rate of growth of labour productivity. This limits the demand for wage goods and contains urban–rural income inequalities. Limiting the demand for wage goods enables a given marketed output of agriculture to provide employment for the maximum number of workers. In addition, it enables industry to increase the share of its output devoted to accumulation. Both these factors contribute to raising the growth rate of employment and output (see the discussion of the coercive model in chapter 4 and of the optimal share of investment in the national income in chapter 5). To operate a rational low wage policy requires a government which pursues an economic policy with a long time horizon, and prevents active working-class opposition (e.g. by ensuring that the trade unions function as transmission belts for government policy and by using sufficient repression). Examples of the rational low wage policy are, that in the USSR for many years after 1928 real wages per worker were below the 1928 level, and that in China real wages appear to have been about the same in 1972 as they were in 1957. Under capitalism a rational low wage policy would encounter two economic problems. First, it would have an adverse effect on domestically generated effective demand. (The importance of this would depend on the ratio of foreign trade to national income.) This is not a problem under state socialism, where the state always generates at least as much demand as is necessary and where economic problems mainly occur on the supply side. Secondly, removal of the incentive provided by falling quasi-rents on old machines, might have an adverse effect on technical progress, innovation and investment. Under state socialism, where technical progress and investment are, in principle, decided by the planners and do not depend on the expectations of firms about future quasi-rents, this is not a significant problem. The two problems encountered by the rational low wage policy under state socialism are as follows. First, it may have an adverse effect on labour productivity. This seems to have happened, for example, in the USSR in the early 1930s. Secondly, it may be impossible to implement because of working-class opposition. This was an important factor in Poland in 1956–60 and in the early 1970s. The Polish Government in those periods had come to power largely as a result of working-class opposition to the previous low growth of real wages, and wished to appease the workers. Similarly, in China the wage increase of 1977 came after prolonged industrial unrest.

Secondly, the huge investment programmes, which have created the industrial capacity to employ a rapidly increasing labour force. The possibility of implementing such programmes partly resulted, as explained above and in chapters 4 and 5, from the rational low wage policy. Thirdly, the use of administrative measures to restrict the influx of rural labour. Fourthly, the existence of the right to work, so that workers cannot easily be dismissed and workers without jobs can expect jobs to be found for them even if their marginal output in them is low or non-existent. This means that part of the 'employment' in the state socialist world corresponds to unemployment benefit in the advanced capitalist countries. That is, it is a means of ensuring an income rather than a means of ensuring output. Fifthly, the early retirement age and expansion of education.

Regional employment

Keynesian regional policy is primarily concerned with the provision by the state of financial incentives to private industry. Socialist regional policy is primarily concerned with the direct provision by the state of the necessary investment.

Regional employment policy in socialist countries has both socio-political and economic aspects. First, it is an aspect of the Leninist nationalities policy. The latter is concerned, not with ensuring purely 'formal' political freedom for formerly subject nationalities but with their rapid social and economic development. Secondly, it is concerned with the efficient utilisation of natural resources. Hence, Soviet regional policy combines both large-scale industrial investment in densely populated formerly backward areas, such as Central Asia, and large-scale natural resource development in sparsely populated Siberia. The enormous expansion of urban employment opportunities in Soviet Central Asia during the period of Soviet power is a major achievement of Soviet power.

One would expect that in a market economy the labour force would have to adjust to the availability of jobs, but that in a socialist planned economy the supply of jobs would be adjusted to the availability of labour. In an empirical study Pryor (1973 pp. 290–7) corroborated this expectation. He found that regional differences in the proportion of the population engaged in mining and manufacturing showed an approximately equal tendency to diminish in the post Second World War period in the state socialist and capitalist countries, but that in the former this was associated with jobs moving to where the people were, and in the latter with the reverse. There are problems with the data used for this exercise, but this is an interesting, if provisional, finding.

Rational utilisation of labour

The efficient allocation of labour can be considered under two heads, static and dynamic. Static efficiency is concerned with allocating a labour force of given productivity between various tasks so as to concentrate labour, especially high-quality labour, in the key sectors. Dynamic efficiency is concerned with raising labour productivity in any task.

An early investigation of the relationship between the sectoral allocation of labour in the state socialist and capitalist worlds was Nove (1964). He compared the USSR in 1959 with the UK in 1951 and found the following significant differences. First, as far as non-manual workers are concerned, the UK had a significantly greater proportion working in distribution, as officials (central and local government) and clerical workers (typists, secretaries, clerks etc.). To a considerable extent this explains the greater ease of shopping in the UK than in the USSR and the fact that business with UK official organisations can be handled by letter. In the USSR it is often necessary to sit for hours in the waiting rooms of various institutions to see some official. It may be said that in the UK the proportion of bureaucrats is greater than in the USSR but bureaucratism is less (because more people enable the work to be done quicker and with less waste of time by the applicant). As far as manual workers are concerned, Nove found a much greater proportion of the Soviet labour force engaged in agriculture, and a smaller proportion engaged in chemicals and metals and engineering. This simply reflected the greater backwardness of the Soviet economy.

This question has also been investigated by Garnsey (1975) and Pryor (1977). Pryor found that, comparing a large number of capitalist and state socialist economies, the proportion in the labour force of white collar workers other than sales personnel, i.e. professional (including technical and related workers), administrative and clerical workers, was mainly determined by the level of economic development. A greater proportion of white collar workers was associated with a higher level of economic development. The proportion was not related to the economic system. He also found that, comparing a large number of capitalist and state socialist countries, the proportion of the population engaged in wholesale and retail trade was significantly higher in the capitalist than in the state socialist countries. Since the participation rate is higher in the state socialist countries, the difference would be even bigger as a proportion of the labour force. The smaller proportion engaged in distribution in state socialism is a deliberate policy by governments which stress the crucial importance in economic growth of manufacturing industry and strive to minimise the allocation of labour to non-productive activities. Pryor also found, and clearly this is closely related to the previous finding, that there was a significant inter-system difference in shopping time, with considerably more time being required for shopping in state socialist countries (especially Poland) than in comparable capitalist countries.

For dynamic efficiency, the socialist countries primarily rely on investment and training. This investment and training have largely taken the form of copying the technology and division of labour prevalent in the capitalist world. Labour productivity in the USSR has always been considerably below that of the most advanced capitalist countries. Hence great stress has always been placed in the USSR on utilising the progressive aspects of Western methods for raising labour productivity. In his well-known pamphlet *The immediate tasks of the Soviet Government* (1918), Lenin wrote that the Taylor system of scientific management

> like all capitalist progress, is a combination of the refined brutality of bourgeois exploitation and a number of the greatest scientific achievements in the field of analysing mechanical motions during work, the

elimination of superfluous and awkward motions, the elaboration of correct methods of work, the introduction of the best system of accounting and control etc. The Soviet Republic must at all costs adopt all that is valuable in the achievements of science and technology in this field. The possibility of building socialism depends exactly upon our success in combining Soviet power and Soviet organisation of administration with the up to date achievements of capitalism. We must organise in Russia the study and teaching of the Taylor system and systematically try it out and adapt it to our ends.

This attitude has persisted down to the present and explains the admiration Soviet officials, planners and economists have for the large Western corporations, which they regard as marvels of the scientific organisation of labour.[4] It also explains the concessions offered by the Soviet Government to Western firms in the 1920s, the import of technology by all the state socialist countries in the 1970s, the R & D cooperation agreements between Western firms and the USSR, the East–West industrial cooperation agreements and the East–West joint ventures. With the Western technology has come the Western organisation of labour without the strong independent worker organisations that exist in the West. M. Dido (1971), the Secretary of the CGIL, Italy's Communist Party dominated labour federation, has discussed this question with specific reference to the huge car plant being built by Fiat at Tol'yatti in the USSR.

The entire project has been carried out on the basis of plans prepared and supervised by Fiat technicians...not only the technical equipment but also the organisation of work is of the Fiat type...it is impossible to distinguish the administrative organisation...whether with regard to working conditions or the absolute priority given to productivity from that of the Turin plant...At Tol'yatti...they have adopted not only Western machines but also Western systems of organisation. To have a minimum of equilibrium, however, such a system presupposes at the very least the existence of a strong trade union force. But at the present moment such a force does not exist, either in the Soviet Union or in the other countries of Eastern Europe.

When asked what disturbed him most about the plant at Tol'yatti, Dido replied that it was hearing the Turin bosses say that 'the trade union demands are unjustified, since even the Soviet leaders pay no attention to them at Tol'yatti'.

[4] The standard Soviet phrase for the efficient utilisation of labour (*nauchnaya organizatsiya truda,* literally 'the scientific organisation of labour') is a literal translation of *l'organisation scientifique du travail,* the French term for Taylorism. In France the phrase *l'organisation rationnelle du travail* was adopted when the reaction against Taylorism set in, but in the USSR the original term, which had Lenin's support, has been retained.

It is no accident that the halting attempts to develop a new technology appropriate to a new, more human, organisation of labour, have taken place not in a state socialist country but in Social-Democratic Scandinavia. The USSR, and the countries which follow her, have *en principe* postponed any attempt to transform the organisation and division of labour till the higher stage of communism, and in practice postponed it till the Greek kalends.

The irony of the endorsement of Taylorism by a 'proletarian Government' which has 'abolished the exploitation of man by man' has not gone entirely unnoticed in the state socialist countries. In 1923–24 there took place in the USSR a very interesting debate on this subject (Bailes 1977). The Taylorist position was defended by the Central Labour Institute, founded in 1920, and its leader A. K. Gastev. It was criticised by 'The Moscow Group of Communists Actively interested in Scientific Management'. In traditional Marxist fashion the latter criticised Taylorism as having the 'aim of transforming the living person into an unreasoning and stupid instrument without any general qualifications or sufficient all-round development'. The views of the Moscow Group were criticised by the head of the trade unions and a number of prominent party figures. At a conference held in 1924 to resolve this dispute, the Central Labour Institute was victorious. Its assumptions and approach were recognised as standards for the whole national economy. The use of piecework as an incentive to greater productivity has remained an important feature of work in the CMEA countries. Disputes about piecework norms have been endemic, sometimes with explosive political consequences, as in Poznan in 1956. Perhaps the supreme triumph of Soviet Taylorism was the Stakhanov movement of the 1930s, which was a state organised rate-busting campaign on an unparalleled scale. One of its organisers was A. K. Gastev.

Some observers have suggested that steps towards a fundamental transformation of the labour process have taken place in China. According to Bettelheim, the transformations that occurred during the Cultural Revolution signified, inter alia, that a struggle was being waged to overcome the division between intellectual and manual labour. Similarly, a new type of technical progress is supposedly taking place in China (Bettelheim 1974b pp. 78–89). Richman (1969 pp. 258–9) confirms that the division of labour is often less pronounced in Chinese than in 'normal' factories. He suggests, however, that this is simply a rational response to the extreme shortage of qualified specialists in a backward country. He also considers that it results in serious inefficiencies, for example, in some of the larger and more complex firms he visited. Richman (1969 pp. 325–6 & 252–3) also confirms the great stress on technical progress resulting from innovations introduced by the workers themselves in China. He suggests, however, that the reason this is worthwhile is because of the current low technological level of Chinese industry. In future, he argues, science-based innovations are likely to become more important. In addition, he considers that stress on the virtues of 'worker engineers' and 'peasant scientists' at the expense of scientific research and development has had serious costs for China (non-utilisation of qualified people, waste of resources in irrational projects). The waste of time at endless political meetings has been stressed by a Soviet scientist who worked in China (Klochko 1964).[5] The main source of technical progress in Chinese industry, of course, is the import of technology from more advanced countries, in the First Five Year Plan from the USSR and in recent years from the leading capitalist countries. This technology, naturally, is associated with the capitalist division of labour.

METHODS

The three chief methods of labour planning in the state socialist countries are administrative, economic and moral.

Administrative methods

In the CMEA countries it is customary to distinguish between 'administrative' and 'economic' methods of plan implementation. By 'administrative' methods is meant instructions from the

[5] According to Klochko (1964 p. 80), 'The primary waste in the organisation of Chinese science was in the wasted time of the people engaged in scientific work, rather than in any failure to utilize a piece of equipment or in carelessness with books. Beautiful, well-equipped labs stood deserted for days on end; thousands of technical books in excellent libraries remained closed while potential readers were at meetings, making confessions, or tilling the soil. This poor country, which had invested immense sums of hard currency between 1955 and 1958 to construct libraries and laboratories, had failed to use these capital investments. Trained personnel were distracted from their duties, and even the equipment was allowed to deteriorate through lack of proper maintenance.'

top of an administrative hierarchy followed by obedience from below. It is the pattern normal in all armies and civil bureaucracies. By 'economic' methods is meant the use of financial sticks and carrots. This is the method normal in market economies.

During the Civil War the Bolsheviks relied heavily on administrative methods and their leaders and intellectuals developed the ideology of reliance on administrative methods, building on the foundations laid by Marx and Kautsky. As far as the founders of Marxism–Leninism are concerned, it is well known that, according to Marx and Engels, commodity production will cease under socialism because society will organise social work directly, without the mediation of the market. It will deliberately allocate the available forces of production according to plan, in accordance with the needs of society. Does it follow from this that the system of organising production in a socialist economy demands a strict central allocation of means of production, labour and consumer goods in physical form? As Brus (1961 p. 40) has noted,

> In so far as we disregard their reservations on the possibility of scientifically determining the forms of the future socialist economy, and draw conclusions from their fragmentary declarations about the subject, we may answer in the affirmative. At any rate, in the works of the creators of scientific socialism it is relatively easy to find such formulations as will confirm these interpretations, but we cannot find any contrary statements, e.g. such as put into the foreground the use of market forms.

In the works of the late-nineteenth-century German Social Democrats the idea that a socialist economy is a natural, non-market, economy is clear, explicit and repeated.

In *The economics of the transition period* Bukharin explained that the transition from capitalism to socialism in the field of labour meant the liquidation of the labour market and its replacement by the allocation of labour by the state. The same thought was expressed by Trotsky in his well-known speech at the 9th Party Congress.

A well-known and much-discussed use of administrative methods was the creation and utilisation in the USSR in 1930–57 of a network of forced labour institutions, the Gulag Archipelago. This partial reïntroduction of serfdom was largely a result of the decision to adopt the coercive model of the role of agriculture in economic development (see chapter 4). Many of the first inhabitants of the camps were farmers deported from their villages at the time of collectivisation. From the point of view of numbers employed, agriculture in the USSR in the 1930s was by far the most important branch of the economy. Reliance on coercion in various construction and mining enterprises was simply a small generalisation, from a quantitative point of view, of the principle, reliance on coercion, on which the main branch of the economy was organised.

Herding labour into camps had the advantage of saving on costs per worker and reducing demand for scarce food, but against this must be set the costs of the guards, officials, punitive apparatus etc., as well as the low productivity of the labour. The use of forced labour camps was copied in China. In May 1951, during the repression of that period, Mao (1977b p. 55) pointed out that large numbers of prisoners under suspended death sentences formed a useful labour force 'which will be conducive to our national construction'. A widespread system of camps for 'reform through labour' and 'education through labour' was established in China, but information about its quantitative significance, evolution over time and economic efficiency, is very sparse. According to a former inmate of reform through labour camps, the Chinese camps are more efficient than the Soviet ones (Pasqualini 1975 p. 12). This may be so, but Pasqualini had no personal knowledge of Soviet camps on which to base the comparison, and in fact there seems to be no firm evidence on this issue.

A necessary condition for the use of coerced labour in the USSR and China was the absence of independent worker organisations.

Another example of the use of administrative methods in the USSR is the allocation of new graduates by the state for the first three years of their working lives.

When the Chinese planned economy was established during the First Five Year Plan (1953–57) one of the things copied from the USSR was the use of economic methods to allocate the labour force. One of the features of the independent, Maoist strategy of development adopted in China from 1958 onwards was the increased use of administrative methods of labour allocation. Physical movement is difficult because it requires the permission of the authorities for a ration card to be transferred from one locality to another. Moreover, housing has to be obtained in a new place. Furthermore, workers may not freely change jobs. By Western standards labour turnover appears to be low. New workers are assigned jobs upon graduating from secondary or technical school or university by the relevant organisation. When an enterprise expands or when new enterprises are established, the additional labour required is recruited from three sources: school graduates, surplus labour drawn from the countryside and surplus labour drawn from other factories.

An important administrative method for implementing the labour plan in all the state socialist countries is keeping files on workers so as to determine their fitness for particular jobs and material rewards. In the USSR, since 1938 each worker has had a labour book, an official document recording his name, age, education, trade, information about his work, transfers from one enterprise to another (with reasons) and details of encouragements and rewards. Enterprises are supposed to engage workers and employees (other than those entering employment for the first time) only on presentation of their labour books, which the enterprise then keeps till the worker is discharged. In addition, the party committees responsible for filling all important posts keep files on actual and possible holders of such posts, and the state security organs also keep personnel files which play an important role in appointments and dismissals. The accumulation of information in the hands of the authorities naturally plays a major role in determining behaviour in a one-employer state.

In China too, the records kept by the authorities play an important role. A major factor governing a cadre's career is his personal file. This is kept within his work unit and records all the important facts about his life including such things as his family and class origins, his technical qualifications, the quality of his work and his attitudes towards various political issues. When a cadre is considered for promotion, this file forms the basis for judgement. Naturally, everyone works hard to avoid getting a black mark on his record. During the Cultural Revolution these files became the centre of considerable debate. Political opponents used them to attack each other and the Red Guards were able to get a lot of confidential information from them about cadres. Several of the most intense local struggles concerned whether a cadre had been correctly labelled during the course of the movement or whether an earlier judgement should be reversed.

Economic methods

The use of economic methods, i.e. of pay, is very common in the socialist countries. In China in 1966–76, the stress was often on group material incentives rather than on individual ones. Material incentives play a very big role, for example, in Soviet regional policy, where pay is much higher and the number of years work required for a pension are much lower, in inhospitable regions, than in the main cities. Similarly, in the USSR, the relative pay of workers in the non-productive sector (e.g. distribution, education and medical care) has traditionally been low, as to direct labour towards the productive sector.

Administrative and economic methods are often used in combination. A very important example is the system of national job evaluation in the socialist countries. This is considered further in chapter 7 below. Similarly, in the CMEA countries, the quantitative planning of the demand for labour and of the output of various kinds of graduates, is normally combined with the planning of relative pay levels so as to attract the appropriate volume and quality of labour.

The way in which the planners manipulate relative pay, and its effects, have been investigated by Hamermesh & Portes (1972). They examined Hungarian data for 1951–67. They found that the planners did raise the relative pay of workers in industries with the fastest rates of growth of output in order to attract labour to them. They also found that this policy was apparently ineffective, since the supply of labour did not appear very responsive to relative earnings. The main influences on the supply of labour appeared to be the outflow from agriculture and the availability of jobs. The conclusion reached by Hamermesh & Portes is that 'the planners were mistaken. They erred in believing that changes in wages of the magnitude they used would affect labour supply.' It is ironical that the mistake of the planners was to take seriously a traditional idea of neoclassical economics, the importance of relative pay in allocating labour.

The use of economic methods is naturally more important in countries where labour is permitted freely to change jobs, e.g. the USSR since 1956 and the smaller East European countries, than in countries with direction of labour, e.g. China.

Moral methods

The use of moral incentives is very widespread in all state socialist countries. In all of them great efforts are devoted during the educational process to internalise the value of hard work for the good of society. The noticeboard with pictures of honoured workers who have worked particularly well, the brigades of communist labour who have pledged themselves to feats of socialist competition, the public meetings at which good workers sit on the platform, the distribution of honours such as 'hero of socialist labour', are familiar features of state socialist life.

So far as nonmaterial incentives are concerned, many of the forms evolved in the Soviet Union have also been used in China; and yet certain techniques have been pushed to greater lengths by the CCP. For example, the mechanism of 'criticism and self-criticism' has been generally employed to a much greater extent than in the USSR. Generally it seems that the Chinese have relied more on nonmaterial incentives and persuasion than the Russians. This reliance on non-material spurs undoubtedly was a factor of great moment in the miscarriage of the Great Leap Forward [Hoffman 1967 p. 119].

A problem with moral methods is that in fact they are often administrative methods with a veneer of non-compulsion. For example in the USSR of the 1970s, the Communist Saturday, when workers work on some Saturdays, supposedly voluntarily, to help in the construction of communism, is actually simply a day's compulsory unpaid work.

How does worker morale and motivation in the state socialist countries compare with that in capitalist countries? To answer this question properly would require an international research programme involving fieldwork in many countries. Such research is not possible in the USSR, China or most of the other state socialist countries. Nevertheless, there is some knowledge in this area, largely arising from the increase in East–West industrial cooperation agreements in the 1970s. A study of the experience of US firms with industrial cooperation agreements with Poland and Romania (Hayden 1976), reported that in these two countries (ibid. p. 108) 'worker morale and initiative [are] close to non-existent'. The account of how the US capitalist corporation Clark Equipment Company, as part of its technology transfer agreement with the Polish concern Bumar Union for the manufacture of heavy-duty planetary reduction axles, had to instill pride of achievement into the indifferent Polish workers by appealing to their patriotism (ibid. p. 49) is deeply ironical. If these accounts are typical, they would seem to indicate that, at any rate in Poland and Romania, worker motivation and morale and pride in work under state socialism compare unfavourably with that normal under capitalism.

It seems that, in general, workers in the state socialist countries continue to regard themselves as wage workers rather than as co-owners of the means of production. Hence there continue to exist such phenomena as worker attempts to limit the work content of a day's labour power,[6] e.g. conflict over piecework norms. These phenomena are startling and unexpected from a Marxist–Leninist point of view. What explains them? There appear to be three chief factors.

First, the adverse effects of state socialism on personal consumption (see chapter 8 below).

Secondly, the lack of control by workers over their working lives. This does not arise from the malevolence of this or that official, but has a definite theoretical explanation. Experience has shown that state (or cooperative) ownership, by itself, is not sufficient to transform the relations of production. As the Soviet sociologist Arutiunian (1973 pp. 109–10) has noted with special reference to Soviet collective farms, though the argument is perfectly general,

> it is necessary to face the essence of the phenomenon of *collectivisation of property*. It is not a once and for all affair. Rather, it *is a long process.* From the legal or, more precisely, the political act of collectivisation to actual collectivisation there is a whole period, perhaps even epoch, of historical development that only begins with the immediate act of collectivisation. The revolution in our country eliminated the order under which property was separated from work and created the conditions for their unification. But such a unification is possible only through a long evolution and a series of intermediate socio-economic forms. The criterion for the unification of the means of production and labour power, materialised and living labour, is the degree of the realisation by the producer himself of the functions of management or, in other words, of the disposition of collectivised property... Empirical studies, however, show that in practice this mechanism [i.e. the formal constitution of a collective farm] by itself does not ensure sufficiently effective participation of each person in the disposition of property.

This important thesis and the general conclusion to be drawn from it, are considered further in chapter 10. Here it is

[6] This is what Taylor called 'soldiering' and what is known in UK management terminology as 'restrictive practices'.

necessary to note only that acceptance of this thesis undermines any expectation of a higher work morale under state socialism than under capitalism. Furthermore, given that new relations of production have not been fully established, the old means of defending worker interests retain much of their usefulness. Workers under state socialism, however, lack the independent worker organisations normal under capitalism, and from this point of view their position is worse than under capitalism. As A. Hegedus, a former Hungarian Prime Minister, has noted (Hegedus 1976a p. 88), during the Stalin period

> The principal function of the trade unions became to bring about the realisation of state plans. Work competition, managed from above and largely manipulated, became their principal contribution to the fulfilment of production plans; their management of this competition, together with the support they gave to the fixing of norms, alienated the working masses from the trade unions and, it may be said, robbed the latter completely of their character as a movement.

This situation has largely persisted down to the present time.[7]

Thirdly, the huge and all-pervading gulf between the words and slogans of the authorities and economic, social and political reality. An example was given above, the Communist Saturday. A compulsory day's unpaid work is treated in the media as if the whole labour force is selflessly working for the common good.

INSTRUMENTS

> The basic method of planning the rational utilisation of labour resources is the balance method.
>
> Litvyakov (1969 p. 166)

The main instrument of labour planning used in the socialist countries is the labour balance. A labour balance is simply a material balance which deals with labour. In the USSR a whole series of labour balances are regularly drawn up, both statistical (concerned with the past) and planning (concerned with various future periods), for the country as a whole and for its subdivisions (e.g. republics and smaller regions). A planning labour balance can be set out schematically as in figure 6.1.

[7] Hegedus has also observed (Hegedus 1976a p. 89) that the Hungarian economic reform is reviving the trade unions as a movement. 'Socialist society is developing in a pluralist direction, and the functions of the state administration and those of the unions are becoming increasingly independent of one another. In comparison with the Stalin era, the trade unions are increasingly taking on the new task of defending the interests of the workers and exercising social control over the administration.' So far this process has been slow and hesitant, and, even in Hungary, perhaps more a hope than a fact.

	Previous period			Planning period		
	Total	of which		Total	of which	
		urban	rural		urban	rural
1. Labour resources (including natural increase)						
of which:						
population of working age (excluding invalids)						
workers of pension age or 15 or less.						
2. Distribution of labour resources						
(a) By type of occupation:						
(1) occupied in the social economy						
(2) full-time students of 16 and above						
(3) household and private gardening						
(b) By branch of the national economy:						
(1) working in the material production sector (by industry)						
(2) working in the non-productive sectors (by sector)						
(c) By social group (workers and employees, collective farmers, cooperative craftsmen, artisans, families of workers, employees and collective farmers occupied in housework and private gardening						

Figure 6.1. *A planning labour balance*

The chief task of the labour balance is to coordinate available labour resources with the requirements for labour. The available labour resources are calculated from statistical and demographic data, account being taken of any special factors (e.g. the increased provision of nursery facilities for children). The required distribution of labour resources is calculated from statistical data and the planned levels of output and labour productivity. Shortages of labour, in general or in specific categories, gives rise to policies (e.g. increase in training, import of foreign machinery, acceleration of mechanisation) designed to overcome them. The labour balance is only a part of the balance of the national economy, and its various sections should be harmonised with the other parts of that balance. For example, the plan for technical progress affects labour productivity and labour requirements in various industries.

Western economists, in particular Keynesians, may be surprised at the emphasis placed in socialist manpower planning on supply side factors. The reason for this is that in the state socialist countries an adequate demand for labour can generally be assumed, and the principal task of manpower planners is to satisfy this demand with respect to quantity, quality and location. It is the supply side, rather than the demand side, that chiefly constrains the growth of the state socialist countries.

Labour coefficients

A relatively new instrument of labour planning in the state socialist countries is the labour coefficient. It is now possible to calculate the direct and indirect labour embodied in each unit of particular outputs. This is particularly interesting for Marxists because it gives empirical content to the Marxist concept of the socially necessary labour embodied in a commodity, or the *value* of that commodity.

An analytical expression for the calculation of full labour inputs was first given by Dmitriev (1898). The first calculation of the analogous concept of full commodity inputs was by Leontief. Leontief's empirical and conceptual work is now regularly employed in the state socialist countries for the compilation of input–output tables in labour units and the calculation of direct and full labour input coefficients.

The first such table was compiled by the Soviet Central Statistical Administration for 1959 and published in 1962. It showed, in terms of labour, the inter-industrial flows, the formation of the final bill of goods, the formation of national product and the costs incurred in the non-productive sphere. This calculation corresponds to the Dmitriev–Leontief full labour coefficients. It showed, for example, that out of 97 million man years expended in the national economy in 1959, about 50 million were ultimately devoted to the production of consumer goods, 30 million to capital formation, exports and other items, and 17 million to the non-productive sphere. Subsequently the

Soviet Central Statistical Administration compiled a similar table for 1966. Although input–output tables in labour terms are regularly compiled in the USSR, and full labour input coefficients have been much discussed and also calculated, it would appear that they have not become an important instrument of labour planning, being confined to various kinds of analytical calculations.

CONCLUSION

Labour planning in the state socialist countries is concerned with facilitating the fulfilment and overfulfilment of the national economic plan by ensuring that the requisite types of labour are available in the right quantities and places and perform the necessary work. This involves, developing the abilities of the labour force, so as to produce the right types of labour, providing full employment so as to avoid waste of resources, ensuring a rational regional distribution of employment and ensuring the efficient utilisation of labour. The main methods used, separately and in combination, are administrative, economic and moral. The main instrument is the labour balance.

In general, the position of workers in state socialism with respect to opportunities for improving qualifications, work intensity, social security, hours of work, security of employment and availability of employment, compares favourably with that in comparable capitalist countries. In some cases, the position of workers does not compare favourably with that in comparable capitalist countries. Notable examples are the Gulag Archipelago and 'reform through labour' and 'education through labour' camps, sent down people, Soviet collective farmers for much of their history and those in political disfavour. The effect of state socialism on industrial safety is impossible to assess fully in the absence of data. For the USSR, the absence of data suggests a poor record. State ownership of the means of production and national economic planning are not sufficient to eliminate unemployment. Urban full employment has been established and maintained in the chief state socialist countries partly by administrative methods, the passport system in the USSR and sending down in China.

No progress has been made under state socialism towards a new, more human, organisation of the labour process. The state socialist countries copy the capitalist organisation of labour without the countervailing power exercised by worker organisations in the West. The fragmentary evidence available about labour morale suggests that, at any rate in Poland and Romania, it compares unfavourably with that normal under capitalism. The absence of independent worker organisations has adverse effects, not only on labour morale, but also on industrial safety and the use of coerced labour.

SUGGESTIONS FOR FURTHER READING

J. Mouly, 'Employment: a concept in need of renovation', *International Labour Review* vol. 116 no. 1 (July–August 1977).

Planning of manpower in the Soviet Union (Moscow 1975).

M. McAuley, *Settling labour disputes in Soviet Russia* (Oxford 1969).

D. Lane & F. O'Dell, *Soviet industrial workers* (London 1978).

P. Wiles, 'Soviet unemployment on US definitions', *Soviet Studies* vol. 23 (April 1972).

K. E. Bailes, 'Alexei Gastev and the Soviet controversy over Taylorism', *Soviet Studies* (July 1977).

J. Timar, *Planning the labour force in Hungary* (New York 1966).

M. Haraszi, 'I have heard the iron cry', *New Left Review* 91.

C. Hoffmann, *The Chinese worker* (Albany 1974).

C. Howe, 'Labour organisation and incentives in industry, before and after the Cultural Revolution', S. Schram (ed.) *Authority, participation and cultural change in China* (Cambridge 1973).

M. D. Fletcher, *Workers and Commissars: trade union policy in the People's Republic of China* (Bellingham, Washington, USA 1974).

B. Silverman (ed.) *Man and Socialism in Cuba: The Great Debate* (New York 1971).

C. Mesa-Lago, *The labour sector and socialist distribution in Cuba* (New York 1968).

H. Scott, *Does socialism liberate women?* (Boston 1974).

D. Davin, *Women-work: Women and the party in revolutionary China* (Oxford 1976).

7

PLANNING INCOMES

Distribution is a method, an instrument, a means, for increasing production.

Lenin (1921)

THEORETICAL BACKGROUND

The actual distribution of income in any country at any time depends on the balance of class forces, the institutional arrangements and indeed the whole history of the country. It is not likely to reflect any uniform principle. Before approaching actual data, however, it is useful to consider alternative principles of income distribution so as to illuminate the actual data and policy debates of various countries. Two well-known, and conflicting, principles of income distribution are those of need, and of desert. The first principle is that income should be distributed in accordance with need, so that, for example, the highest incomes should go to cripples and those with many dependants and the lowest to healthy people with no dependants. The second principle is that income should be distributed in accordance with the contribution that has been made to society so that, for example, the highest incomes go to inventors, prospectors, engineers, coal miners and farmers, and the lowest to the blind, children and the idle.

The Marxist view of distribution under socialism is that the aim of the socialist movement is to create a society in which distribution is on the basis of need, but that in the years immediately after the revolution it will still be necessary to base distribution on work performed, i.e. on desert. This was clearly explained by Marx in his *Critique of the Gotha Programme* (1875), in which he wrote that,

What we have to deal with here [immediately after the revolution] is a communist society, not as it has *developed* on its own foundations, but on the contrary, just as it *emerges* from capitalist society, and which is thus in every respect, economically, morally and intellectually, still stamped with the birthmarks of the old society from whose womb it emerges. Accordingly, the individual producer receives back from society – after the deductions have been made – exactly what he gives to it...he receives a certificate from society that he has furnished such and such an amount of labour (after deducting his labour from the common funds), and with this certificate he draws from the social stock of means of consumption as much as costs the same amount of labour...

Hence, *equal right* here is still in principle *bourgeois right*, although principle and practice are no longer at loggerheads, while the exchange of equivalents in commodity exchange only exists *on the average* and not in the individual case.

In spite of this advance, this *equal right* is still constantly stigmatised by a bourgeois limitation. The right of the producers is *proportional* to the labour they supply; the equality consists in the fact that measurement is made with an *equal standard*, labour.

But one man is superior to another physically or mentally and so supplies more labour in the same time, or can labour for a longer time; and labour, to serve as a measure, must be defined by its duration or its intensity, otherwise it ceases to be a standard of measurement. This *equal* right is an unequal right for unequal labour. It recognises no class differences, because everyone is only a worker like everyone else; but it tacitly recognises unequal individual endowment and thus productive capacity as natural privileges. *It is, therefore, a right of inequality, in its content, like every right.* Right by its very nature can consist only in the application of an equal standard; but unequal individuals (and they would not be different individuals if they were not unequal) are measurable only by an equal standard in so far as they are brought under an equal point of view, are taken from one *definite* side only, for instance, in the present case, are regarded *only as workers*, and nothing more is seen in them, everything else being ignored...

But these defects are inevitable in the first phase of communist society as it is when it has just emerged after prolonged birth pangs from capitalist society...

In a higher phase of communist society, after the enslaving subordination of the individual to the division of labour, and therewith also the antithesis between mental and physical labour, has vanished; after labour has become not only a means of life but life's prime want; after the productive forces have also increased with the all-round development of the individual, and all the springs of cooperative wealth flow more abundantly – only then can the narrow horizon of bourgeois right be crossed in its entirety and society inscribe on its banners: From each according to his ability, to each according to his need!

These ideas have remained orthodox in all the socialist countries but have been interpreted in very different ways at different times and in different countries. In the USSR they were used in the 1930s to justify an attack on egalitarianism and a widening of differentials. Since the mid 1950s they have been used to support a new approach to wages and wage differentials. In this latter period the socialist distribution principle has been interpreted as requiring equal pay for equal work and this has been used to justify greater equalisation of incomes, the rationalisation of wage scales within industries and plants, the use of comparison and job evaluation to a much greater extent than in the capitalist world, and a reduction in urban–rural differentials. The communist principle of distribution according to need is supposed to be realised by the transfer payments and free public services. In China, where the bulk of the population is engaged in agriculture, distribution between collectives (such as teams, brigades and communes) appears to be largely based on work performed (and natural conditions), and within collectives on both work and need (Hoffmann 1967, Riskin 1975).

The emphasis placed on distribution according to need is an important feature of Chinese agriculture. For approximately the first three and a half decades of their existence, the incomes of Soviet collective farmers derived from their private plots and the number of labour days they worked for the collective farms. Both of these are examples of distribution according to desert (subject to tribute exacted by the state and differences in natural conditions). In China, when communes were first organised (1958), distribution within them was on the basis of need. Communal mess halls were organised and communal meals provided for all, free of charge, regardless of work done. This system of free supply was much praised in the Chinese media in 1958 as an example of communist distribution. It appears, however, to have had an adverse effect on work incentives and hence to have been one of the factors contributing to the crisis of 1959–61. 'Why should we work hard if we will eat well anyway?' seems to have been a widespread thought. Hence completely free supply was soon abandoned.

Partial distribution on the basis of need, however, was revived during and after the Cultural Revolution. In the early 1970s it typically worked as follows. The basic accounting unit was the team. (A team is a group of households, on average about 30–35, which is the basic collective unit of production and distribution in rural China. It is a sub-unit of a brigade, which itself is a sub-unit of a commune. It is intended to combine incentives to produce – the members are neighbours and often relatives as well – with the advantages of collectivist agriculture. The nearest Soviet equivalent would be the so-called link (*zveno*), which has had a long and controversial history in the Soviet Union but which has never been very important.) Out of its gross output the first claimant was the state, which received a tax in kind, often about 6% of gross output. (In addition, the team also had an obligation to meet its sales quotas to the state and its commercial contracts with the state trading organisations, if any. For these deliveries, however, unlike the tax, the team was paid. It could also make over-quota sales to the state, for which, in the case of grain, it received higher prices. The system of quotas applied to the main outputs, that is grain and industrial crops (such as cotton). The system of contracts applied to goods of lesser importance such as vegetables, fruit and meat.) The second claimant was the reserve fund. Into this say 20% of gross output would be paid to cover grain reserves, seed and other working capital, investment and welfare (e.g. sickness and old age benefits and burial expenses). The balance was split into approximately equal portions (the ratio between the two portions differing in different areas) and distributed (in kind and cash) in two different ways. The first was equally distributed among the members of the team as that member's grain ration. The second was divided among the members of the team in accordance with the number of work points earned. Team members also had the income from their private plots and also remittances from relatives (e.g. sons working in industry) where applicable.

This system has two important things in common with the Soviet one from collectivisation down to 1966 (when something akin to a wage system was introduced into Soviet collective farms). First, peasant incomes are a residual item of the farm accounts and not a prior charge like the wages of workers in state industry. The income of the farmers varies directly with their output. In this respect their position is like that of primary producers in the capitalist world. Unlike the latter, however, they do not suffer from violently fluctuating prices. Secondly, payment for work done takes the form of labour days or work points which depend on work performed and whose value is not known until long after the event. It has one special feature, however, a greater stress on distribution according to need (i.e. the grain ration and the welfare benefits). The Chinese system requires two special inputs, numerous rural cadres and extensive political education campaigns aimed at replacing the old family-centred psychology by a new collectively-oriented one. As pointed out in chapter 4, given the currently available output statistics, its effect on output does not seem especially favourable. Its effect on distribution, however, appears to have been dramatic, if one compares it with pre 1949 China or other Asian countries, as is shown later in this chapter.

SOCIALIST INCOMES POLICY

Marxists consider that the decentralised system of income determination that exists under capitalism is just another aspect of the anarchy of production that must be replaced under socialism by a planned and centralised system. All the state socialist countries operate what in Western terminology would be called permanent incomes policies. Important aspects of these policies are, price control, the planning of foreign trade, the elimination of large property incomes, compulsory arbitration, national job evaluation, steady growth of real incomes, uniform regional net advantages, the production mindedness of trade unions, full employment, a proletarian Government and a non-permissive approach to breaches of labour discipline.

Price control is a basic part of incomes planning in state socialist countries. By keeping prices under control a major source of pressure for wage increases is removed. The success of the state socialist countries in the past two and a half decades in maintaining stable prices, as measured by official statistics, is shown in table 7.1.

The official statistics summarised in table 7.1 indicate that the state socialist countries (other than Yugoslavia) have been extremely successful in preventing prices spiralling upwards. It is well known that these figures actually exaggerate the success of the state socialist countries because of their treatment of 'new' goods, free market prices and other factors (Vainshtein 1969 pp. 132–7). To what extent should they be adjusted to allow for this? Hsiao (1971) has undertaken such an adjustment for China in 1952–57. According to her calculations, the actual average rate of inflation in China in 1952–57 was not 1.7% p.a. as shown in the official statistics, but double that, at 3.5% p.a., when allowance is made for repressed inflation. Her calculations also show that the official statistics give a misleading impression not only of the average rate of inflation but also of year to year fluctuations. For example, according to her calculations, both 1953 and 1956 were years of sharp inflationary pressures, with

Table 7.1. *Consumer price indices*

Year	Bulgaria	Czechoslovakia	DDR	Hungary	Poland	Romania	USSR	Yugoslavia	China
1952	—	—	—	—	—	—	—	—	100.0[a]
1953	—	—	—	—	—	—	—	—	103.2
1954	—	—	—	—	—	—	—	—	105.5
1955	100.0	100.0	100.0	100.0	100.0	100.0	100.0	100.0	106.3
1956	—	—	—	—	—	—	—	—	106.3
1957	—	—	—	—	—	—	—	—	108.6
1958	—	—	—	—	—	—	—	—	108.3
1960	90.6	91.3	89.5	100.1	110.3	103.0	100.7	130.2	—
1963	—	—	—	—	—	—	—	—	118.2[b]
1965	96.3	90.8	89.4	103.8	116.3	102.1	101.5	248.3	—
1970	96.6	97.5	89.2	109.5	121.7	104.1	101.2	407.0	—
1972	—	—	—	—	—	—	—	—	118.2
1974	99.7	97.3	88.4	120.5	125.9	107.4	101.2	792.4	—

[a] For 1952–58 the figures are for nation-wide average retail prices.
[b] This figure is for retail prices in eight cities and is not fully comparable with the data for 1952–58.

Source: Official statistics. For China the figures for 1952–58 are from Chen (1967), p. 409, for 1963 from Howe (1973a), p. 33 and for 1972 from Howe (1973a), pp. 33–4.

inflation of 14% in the former and 12% in the latter. Nevertheless, the average rate of inflation shown by her calculations is remarkably low bearing in mind the institutional changes taking place in the economy at this period (the socialisation of the economy), the very rapid inflation prior to 1952, the big investment programme and the rapid rate of industrial growth.

On the whole it seems reasonable to accept the view, which is confirmed by casual impressions, that although the official statistics are not comparable with those for other countries, nevertheless the average rate of increase in retail prices in the CMEA countries since 1955 and in China since 1952 compares very favourably with that of the OECD countries in general and especially with the UK, France, Italy and Japan. This has helped immensely with the implementation of incomes policy. The difficulties which spiralling prices cause for incomes policy are clearly shown by Soviet experience in 1928–40. In that period the USSR experienced a massive inflation, with state retail prices rising tenfold (Holzman 1960). A major reason for this was the huge rise in food prices which forced up wages.

The planning of foreign trade has the advantage of insulating the economy somewhat from shocks originating on the world market. Both sudden sharp price fluctuations and sudden falls in effective demand can be avoided by planning foreign trade on a medium-term basis. This enables the planners to avoid either sharp money wage increases (in response to an increase in prices) or sharp real wage cuts (in response to a sudden deterioration in the terms of trade). This naturally facilitates the planned development of incomes.

Marxists have always laid great stress on the absence of the distinction between property owners and proletarians as a necessary condition of a harmonious society. An important difference between the state socialist and capitalist worlds is the absence in the former of the small minority of individuals with huge holdings of means of production that plays such an important role in the latter. In the USSR, for example, there is still some property income, e.g. interest on savings bank deposits and some rent, but the amounts involved are relatively small. In addition, conspicuous consumption is absent, and the luxuries enjoyed by top officials, although substantial, do not compare favourably with those of Western millionaires and are less visible. It is noteworthy that in China too, where income differentials are substantial, visible signs of consumption differences are negligible (Whyte 1975). The dysfunctional effect of conspicuous consumption, often deriving from property income, in securing worker agreement to incomes policy, is well known. 'Why should we make sacrifices when at Ascot people are living off champagne and caviare?' is a familiar remark.

In any system labour disputes are bound to occur. In the West these are resolved by collective bargaining, with the strike and unemployment being the chief weapons in the hands of the parties. The Soviet system of compulsory arbitration (McAuley, M. 1969) provides a method of settling factory level disputes without interrupting production or wasting resources.

Experience with incomes policy in various countries shows that the conscious determination of relative incomes is very difficult. The Soviet system for dealing with this is that of national job evaluation (Handy 1971). This is a system whereby, in principle, all jobs and all workers are graded, the jobs by function and the workers by skill. The wages actually received by any worker, above the minimum wage, depend on his occupation and grade, the grade of the job, the work norms, the level of output (if on piecework) or the length of time worked (if on a time system), and the receipt of bonuses and regional coefficients (if any). The underlying idea is to replace the determination of relative incomes by market forces, by their determination in a rational, objective fashion, and to stimulate the raising of the qualifications of the labour force, production and productivity. Although the 'scientific', 'objective' nature of the resulting income distribution is something of a myth, national job evaluation does establish a relatively reasonable relationship between the wages of similar workers, in the same plant and in different plants and industries, quite unlike the chaotic system in most capitalist countries. National job evaluation probably only makes sense as part of a homogeneous economic system. It would stand little chance of success if it were imposed, on its own, on the fragmented structure of industry common in many capitalist countries. Indeed, it arose, in large part, as a reaction against the fragmented ministerial wage system that existed in the USSR during the Stalin period.

The steady growth of real incomes is an important feature of socialist incomes policy, for two reasons. First, it ensures greater acceptability for the economic institutions. In the USSR, the past twenty-five years have seen an enormous increase in real incomes. The housing situation has greatly improved, the quantity, quality and availability of food has greatly increased, as has that of clothing and other manufactured consumer goods. Except for the effects of bad harvests (such as meatless days in 1976)[1] there has been a continuous, and very substantial, increase in real incomes for a quarter of a century. This naturally lends the present system of determining incomes great legitimacy. Secondly, it provides the necessary room for flexibility, that is for increases in the relative pay of some groups (e.g. farmers, teachers, doctors) without lowering the real pay of others.

As far as income relativities are concerned, Adam Smith and his successors stress the allocative function of wages and the need for differentials so as to equalise the net advantages of all occupations. Keynes and his successors stress the availability of jobs and the segmented nature of the labour market and argue that differentials are largely historic and arbitrary. The experience of the state socialist countries suggests that the Keynesian doctrine is largely correct as far as relative occupa-

[1] A meatless day is, generally, one day a week on which no meat is sold in shops or served in restaurants. The purpose is to reduce demand without raising prices. In the USSR meatless days appear to have persisted into 1977.

tional earnings are concerned, and the classical doctrine is largely correct as far as relative geographical earnings are concerned. Manpower planning, both current and in the field of education, can control the number of people qualified in particular specialisms. This can ensure that there are sufficient people with the requisite qualifications for any category of employment. Although changes in relative earnings may affect the relative attraction of careers as perceived by schoolchildren and their parents, the gestation period is very long. Hence relative earnings can be changed significantly without in the short run much affecting labour availability. On the regional plane, however, things are very different. In the USSR, the higher earnings to be obtained in the towns would have caused such a mass movement from the villages if free movement of labour had existed, that administrative measures had to be used for decades to prevent this. Similarly, in China the use of administrative methods to prevent an excessive influx of labour to the towns is a permanent feature of the economy. Furthermore, administrative measures have to be used in all the state socialist countries to control emigration. In the USSR the desirability of certain cities because of their amenities so failed to be offset by lower earnings that administrative measures had to be used to control access to them. Similarly, in the USSR the inhospitability of many regions (such as the Far North and Far East) has required very substantial regional coefficients for them to recruit and hold labour. In addition, an unplanned migration of labour has taken place to certain areas (such as the North Caucusus, Transcaucasia and Central Asia) where uniform national wage scales failed to reflect the advantages of abundant sunshine, fruit and vegetables. The need to equalise regional net advantages is naturally more important in a continental country, such as the USA, Canada, the USSR or India, than in a small country.

West European trade unions, like the Social Democratic movement in general, are primarily concerned with distribution. They seek to raise labour's share in the output of capitalism, to protect workers from changes in work organisation that would have an adverse effect on them, and to increase state expenditure on free or subsidised public services (e.g. education, medical care, housing). Trade unions in state socialist countries also seek to protect their members in factory or shop level disputes and represent their interests. That they do actually play a positive role in protecting their members is shown for example, rather ironically, by the fact that in China they were dissolved during the Cultural Revolution on the grounds that they supported and protected their members, the permanent workers, who were a privileged elite compared to the temporary workers and peasants. Nevertheless, they are primarily organs of the state concerned with increasing production. (The need for resistance to changes in work organisation is of course much less for workers in the state socialist countries than in most capitalist countries because of the much greater degree of job security which the former enjoy.) Their main function is to stimulate the increases in productivity that, given the distribution of the national income, are the only source of increasing real wages. The transition of Soviet trade unions from trade unionism to production mindedness was part of a revolution from above which took place in the USSR in 1928–34.

Full employment is an important aspect of incomes policy in all state socialist countries. Full employment (which can always be ensured by a Government prepared to reduce sufficiently the current real income of those who would anyway be employed) is a traditional objective of the labour movement and its attainment removes a major obstacle to labour cooperation in the reorganisation of production.

The proletarian character of the Governments of the state socialist countries is an important aspect of their incomes policy. This proletarian character is self proclaimed, reflected in some real policies (e.g. full employment, security of employment, relatively equal income distribution, relatively stable prices) and also in the personal backgrounds of many of the top leaders. In the UK, the non-proletarian character of the Conservative Party is the main reason why, for that party, incomes policy is not a feasible policy (as Heath discovered and Thatcher accepted).

The ultimate sanction in any society is repression. In the UK, at the present time, the control of shoplifting, the Irish Republican Army, the heroin trade and other types of activity deemed anti-social is in the hands of the police and the army. Similarly, in the state socialist countries strikes are in general dealt with by the arrest of 'ringleaders' and 'agitators', as Polish experience in 1976 once more indicated.

Of the conditions listed above, which are necessary and which are sufficient for the maintenance of a permanent incomes policy? This is difficult to judge. Experience up till now suggests the conjecture that all the conditions taken together are sufficient, and that five of them, price control, steady growth of real incomes, full employment, a proletarian Government and a non-permissive approach to breaches of labour discipline, are necessary.

INTER-SYSTEM COMPARISONS

International comparisons of the distribution of income are very difficult both because of the poor quality of the data and because of the existence of numerous different measures of income distribution which can be used for comparative purposes. Nevertheless, there has been some work in this area, notably by Pryor, Wiles and Khan.

Pryor (1973 chapter 3) found that, comparing Western countries with East European countries, three variables played a statistically significant role in explaining the pre-tax distribution of non-agricultural labour incomes. They were, level of development, size of population, and economic system. The degree of inequality declined as the level of development rose, increased as the population rose, and was less for Eastern than for Western countries. The effect of property incomes was to increase the advantage (from an egalitarian point of view) of the East European countries.

Wiles considered the effects of taxation and used a different measure of income distribution. His findings are summarised in table 7.2.

From the data in the table the following points emerge. First, the three most unequal countries (USA, Canada, Italy) are all capitalist. Secondly, the most equal country (Sweden) is also capitalist. Thirdly, two capitalist countries (Sweden and the UK) are more equal than the USSR. Fourthly, the state socialist countries are more equal than one would expect on the basis of the international relationship between level of development and size of population, and inequality. Accordingly, two conclusions may be drawn. First, state socialism is neither a necessary nor a sufficient condition for a more equal distribution of income than any capitalist country. It is not necessary, because Sweden does without it. It is not sufficient, because even with it the USSR is more unequal than Sweden or the UK. Secondly, in making international comparisons, state socialism is one of the factors associated with greater income equality. This corroborates Pryor's findings. It is important to note that these conclusions might change in the event of changes, in the situation in various

Table 7.2. *Ratios of income per head in selected countries (ratio of top 5 per cent to bottom 5 per cent)*

	Before tax	After tax
UK (1953–4)	5·7	5·0
UK (1969)	5·9	5·0
USA (1968)	13·3	12.7
Italy (1969)	11.2	—
Hungary (1967)	4.2	4.0
Czechoslovakia (1965)	4·5	4·3
Bulgaria (1963–5)	3.8	—
USSR (1966)	6.0	5·7
Sweden	—	3·0
Denmark	—	6.0
Canada	—	12.0

Source: Wiles (1974a) pp. 48 and xiv.

countries, in the quality of the data, and the measure of income distribution used.

The data on Soviet income distribution has been reexamined by McAuley (1977). He reached three interesting and important conclusions. First, that Wiles had overestimated inequality in the USSR. In fact, according to McAuley, income inequality in the USSR in the late 1960s was about the same as that calculated by Wiles for Hungary and Czechoslovakia. Secondly, in the late 1960s more than two fifths of the Soviet population were still living in poverty.[2] Thirdly, that since 1956 the USSR has experienced a major reduction in inequality. This had already been noted by Wiles (1974a p. 25), who had observed that 'the statistical record since Stalin is a very good one indeed. I doubt if any other country can show a more rapid and sweeping progress towards equality.' A very significant factor in this reduction in inequality has been the repeated increases in the minimum wage. McAuley's investigation adds to knowledge but does not upset the two qualitative conclusions reached above on the basis of the Wiles data. It does, however, emphasise the fragility of conclusions about international comparisons of the distribution of income with the presently available data.

It is important to note that the income distribution statistics

[2] 'Poverty', of course, is a relative and culture-bound concept. In the United States, for example, half a million families below the 'poverty' line own two or more cars. The measure of 'poverty' used by McAuley is a Soviet one, developed by Soviet specialists for Soviet conditions.

analysed by Wiles and McAuley concern normal money income only and exclude both top money incomes and non-money incomes such as imputed rent from owner-occupied dwellings, the subsidy element in state rents and free medical and educational services. Since there are systematic differences between the value of the subsidy element in state rents and free educational and medical services, between social groups, measurement of money incomes only might give a distorted picture of the distribution of real income. For example, in the USSR, there are very great differences between the quality of medical care available in Russian villages and that provided in the special facilities available to top party and state officials, members of the Academy of Sciences and the Union of Writers, officers in the armed forces and state security organs, foreigners and other elite groups. Whereas in the West the labour movement regards the free provision of medical services as a means of equalising real incomes, it is entirely possible that in the USSR, where the facilities are financed out of indirect taxation and differentially provided, charging the user for medical services on the basis of costs would increase equality. A similar situation exists with respect to housing.

The existence of important real income differences not reflected in the published data used by Wiles and McAuley does not mean that there is no information available on these differences. In an important paper, Matthews (1975) investigated the question of whether there existed in the USSR an elite with real incomes much above the rest of the population. His investigation is summed up in table 7.3.

Table 7.3 shows an elite group of 0.2% of the employed population, with real incomes much above the average. Matthews' paper is only an initial investigation of this important subject. It has been taken further in his (1978).

Combining the evidence collected by Wiles, McAuley and Matthews, the following picture of the USSR about 1970 emerges. It was a society in which the great mass of the population was quite equal and a large proportion of it was below the poverty level, and there was a small (about 0.2%) elite. Two important differences between the Western and Soviet distributions of income stand out. First, the Soviet elite is much worse off in terms of wealth and independence from the state, than are Western elites. Secondly, the USSR lacks the large middle class which plays such an important role in the capitalist world. The

Table 7.3. *Elite occupational groups in the USSR in 1970*[a]

	Thousands	%
Party officials	95	38
State, Komsomol and trade union officials	60	24
The intelligentsia[b]	43	17
Enterprise managers	22	9
The military, police, diplomatic service	30	12
Total	250	100

[a] Persons earning 450 roubles a month or more and having access to substantial non-cash benefits. (Average wages in the USSR in 1970 were 122 roubles per month.)

[b] I.e. academicians, heads of higher educational institutions, institutes, faculties and laboratories; head doctors; senior legal officials; editors and senior journalists; leaders in arts and artistic bureaucracy.

Source: Matthews (1975) p. 13.

two differences are an important factor explaining the fragility of the state socialist regimes (Hungary in 1956, Czechoslovakia in 1968, the insistence in the USSR on complete pre-publication censorship) and the nature and social basis of the economic reform widely discussed throughout Eastern Europe in the 1960s.

For China as a whole there are simply no statistical income distribution data available at all. There are, however, the casual observations of visitors, numerous official documents, and some calculations for the rural sector only. According to authors such as Richman (1969 pp. 231–40) and Eckstein (1977 pp. 298–304), during the First Five Year Plan (1953–57) earnings differentials in industry were substantial and modelled on contemporary Soviet practice, but in subsequent years, under the influence of campaigns such as the Great Leap Forward and the Cultural Revolution, they were reduced. Nevertheless, according to these authors, in the mid 1970s there were still substantial income differences within industry, between urban and rural areas, and inter-regionally. These differences, they suggest, were probably less pronounced than in the mid 1950s, when differences were probably less than those of the mid 1930s. Howe (1973a) and Whyte (1975), on the other hand, suggest that the Cultural Revolution had little effect on income differences. It even seems that during the Cultural Revolution there was a policy of not using financial sanctions to deal with political and ideological errors. Chen (1973) has described how Peking cadres, sent to live in villages to overcome their errors, continued to receive their salaries as usual, but were forbidden to tell local people how much they received. Under social pressure not to engage in conspicuous consumption, many of them accumulated substantial savings while they were reforming themselves! A clear picture of income differences in China and their evolution over time is impossible in the absence of data.

An interesting example of the importance of income differences in China prior to the Cultural Revolution is provided by the schools. At this time only a small minority of the relevant age group went to secondary schools due to a shortage of facilities. In the early 1960s the authorities pursued a policy of concentrating resources on a minority of successful schools. The idea was to ensure that sufficient qualified people would be produced to meet the needs of the national economy. The privileged position of the pupils at these schools was pronounced. Schooling was not free. Tuition fees were not high, on average they were about 5 or 6 yuan a year, at a time when average wages were about 50 yuan a month. Nevertheless, they were not insignificant, particularly if there were several children in a family, bearing in mind that textbooks and stationery also had to be paid for, and that there was an opportunity cost of secondary schooling in terms of wages forgone. Furthermore, the better schools tended to charge more. In 1966 Watson (1975 p. 127) visited a boarding kindergarten in Chengchow which charged 13.50 yuan per month for each child, and one in Peking which charged 25 yuan. In important cities, a number of the well-endowed schools took children almost exclusively from the families of leading cadres. A well known example was the Number 2 Primary School in Peking where many of China's leaders sent their children and grandchildren. The existence of these selective facilities, the substantial charges they made, and the fact that only a small minority received any secondary education, were all aspects of massive inequality by West European standards.

Similarly, unequal access to medical care, both as regards payment and quality, has been a permanent feature of Chinese society since 1949 (and also one of the issues in the GPCR). Only party and state cadres and insured workers have had free medical care. These two groups appear to have amounted to less than 25% of the urban population throughout. The remainder of the urban population has had to pay for curative care or do without. The quality of care has varied substantially, with that available to top cadres being higher than that to temporary workers. Prior to the GPCR (and probably also today) each large hospital had several single rooms, furnished with sofas and chairs and very comfortable, for cadres of rank 13 upwards. (Since 1956 the Chinese bureaucracy has been graded into 30 ranks.) In the rural areas, medical care has generally been scanty, of low quality, and had to be paid for. During the GLF free medical care was introduced into the rural areas, but this programme disintegrated in the economic stringency that followed. In the GPCR local rural medical insurance was generally introduced, with small payments for use to discourage waste, and large numbers of paramedical personnel ('barefoot doctors') trained. Both programmes appear to have continued to the present. Although the People's Republic has been unable in the first three decades of its existence to meet its founders' goal of free high quality care for all, it has greatly increased standards for all as measured by (estimated) mortality and morbidity statistics, and greatly improved the access to, and quality of care available to, the poor and middle rural inhabitants.

However, if comparison is made with other developing countries, which have retained private ownership of the means of production, the general impression (it can be no more in the absence of data) is that China has successfully truncated the extremes of the income distribution. Since China is mainly an agricultural country, the most important factor determining distribution is the abolition of inequalities in land ownership, so ending the division between land owners and rural proletarians. As was pointed out in chapter 4, this means that the effects of adverse conditions are shared more or less equally, and do not fall mainly on one group. the wholly or partly landless labourers. Since malnutrition and famine largely result from failures of distribution rather than failures of production, this is a most important consideration.

For the distribution of *rural* incomes in China there is some data, though it is not of the highest quality. According to Khan (1976) in China in the 1930s the ratio of the income of the top twenty per cent of rural households to the bottom twenty per cent was about 8. As a result of land reform this income inequality was at least halved and income inequality in rural China has remained at the relatively low level established by land reform. His results and some comparative data for other countries is set out in table 7.4.

In the 1970s it became fashionable, especially in World Bank (IBRD) circles, to argue that economic growth that did not benefit

Table 7.4. *Income inequality in rural Asia*

Country	Date	Ratio of per capita income of the top 20 per cent to that of the bottom 20 per cent
China	1930s	7 or 8[a]
	1952	3
	c. 1965	4[b]
India	1963–65	6
Pakistan	1963–64	6
West Malaysia	1957	7
	1970	14
Sri Lanka	1963	14
	1973	8
Philippines	1965	9
	1970–71	12
Bangladesh	1963–64	5

[a] These are estimates produced by two different researchers. In view of the poor data their close agreement is more remarkable than their disagreement.
[b] Khan suggests that the apparent increase in inequality between 1952 and 1965 was probably an illusion resulting from the poor data.
Source: Khan (1976).

the rural poor was quite unacceptable. Great efforts should be made, it was argued, to alleviate rural poverty by combining economic growth with an equitable distribution of income. This doctrine appears to have been implemented in the Chinese countryside from the establishment of the People's Republic onwards. A reasonable rate of economic growth has been combined with a relatively equal distribution of income. If the data in table 7.4 are reliable, it would seem that income distribution in rural China, in the whole period since land reform, has been significantly more equal than in much of the rest of rural Asia. How has this been achieved?

The main factor is obviously land reform, which equalised the distribution of rural incomes, and the Maoist model of collectivisation which has maintained this equalisation. Another factor is the emphasis on distribution according to need (e.g. the grain ration to which each household is entitled, low cost basic services such as medical care and education, and welfare benefits for the needy). The price policy pursued, which has been consciously pro-poor, with low prices for basic necessities and high prices for luxuries, has also been a factor. For example, in China the prices of foodgrains and cotton textiles are much lower, relative to the price of bicycles, than in India.

It is most important to note that what has been achieved in the state socialist world is not relative equality in general, but relative equality in the distribution of income and wealth, and this has been achieved by methods which have required very substantial inequalities of power. This illustrates the general proposition that money income and wealth are much less important factors in social stratification in the state socialist countries than in the capitalist world, because of the overwhelming importance of the state in the former. In the USSR, the millionaire Ostap Bender was unable to do anything with his wealth. The state security officer Erchov, on the other hand, was able to get the woman he wanted without any trouble, even though she was someone else's wife. He simply instructed the couple to divorce and her to marry him.[3]

Similarly, China is a country where the entire society has been transformed by a continous process of social change from above. The mass of the population has been subordinated to the cadres, and cadres at each level to their superiors. Being a cadre has often been a thankless task. Nevertheless, the great inequalities of power between cadres, and between cadres and the masses, have always been present. Without them it would have been impossible to carry out the social transformation which has in fact taken place. As one work point recorder put it during the Socialist Education Movement (Chen 1969 p. 218), 'The handle of the sword is always in the hands of the cadre. We are powerless.' As was pointed out in chapter 4, an example of these inequalities of power, and of their importance, is provided by the Great Leap Forward. This forced the mass of the population to perform greatly increased work, much of it wasted, and was a major factor causing the deaths from malnutrition and starvation which took place in 1960–62.

Why does inequality persist under state socialism? There seem to be four main reasons, the division of labour, the family, the sexual division of roles and the role of the state in state socialism. The division of labour has persisted, so that, for example, some people are high officials and others are agricultural labourers. The family has persisted, so that, for example, some children come from intelligentsia families and have the advantages that

[3] Ostap Bender is the central character in Ilf and Petrov's famous novel *The golden calf*. By devious means he eventually becomes a millionaire, but the only thing he is able to do with his money is to travel on trains. All other goods are available on allocation only. State security officer Erchov is one of the characters in V. Serge's novel *The case of Comrade Tulayev.*

go with this in settled societies, while others come from worker or peasant families. The sexual division of roles ensures that most top jobs are in the hands of men, while many of the most arduous jobs are undertaken by women. The dominant role of the state in state socialism has ensured that those holding high official positions have attractive and well-paid jobs while others, especially those in political disfavour, have dreary, poorly paid jobs, no jobs at all or die from repression or starvation.

CONCLUSION

The Marxist view of incomes planning under socialism is that on the morrow of the revolution it is necessary to eliminate parasitical incomes and base distribution on work performed, but that the ultimate objective of the socialist movement in this field is distribution according to need. All the state socialist countries operate what in Western terminology would be called permanent incomes policies. The experience of the state socialist countries suggests that the following are sufficient conditions for a permanent incomes policy: price control, the planning of foreign trade, the elimination of large property incomes, compulsory arbitration, national job evaluation, steady growth of real incomes, uniform regional net advantages, the production mindedness of trade unions, full employment, a proletarian Government, and a non-permissive approach to breaches of labour discipline.

Satisfactory comparisons between the distribution of incomes under state socialism and capitalism are not yet possible, largely owing to the absence of data for China. It seems very probable, however, that the distribution of income in the state socialist countries is significantly more equal than in capitalist countries at comparable levels of development. Furthermore, countries with state ownership of the means of production naturally do not have the small minority of individuals with huge holdings of means of production normal under capitalism. In addition, the elite in the state socialist countries is significantly worse off than the elite in capitalist countries. State socialism is neither a necessary, nor a sufficient, condition to ensure a more equal distribution of income than any capitalist country. It does, however, appear to be one of the factors, along with level of development and smallness of the population, associated with greater equality in the distribution of income.

The available empirical evidence about the distribution of income in the USSR around 1970, suggests that the great mass of the population was quite equal and a large proportion of it below the poverty line, and there was a small elite. The most striking changes in the Soviet income distribution over time are the very big increases in inequality in the first two five year plans (1928–37) and the very big reduction in inequality since the twentieth party congress (1956). As far as China is concerned, the widespread impression of an extremely equal society appears to be quite wrong from the viewpoint of Social Democratic Western Europe, but correct from the viewpoint of countries such as Mexico. The main feature of China's income distribution is a distribution of rural incomes which, since land reform, has been significantly more equal than in China in the 1930s or in much of the rest of contemporary rural Asia.

The main reasons for the persistence of inequality under state socialism appear to be the division of labour, the family, the sexual division of roles and the role of the state in state socialism.

SUGGESTIONS FOR FURTHER READING

P. Wiles, *Distribution of income: East and West* (Amsterdam 1974).

Incomes in postwar Europe (UN ECE Economic Survey of Europe in 1965: Part 2 chapters 7–11).

D. Lane, *The end of inequality?* (London 1971).

F. Parkin, *Class, Inequality and Political Order* (London 1971).

W. Brus, 'Income distribution and economic reforms in Poland', *Il Politico* vol. XXXIX no. 1 (1974).

A. McAuley, 'The distribution of incomes and earnings in the Soviet Union', *Soviet Studies* (April 1977).

M. Matthews, 'Top incomes in the USSR: towards a definition of the Soviet elite', *Survey* vol. 21 no. 3 (1975).

M. Matthews, *Privilege in the Soviet Union* (London 1978).

Michael Ellman, 'What are the conditions for a viable incomes policy? The Soviet experience', S. Markowski (ed.) *Reverse Sovietology* (forthcoming).

C. Howe, *Wage patterns and wage policy in modern China 1919–1972* (Cambridge 1973).

A. R. Khan, 'The distribution of income in rural China' (mimeo, ILO Geneva 1976).

M. K. Whyte, 'Inequality and stratification in China', *The China Quarterly* (December 1975).

A. McAuley, *Economic welfare in the Soviet Union* (London 1979)

8

PLANNING CONSUMPTION

Wages are low and the living standard is not high. We only get enough clothing and a full stomach. To develop the economy this situation must be maintained for some time to come.

Teng Hsiao-ping (China 1975 p. 20)

INTRODUCTION

In the Soviet five year plans of the 1970s the planning of consumption is implicit in the plans for the consumer goods industries and agriculture, and explicit in the section of the plan entitled 'The further increase in the material and cultural standard of living of the people'. The latter has sections on money wages and the social wage (education, medical care, housing subsidies, pensions, student grants, family income supplements), retail trade, domestic services (laundries, cleaners, garages, baths, hairdressers etc.), housing, education and culture, and medical care. The total planned volume of consumption is determined by the planned growth of the national income and its division between consumption and non-consumption (investment, defence). Money wages and the social wage are distributed, according to Soviet theory, on different principles. Money wages depend on the quantity and quality of labour performed. The social wage is stated to be based on need. The key indices of this section of the Soviet Ninth Five Year Plan (1971–75) are set out in table 8.1.

Consumption in the state socialist countries has not been planned in a uniform way throughout the whole period of their existence. On the contrary, it has depended very much on the stage of economic development which they have reached. In any country consumption must depend on, and be deter-

Table 8.1. *The plan for raising the standard of living in the USSR 1971–75 (key indices)*

	Units of measurement	1971	1972	1973	1974	1975
Real incomes per head	% of 1970	104.7	111.0	117.3	123.8	130.8
Average wages	% of 1970	102.8	107.5	112.3	117.5	122.4
Average pay of collective farmers	% of 1970	102.8	109.2	117.5	124.2	130.6
The social wage	% of 1970	107.2	114.1	121.1	130.5	140.6
Volume of domestic services	% of 1970	116.7	131.7	151.4	173.8	200.3
Children in pre-school institutions	000s	9,527	9,764	10,227	10,705	11,228
Admissions to higher educational institutions	000s	902.3	913.6	919.7	943.5	977.0
Hospital beds	000s	2,730	2,797	2,857	2,925	3,000
Housing completed	millions m^2	116.6	115.1	115.3	116.2	116.8

Source: *Gosudarstvennyi* (1972) pp. 353–4.

mined by, the production of that country at that time. S. P. Chertopolokhov (1975 pp. 47–9), of the Leningrad Higher Party School, has distinguished five stages in the formation, development and degree of satisfaction of wants in the USSR since 1917.

The first stage (1917–20), was one in which consumption was squeezed below the level necessary for the reproduction of labour power, in the interest of the survival of socialism. The urban population fell sharply and many people starved to death. This was a result of the Civil War and invasion and the policies of War Communism. Even under these extreme conditions the organs of Soviet power and the trade unions tried to organise the distribution of consumer goods on a scientific basis. Price indices and subsistence minima were calculated, and budget surveys undertaken. The subordination of consumption to the survival of state socialism can be illustrated by the following fact. At one time during the Civil War, the rations for workers provided only 24% of the calories which the calculation of requirements showed to be necessary.

The second stage (1922–37) was marked by a gradual transition to the satisfaction of subsistence requirements. It begins with the transition to NEP and ends with the abolition of rationing and the relatively good years 1935–37.

The third stage, which lasted till the late 1950s or early 1960s, was one in which the study and planning of consumption was largely neglected. Priority was given to the planning of the defence and investment industries.

The fourth stage (*c.* 1960 onwards) was one in which the task of satisfying consumption at the level of the consumption norms was posed. From 1962 rational budgets (i.e. budgets providing for the satisfaction of basic needs at minimum cost) were calculated both for individual workers and for families with four members. Rational consumption norms were first worked out on a large scale in 1956–57. They were made more precise in 1968 as a result of the work of a special commission created for this purpose by the USSR Academy of Sciences. The USSR is still at this stage, trying to ensure the attainment of the norms by the whole population. This must be done first in a quantitative way, and then qualitatively as well.

The fifth stage, which has not yet begun, will be marked by the

> full reasonable satisfaction of the existing diversity of wants. In this connection there arises the question of what one understands by 'the reasonable satisfaction of wants'. The very concept of 'wants' assumes already a definite limit to the availability of the goods used for consumption, and an abundance of goods does not mean that any wish of an individual can be wholly satisfied. A reasonable satisfaction of wants assumes such a level of consumption of material and cultural goods as to provide for the rational reproduction of labour power under the given conditions of production. Such a reproduction of labour power assumes the all round development of the personality, the full uncovering of the abilities of each individual and the transformation of labour into a vital need.

Chertopolokhov's argument makes clear five important points. First, the planning of consumption in the USSR has not been the same throughout Soviet power but has evolved in the course of economic development. Secondly, the extent to which wants could be satisfied has depended on the development of production. The transition to the fourth stage was only possible because of the success of socialist industrialisation. Thirdly, Soviet planning envisages a day when all 'reasonable' wants will be satisfied. Fourthly, Soviet planners reject the Western view that the output of an economy ought to be determined by the expenditure of individuals. Fifthly, the main method of planning the consumption of particular goods and services is that of norms.

PLANNING BY NORMS[1]

Consumption planning is concerned with the planning of incomes, expenditures and the production of consumer goods, and with ensuring the consistency and efficiency of these plans. The main instrument used for harmonising planned incomes with planned expenditures is the balance of money incomes and expenditures of the population.

In order for the latter to balance, it is necessary that wages issued in those sectors of the economy not producing wage goods (investment, social consumption, defence) be soaked up by direct or indirect taxes or by savings (Dobb 1960 p. 91). If only indirect taxation is used, then the average mark-up (p) of retail prices over costs should be determined by the formula

$$p = \frac{W_{sc} + W_i + W_d}{W_{pc}}$$

where W_{sc} is the wage bill in social consumption,
W_i is the wage bill in the investment industries,
W_d is the wage bill in defence, and
W_{pc} is the wage bill in the industries producing goods for personal consumption.

For example, if one third of wages are issued in social consumption, investment and the defence sector, and two thirds in the personal consumption sector, then in the absence of savings and direct taxation the average mark-up should be 50%. Two corollaries of this proposition are as follows. First, the higher the ratio of the wage bill in the non-personal consumption sectors to the wage bill in the personal consumption sector, the higher the mark-up must be. Secondly, in a socialist economy the effect of an increase in savings is that it permits the price level to be lower than it otherwise would be. If the equation is violated this will result either in excess stocks (if the mark-up is too high) or in shortages and queues (if the mark-up is too low).

In calculating the volume of particular goods and services required, the planners use two main methods. One is forecasts of consumer behaviour, based on extrapolation, expenditure patterns of higher income groups, income and price elasticities of demand and consumer behaviour in the more advanced countries. The other method is that of plan norms. The first

[1] The material in this section is mainly taken from Weitzman (1974).

Table 8.2. *USSR daily nutritional norms*

Age, sex and labour category	Calorific requirements (in kilocalories)	Intake of nutritional substances (in grams)		
		Proteins	Fats	Carbo-hydrates
Children to 1 year	800	25	25	113
Children 3–6 years	1,900	65	69	241
Youths 15–17 years	3,300	113	99	467
Working-age adults				
Group 1 (mental labour, e.g. students and office workers)				
Men	3,000	102	97	410
Women	2,700	92	87	369
Group 2 (light manual labour)				
Men	3,500	102	113	478
Women	3,200	109	103	437
Group 3 (heavy physical labour)				
Men	4,000	137	129	546
Women	3,600	123	116	492
Group 4 (very heavy physical labour)				
Men	4,500	146	145	615
Non-working pensioners	2,500	85	74	351

method attempts to foresee consumer demand, the latter to shape it.

A norm is simply the quantity of a particular good or service required per head of the population. Although the method of norms is an alternative to the price mechanism for the determination of output, it is in fact quite widely used in Western countries. It is used in areas where distribution on the basis of purchasing power has been replaced by distribution on the basis of need. Examples are, the provision of housing, hospitals, schools and parks. Calculations of the desirable number of rooms, hospital beds and school places per person are a familiar tool of planning in welfare states. The use of norms in consumption planning is illustrated in tables 8.2 and 8.3. Table 8.2 shows nutritional norms and table 8.3 the relationship between them and actual food consumption in the USSR and selected capitalist countries. This type of data clearly provides important

Table 8.3. *Actual and normative food consumption in the USSR and actual food consumption in selected capitalist countries (kilograms/head/year)*

'ood category	USSR Norm	USSR 1970 actual	USSR 1970 % of norm	USA average 1960–62	UK average 1960/61–1962/63	Italy average 1960/61–1962/63	France average 1960/61–1962/63
d (in terms of r), groats, aroni products	120	149	124	74	87	145	104
oes	97	130	134	48	98	50	99
tables and melons	146	83	57	125	58	139	149
and berries sh)	91	n.a.	n.a.	86	44	88[a]	62
l fruit	3.6	n.a.	n.a.	1	3	1	1
r	37	39	106	49	53	23	32
table oil and garine	7	7	93	15	10	13	10
and meat lucts	82	48	59	96	61	31	77
and fish products	18	15	85	5	10	7	11
and milk products	434	307	71	291	462	217	367
	17	9	53	19	15	9	11

[a] Includes olives.
Note: Figures have been rounded.

information for the planning of agriculture, the food-processing industry and foreign trade.

Tables 8.2 and 8.3 illustrate two important facts about the method of norms. First, where there is an objective, scientific basis for the norms, as in nutritional science, then the norms provide valuable information for the planners. Secondly, that the possibility of *substitution* between products causes serious difficulties for the norm method.[2] This is shown most clearly by table 8.4.

Why is it 'rational' for Soviet men to have 7 pairs of shoes? Why not 4 or 12? Why is it 'rational' for Soviet women to have 15 dresses? Why not more, or less? Perhaps women prefer fewer dresses and more trousers? It is clear that these clothing stock norms have little basis and are largely arbitrary. What is the 'rational' number of cars per person?

[2] Even in the field of nutrition, the substitutability of many foods from a nutritive ingredients point of view, casts considerable doubt on the 'scientific' basis of the norms.

Table 8.4. *USSR rational wardrobe and 1961 US Heller budget clothing stocks (no. of pieces/head)*

	USSR rational wardrobe		USA Heller budget I[a]		USA Heller budget II[b]	
	Men	Women	Men	Women	Men	Women
Coats	2.6	2.6	1	2	1	3
Raincoats	0.4	0.4	1	1	1	1
Jackets and sweaters	2.0	3.0	2	1	4	2
Suits	5.0	2.0	2	1	4	2
Trousers	2.0	n.a.	2	2	2	4
Dresses	—	15.0	—	9	—	13
Socks and hosiery (prs)	9.0	9.0	11	10	13	10
Leather shoes (prs)	7.0	10.0	3	5	5	8

[a] Family of a wage earner.
[b] Family of a white collar worker (professional or executive).

What happens when the quantity of a particular good or service which the public actually wishes to buy differs from the 'rational' quantity provided by the planners in accordance with the norms? One possibility is to change the norms. For example, experience in the USSR in the 1960s showed that the norms for the purchase of consumer durables (televisions, refrigerators, washing machines, cars etc.) were too low and they were raised (Buzlyakov 1969 p. 172). Another possibility is to advertise the goods so as to boost sales. Hanson (1974) noted that in recent years in the USSR and Poland there has been an increasing tendency to use advertising to boost sales of those consumer goods for which buyers' markets exist. Another possibility is to alter prices to bring demand into line with supply. If demand is too low prices may be cut or easy credit offered. If demand is too high prices may be raised. Altering prices, however, has not only allocative but also distributive consequences.

An interesting example of the importance of the latter were the riots in the working-class towns of north Poland which led to the fall of Gomulka in December 1970. One cause of these riots was the Government's decision in December 1970 to raise food prices substantially. This decision had been preceded by an interesting economic discussion (Mieczkowski 1975 pp. 154–71, Nuti 1971). The discussion was initiated by J. Pajestka, the Vice-President of the Polish Planning Commission. He argued

Table 8.5. *Polish consumption structure in 1967 (in %)*

	Total	From personal incomes	From social funds
Food	40.0	44.5	14.2
Drink	9.3	10.6	—
Tobacco	3.1	3.5	—
Clothes and shoes	13.6	15.5	—
Fuel and power	2.3	2.7	—
Housing	7.3	7.7	4.1
Hygiene and health	7.7	3.3	40.1
Culture, sport and tourism	9.8	5.4	41.5
Transport and communications	4.5	5.1	—
Other	1.5	1.7	0.1
Total	100.0	100.0	100.0

Source: Nuti (1971).

Table 8.6. *Social cost – retail price ratios (Poland in 1970)*

1. Food	1.288	
1.1 Meat and poultry		1.732
1.2 Fish		1.287
1.3 Fat		1.288
1.4 Sugar		0.867
1.5 Fruit and vegetables		0.864
2. Clothes and shoes	0.726	
2.1 Fabrics		0.817
2.2 Ready to wear		0.677
2.3 Shoes		0.673
3. Durable goods	0.748	
3.1 Means of transport		0.808
3.2 Electrical goods		0.732
4. Chemical manufactures	0.710	
5. Paper products	0.791	
6. Transport services	1.391	

Source: Nuti (1971).

that the expenditure pattern of Polish consumers was being distorted by an irrational price system. Some relevant data is set out in tables 8.5 and 8.6.

The tables show that in 1967 more than half of the personal expenditure of Polish consumers went on food and drink. Pajestka suggested that this high share of food expenditure was partly a result of selling food too cheaply. Given the relative social

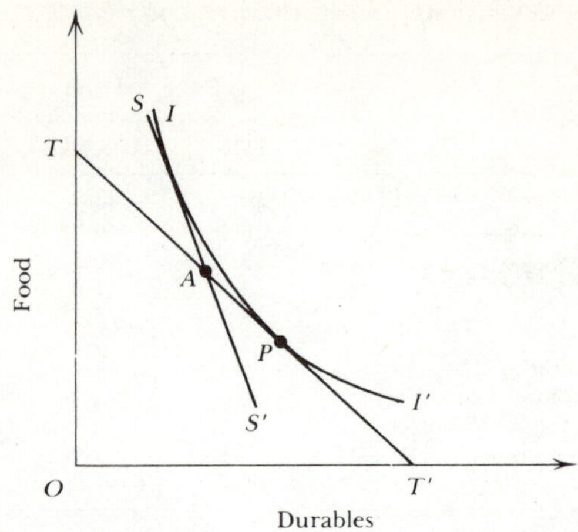

Figure 8.1 Changing relative prices to improve welfare.

costs of producing the different commodity groups (see table 8.6), he argued, it would be more efficient to consume less food and more durables. The argument is illustrated in figure 8.1.

Consider an economy which can produce either food or durables or some combination of the two as given by the transformation line TT'. If market prices equal this rate of transformation consumption would be P. Consumers would be on the indifference curve II'. If actual prices underprice food relative to durables, then the actual consumption point is A. A is on a lower indifference curve than P. Hence welfare maximisation requires that consumers be confronted by the rational price TT' rather than the cheap food price SS'.

This argument rests on two assumptions. First, it assumes that food and durables are substitutes. If they were not it would be impossible to make welfare comparisons between P and A. Secondly, it ignores the fact that if food and durables are consumed in different proportions by different social groups, a change in their relative price will change the distribution of real income between the groups.

These are two of the reasons why in the USSR only very limited use is made of price changes (e.g. for seasonal fruits) and emphasis is placed on quantity changes in bringing supply and demand into equilibrium.

Summary

The method of norms is the main method of consumption planning used in the state socialist countries. Its main weaknesses are the arbitrary nature of many of the norms and the phenomenon of substitutability. The norms can be implemented, inter alia, by quantity and price adjustments. The use of the latter can raise distributive problems.

SUPPLY AND DEMAND

> In the USSR the growth of consumption (purchasing power) of the masses continually outstrips the growth of production and pushes it ahead, but under capitalism, on the other hand, the growth of consumption (purchasing power) of the masses never catches up with the growth of production and continually lags behind it, which condemns production to crises...[In the USSR] the growth of the domestic market will advance beyond the growth of industry and push it forward towards continuous expansion.
>
> J. Stalin (1955b pp. 300 and 332)

A characteristic feature of consumption in the CMEA countries is the existence of shortages and queues. This has characterised the entire history of the USSR since its creation. What explains it? There are four chief explanations, not mutually exclusive, macroeconomic, microeconomic, distributive and social. Consider each in turn.

The macroeconomic argument is that shortages and queues are symptoms of suppressed inflation. The volume of purchasing power in the hands of the public is in excess of the volume of consumer goods and services available. In the 1920s shortages and queues were officially explained in the USSR as resulting from a 'goods famine'. This phrase suggested that the shortages and queues were a result of physical factors (low output and productivity) akin to the results of a bad harvest. This notion was criticised by a number of Soviet economists. In articles published in 1925 and 1926 Shanin and Novozhilov argued, in effect, that the shortages resulted from violation of the macroeconomic equilibrium equation on page 201 above. The incomes being generated in the economy were in excess of the market value of consumer goods output. Looking at the matter from a static point of view, Novozhilov argues that the solution was to raise prices so as to restore equilibrium. Looking at the matter from a dynamic point of view, Shanin argued for a rapid expansion of the output of consumer goods and for only a small allocation of investment resources to producer goods. These ideas were decisively rejected by the party, which launched instead a rapid expansion of employment in, and output of, producer goods industries. This naturally exacerbated the situation. Rationing of all producer goods and many consumer goods, together with restricted access retail trade, had to be introduced to keep the situation under control.

Thirthy-three years later, Novozhilov (1959 pp. 199–200) reverted to his earlier theme. He argued that the underpricing of goods leads to the expenditure of 'time and effort on the search for scarce goods and standing in queues. At the same time unproductive and even criminal actions (speculation in scarce goods, under the counter sales by assistants of the scarce goods etc.) become a source of unjustified enrichment.'

The views of Novozhilov and other Soviet economists who share his position on this issue, have remained unorthodox. The idea of the price mechanism as the most efficient way of allocating scarce goods between consumers, has been repeatedly rejected by the authorities. They have argued that the way to overcome shortages is not to raise prices but to expand output. For example, a deputy chairman of Gosplan has argued (Bachurin 1969 p. 15) that,

> It is very easy, it turns out, to overcome a shortage of this or that product – it is sufficient to raise their prices... [However] the raising of prices consciously places limits on the possibilities of satisfying the needs of members of society instead of devoting all our efforts to their satisfaction by means of growth (increasing investment) and raising labour productivity.

The classic exposition of the orthodox Marxist–Leninist point of view is contained in a speech by Stalin at the 16th Party Congress (1930), an extract from which is quoted at the head of this section. In that speech he contrasted the relationship between demand and supply under capitalism and under socialism. Capitalism is characterised by over-production and lack of demand (unemployed labour and machinery; schemes to keep goods off the market by destruction, reductions in output or eliminating competition). Under socialism, on the other hand, demand runs ahead of production and provides a stimulus to it. Instead of raising prices to reestablish equilibrium, he advocated cutting prices so as to increase real wages (as was done in 1948–54).

The idea that the CMEA countries suffer from permanent suppressed inflation has become part of the conventional wisdom. In a study of Soviet retail trade in 1932–69, however, Skurski (1972) argued that the situation in Soviet distribution had changed substantially over time. In 1932–47 there was a permanent sellers' market, with considerable formal rationing. In 1948–57 there was still a sellers' market but with an increased availability of goods. 1958–64 marked a transitional period in which a buyers' market was developing for the majority of non-food consumer goods, and 1965–69 saw the retail system adopting to the new situation. This does not mean that at the end of this period all the goods consumers wanted were freely available. It simply means that for the majority of non-food consumer goods available, the total volume of goods sold was equal to the volume consumers wished to buy given their incomes and the prices of the goods. More generally, Portes (1974) has argued that for the last twenty years the conventional wisdom may well be erroneous for Eastern Europe as a whole. Shortages and queues may well be symptoms not of macroeconomic disequilibrium but of microeconomic disequilibrium.

The microeconomic argument is that the CMEA countries suffer from incorrect *relative* prices. It is entirely possible for the macroeconomic balance equation on p. 201 to be met, but for the prices of individual goods to differ substantially from the supply and demand equilibrium levels. Indeed, one might well expect this normally to be the case, since the planners combine planned balancing of incomes and expenditures by means of the balance of money incomes and expenditures of the population, with a policy of stable prices. The microeconomic explanation has the advantage over the macroeconomic one of explaining the existence side by side both of shortages and excess stocks.

From a Marshallian point of view, the permanent existence in the USSR of shortages, queues and 'scarce goods' (i.e. goods that people want and which are produced but which are unavailable at a particular place at a particular time) and the replacement of shopping by 'obtaining with difficulty',[3] are a result of rejecting the distinction between the short run and the long run. In the long run it *is* appropriate to bring supply and demand into balance by adjusting output. In the short run, however, the appropriate adjustment mechanism is the alteration of prices.

[3] The word *dostat'* (literally 'to obtain with difficulty') is often used to describe buying goods in the USSR.

Joan Robinson has often argued that this distinction would be useful for a socialist economy (e.g. Robinson 1960 part 5), but this has never been the Marxist–Leninist view.

The distributive explanation concentrates on factors specific to the distribution sector. For example, as was pointed out in chapter 6, the CMEA countries deliberately keep down the proportion of the labour force engaged in distribution and this is a major factor in explaining why shopping there takes longer than in comparable capitalist countries. Similarly, they also reduce investment in distribution. Research in Poland (Turcan 1977) suggests that the system of responsibility for lost goods is also very important. In the 1940s regulations were introduced in Poland making those employed in distribution personally responsible for losses, however incurred. The system is changing, but the most common arrangement at present is that staff are responsible for losses due to dishonesty and for losses exceeding 1 % of the stock value. In these circumstances the staff must pay for the losses incurred. If a member of the staff steals and though convicted is unable to pay, it is the responsibility of the remainder of the staff to pay for the losses, i.e. there is a common responsibility for looking after state property in shops.

Given this system of personal responsibility, stocktaking and checking the receipt of goods are matters of considerable concern to those employed. According to Ministry of Finance regulations there must be at least one stocktaking every year, but if any sales assistant leaves the shop, a member of the remaining staff has the right to insist that a stocktaking be carried out. In view of this, the unexpected closure of shops, the lack of interest in selling, keeping customers away from products, queues for baskets in supermarkets etc. all become explicable. The sales assistant's job is partly that of a store detective or security guard. The staff are at least as interested in preventing theft as in selling.

Turcan's research is extremely suggestive. Whether or not the same system exists in the other CMEA countries is not known to the author. It may well do so. Obviously factors internal to distribution (low levels of employment and investment, the system of responsibility for preventing loss) are an important factor explaining shopping difficulties in the CMEA countries.

The social explanation is that increasing the relative prices of the scarcest goods is impossible because this would lead to riots and strikes. Experience in the USSR in 1962 and in Poland in

1970/71 and 1976 certainly suggests that large state price increases for basic food products are likely to produce an explosive political situation. Many workers evidently prefer shortages and queues, or rationing, to the free availability of goods that only those with money can afford. Hence Poland rationed sugar in 1976 and the USSR in the 1970s has enormous food subsidies combined with meatless days and poor availability of food in many areas. The situation is exacerbated by the policy of leaving prices stable for years, so that the necessary readjustments are very large. In Hungary in recent years it has proved possible to alter the relative price of basic foodstuffs. Advance explanations were issued, small but frequent changes made and compensating income adjustments made.

It seems clear that all four explanations have been important as causes of shortages and queues in the CMEA countries, the balance between the different explanations varying over time and between countries.

An interesting and important result of the inability of the official economy to meet all consumer needs is the existence in the USSR of a large and flourishing non-state, or parallel, market. In a useful paper, Simes (1975) provided a good survey of it. He noted that the non-state, or parallel, market

> offers not only better (usually foreign-made) clothing or rare editions of popular authors, but also gives those Soviet citizens, who are in a position to pay, an opportunity to obtain better medical care, a higher standard of education and training, better vacations, better interior decoration for their apartments, better baby-sitting facilities, better transportation, even identification papers, diplomas and other documents. More than that, not only private individuals, but government firms, agencies and collective farms frequently use the services provided

by the parallel market. 'People active in the parallel market vary from petty speculators selling fashionable clothes, to people of real influence and wealth, such as the famous Georgian underground capitalist Laziashvili, whose connections included several top officials.' Western analogies are not only war-time black markets, but also the cash-only markets normal in countries with high tax rates (e.g. household repairs, private lessons) and/or profitable illegal commodities (e.g. habit forming narcotic drugs).[4]

[4] It would be interesting to compare the size and economic and social significance of the criminal economies in the USSR and USA. In both countries they are large, significant and well integrated into the legal economy.

The view is widespread in Eastern Europe that the way to improve the position of personal consumption is by a basic reform of the economic mechanism, which marks a general transition from a sellers' market to a buyers' market, abolishes current planning, restores to enterprises or associations the right to determine for themselves their inputs and reintroduces competition. Joan Robinson has often argued that this is a mistaken line of development because it risks recreating the ills of producer sovereignty which in her view normally characterise capitalism. 'The true moral to be drawn from capitalist experience', she has written (Robinson 1964 p. 521)

> is that production will never be responsive to consumer needs as long as the initiative lies with the producer. Even within capitalism consumers are beginning to organize to defend themselves. In a planned economy the best hope seems to be to develop a class of functionaries, playing the role of wholesale dealers, whose career and self-respect depend on satisfying the consumer. They could keep in touch with demand through the shops; market research, which in the capitalist world is directed to finding out how to bamboozle the housewife, could be directed to discovering what she really needs; design and quality could be imposed upon manufacturing enterprises and the product mix settled by placing orders in such a way as to hold a balance between economies of scale and variety of tastes.

Joan Robinson has also argued that not only should consumer sovereignty via the wholesalers be established in socialist countries but that such a system is functioning in China (Robinson 1975 pp. 4–6). 'The Chinese system depends on a high level of morality (or "political consciousness") in every sphere from top to bottom. If this has been lost in Eastern Europe it cannot be recovered merely by changing the relations between commerce and industry.' Richman (1969 pp. 882–3) has confirmed that there is greater direct contact between trade and production in China than in the USSR. He has suggested that in general there is a greater stress on the satisfaction of consumer needs in China than in the USSR. One reason for the lesser importance of shortages and queues in China than in the CMEA countries, is the existence of formal rationing in China.

Formal rationing (as opposed to informal rationing via shortages and queues or rationing via the price mechanism), has been extensively used in the state socialist countries. In the USSR there was rationing in the Civil War, in 1928–35, and during the Great Patriotic War; in China basic commodities have been rationed since the early days of the People's Republic; in Poland the rationing of some foodstuffs was introduced in 1976 and in Cuba rationing is extensive and has lasted many years. Formal rationing has a number of advantages compared with the free market allocation of consumer goods. First, it enables commodities to be allocated on an egalitarian basis. Secondly, it facilitates control over population movement. For example, in China rural people cannot freely migrate to cities and look for jobs. They must first apply for permission and receive a ration book usable in the relevant city. Thirdly, it enables goods to be allocated in accordance with paternalistic criteria. For example, whereas distribution via the market may lead to children going without milk as parents spend their earnings on alcohol or tobacco, rationing can attempt to prevent this. Fourthly, it enables goods to be allocated on the needs principle, rather than on the desert principle. Fifthly, it enables discrimination to be made between deserving groups of the population who receive rations (e.g. manual workers) and undeserving ones (e.g. white collar workers, intellectuals or enemies of the people) who are left to starve.[5]

It also has a number of problems. First, extensive use of rationing undermines material incentives. This may have an adverse effect on labour productivity. Secondly, in general a person who receives rations is worse off with rations than with an equivalent quantity of money. The reason is that the relative quantities in which the person receives the various rationed goods is likely to differ from the relative quantities in which he/she would have bought the commodities. Unless the rations are only for a small number of very basic goods, or there are stringent punitive sanctions against this, this disadvantage of rations relative to universal purpose coupons (i.e. money) is likely to manifest itself in a formal or informal market in which rations for different commodities are exchanged against each other or for money.

The balance between the advantages and disadvantages of formal rationing depend on the concrete circumstances of particular countries at particular times.

It is not necessary to introduce formal rationing in order

[5] In 1948 Zhdanov (then a leading member of the Soviet Politburo) told Djilas how his (Zhdanov's) criticism of the writer Zoshchenko had been taken in Leningrad. The local authorities simply took away Zoshchenko's ration coupons and did not give them back till after Moscow's magnanimous intervention (Djilas 1962 p. 150).

to replace flexible prices and quantities, by administrative methods, in equilibrating supply and demand. A recent Soviet book on consumer demand (Levin & Yarkin 1976 pp. 284–9) considers a number of other administrative methods for regulating demand. They include, limiting the number of units sold per customer, only selling goods against preliminary orders, which may take a long time to be fulfilled (for example some types of refrigerators, suites of furniture and carpets), and distributing particularly scarce goods (e.g. cars) via employers rather than via the retail system. The fact that such methods are discussed in a book published in 1976 indicates that in the USSR the general availability of all goods in all places is still only a dream for the distant future.

Rationing may exist not only for consumer goods but also for producer goods. The replacement of competition and flexible prices and quantities by rationing, as the allocation mechanism for producer goods, has been a permanent feature of the Soviet economy since the end of the 1920s. Although abolished in Yugoslavia and Hungary, it also exists (with certain modifications) in all the other state socialist countries. What effects on the economy are there of eliminating competition between firms, allocating producer goods via a rationing system and balancing supply and demand for consumer goods by increasing supply and maintaining prices stable (or even, if possible, reducing them)? The standard analysis of this question is by Kornai (1971 part III). His argument is summed up in table 8.7.

Looking at table 8.7 it is easy to see why capitalism is normally characterised by pressure. It brings rapid technical progress and benefits the upper income groups (as consumers). The costs (unemployment, insecurity of employment, inequality) primarily fall on the working class. It is equally clear why war-time capitalist economies move over to suction. It increases the volume of output; mobilises hitherto wasted inputs; and facilitates social peace by offering the workers full employment, security of employment, and greater equality. One can also see why the orthodox Marxist–Leninist view is that suction is preferable to pressure. It raises output in the short run, eliminates unemployment and insecurity of employment, and its adverse effects on consumption do not affect the elite because of the existence of special shops, sanatoria and hotels for the elite, where pressure rules. These special facilities also play a useful role in rewarding conformity. The ill effects of suction on consumption

Table 8.7. *Pressure and suction compared*[a]

Area	Pressure	Suction
Output	In the short run brakes the increase in volume.	In the short run stimulates the increase in volume.
Inputs	Partial idleness of resources. Free combination of inputs.	Tight utilisation of resources. Forced substitution of inputs.
Technical progress	Stimulates introduction of revolutionary new products.	Does not stimulate introduction of revolutionary new products.
Quality	Stimulates improvements of quality and a high level of quality.	Does not stimulate improvements of quality or a high level of quality.
Competition	Sellers compete for buyers. Even the monopolist behaves 'like a competitor'.	Buyers compete for sellers. Even when there is a multiplicity of producers each producer behaves 'like a monopolist'.
Adaptation	Producers adapt to consumers in the short run. Producers attempt to establish product differentiation, brand loyalty and mould consumers.	Consumers adapt to producers in the short run. Sharp price adjustments needed occasionally.
Uncertainty	Burden of uncertainty carried by the seller.	Burden of uncertainty carried by the buyer.
Selection	Selection is made by buyer.	Selection is made by seller or central administrative organ.
	Generally progressive selection criteria.	Generally indifferent or counterproductive selection criteria.
Information flow	Generally the seller informs the buyer.	Generally the buyer seeks to obtain information about buying possibilities.
Social consequences	Generally unequal income distribution. Leads to demands for full employment. Efforts to deceive consumers. Waste of resources on advertising and marketing.	Generally equal income distribution. Leads to demands for economic reform. Creation of a market for elite where pressure rules. Creation of a black market where goods can be obtained – at a price.

[a] 'Pressure' and 'suction' correspond to a buyers' market and a sellers' market respectively.

Source: Adapted from Kornai (1971) p. 302.

are a major reason for the support for economic reform by wide strata of the population in Eastern Europe.

Pressure in an economy divided into classes is accompanied by envy and class struggle. Suction, on the other hand, can give rise to widespread low morale and demoralisation.[6]

Kornai's argument stresses the advantages of competition and flexible prices and quantities, in a buyers' market, for stimulating technical progress and high quality. This corroborates the arguments of Schumpeter and J. M. Clark that the great merit of the competitive market economy is not that stressed by neo-classical economics, of driving prices down to costs and costs to a minimum. Rather it is the stimulus it provides to new goods and technical progress.

THE EFFECT ON CONSUMPTION OF THE TRANSITION FROM CAPITALISM TO STATE SOCIALISM

Judging by historical experience, the transition from capitalism to state socialism might be expected to have both positive and negative effects on consumption. On the negative side the following would seem to be the most important.

First, the costs of revolution (Bukharin 1920 chapter 6, Sakharov 1969).[7] Revolutions result from internal and external political conflicts which have a major cost in terms of lives lost, physical destruction and loss of working time. This will reduce living standards.[8] In addition, the new regime may have to devote considerable resources (which might otherwise have been consumed) to repressing its internal enemies and/or fighting, or preparing to fight, its external enemies.

[6] One phenomenon which accentuates popular dissatisfaction and demoralisation in Eastern Europe is the special shops where scarce, high quality and luxury goods can be obtained – for convertible currency only. This system, which was initiated in the USSR in the early 1930s, creates a privileged stratum with access to attractive consumer goods inaccessible to the mass of the population. The latter are naturally resentful.

From the point of view of the authorities, sales in these shops are exports. Exports are necessary to pay for imports of machinery and grain and to service debts. Popular dissatisfaction and demoralisation, on the other hand, are so endemic that a little more seems to the authorities of little significance.

[7] For a discussion of the costs of revolution in Cambodia see Ponchaud (1978).

[8] Wiles (1974 p. 104) has noted that 'nothing harms the poor so much as a failed revolution, for that gives us the costs without the benefits... I would put the odds against a revolutionary attempt, taken at random from human history, at three to one. This is a much more serious conservative argument than the futurity discount or the costs of a successful revolution.'

Secondly, there is the loss of the output of small-scale private enterprise. The suppression of artisans, small workshops, petty trade and small-scale private services can have a serious adverse effect on popular welfare.

Thirdly, once the state is transformed into the main engine of economic development, mistakes in economic policy can have a major – sometimes catastrophic – effect on consumption. Such mistakes are quite common.

Fourthly, the high share of investment in the national income of state socialist countries has an opportunity cost in terms of consumption forgone. Huberman and Sweezy (1969 p. 107) noted that this 'goes far to explain the extreme austerity of life in Cuba today, so much commented on by all visitors to the island'.

Fifthly, the establishment of a suction economy will lead to widespread queues, shortages and popular dissatisfaction.

On the positive side the following effects would seem to be the most important.

First, there are the gains to the poor from the distribution among them of the confiscated stocks of consumer goods of the rich (e.g. housing).

Secondly, to the extent that the level of production is not adversely affected, it is possible to redistribute the income which formerly accrued to the rich.

Thirdly, employment can be increased sharply.

Fourthly, security of employment can be introduced.

Fifthly, education and medical services can be extended to wider strata of the population and rapidly expanded.

Do the pluses outweigh the minuses, or vice versa? According to Huberman and Sweezy (1969 p. 108), writing about Cuba, but whose argument is perfectly general, the pluses clearly outweigh the minuses.

> we must emphasise that Cuban austerity is not like that in the underdeveloped countries of the 'free world'. In the latter the burden of austerity is borne by the workers, peasants, unemployed, etc., whose incomes are extremely low or non-existent and who usually make up from 75 to 90 per cent of the population. The middle strata live in relative comfort and the ruling oligarchies in outrageous luxury. The shops are full only because the price–income system keeps the vast majority from buying what is in them. To the superficial observer there appear to be no shortages; to most of the people there are nothing but shortages. How right was the Cuban boy who said to Yose Yglesias: 'If everyone in Mexico could afford to buy a pair of shoes, how many do you think would be left in the stores?'
>
> The point is that in Cuba everyone *can* afford to buy a pair of shoes,

and there are never any left in the stores. And the same goes for nearly all other consumer goods. The explanation is twofold: First, the minimum wage in Cuba is 85 pesos a month and a large percentage of workers get two or three times as much. Moreover, there is a labour shortage so that every able-bodied person can get a job and many families have two or more wage-earners. Second, average rents are very low, education and health and some other services are free, and rationed goods are cheap. The result is a large volume of 'free' purchasing power chasing after a very limited supply of goods. In these circumstances, the shortages which are hidden in other countries rise to the surface for all to see. What's more, they affect the entire population including the top management and the middle strata who would be comfortably off in other countries. In other words, *everyone* feels the shortages, and this sometimes gives the impression that they are a lot worse off than they really are.

For the truth is that the shortages which all Cubans have to bear are not nearly as bad as those which afflict the great majority of Latin Americans.

This verdict, however, is simply the opinion of two observers. To throw more light on the situation it is useful to calculate a synthetic social indicator, standardised for differences in economic development. This permits a simple numerical comparison between welfare levels in the two systems. An attempt to do this has been made by the Yugoslav economist Horvat, whose work is reproduced in table 8.8 below.

The table was constructed in the following way. The sixty most developed countries for which there are statistics were ranked by various criteria. All the state socialist countries among them are listed in the above table. Column 5 ranks the number of tertiary students per ten thousand of the population. Column six is the arithmetic average of the rank of hospital beds per ten thousand of the population and the rank of physicians per ten thousand of the population. Column seven is the average of columns 4, 5 and 6. Columns 8 and 9 give the differences, for each country and for the whole group of countries, between the ranking by GNP and that by basic welfare. For example, a figure of +5.0 in D_2 indicates that a country in 1970 had achieved a basic welfare level five places ahead of the world average for a country with its GNP per capita. Conversely a figure of −5.0 in D_2 indicates that a country in 1970 had only achieved a basic welfare level five places behind the world average for a country with its GNP per capita.

The table shows clearly that, using Horvat's method, both in 1968 and 1970 the state socialist countries had achieved signifi-

Table 8.8. *Social indicators of the state socialist countries (ranks of indicators)*

Country (1)	Per capita GNP in 1968 (2)	Per capita GNP in 1970 (3)	Life expectancy (4)	Students (5)	Health service (6)	Basic welfare (7)	Difference D_1 (8 = 2 − 7)	Difference D_2 (9 = 3 − 7)
GDR	15	12	6	36	3	15.0	0.0	−3.0
Czechoslovakia	19	16	19	22	5	15.3	3.7	0.7
USSR	22	20	26	5	1	10.7	11.3	9.3
Hungary	23	23	27	37	9	24.3	−1.3	−1.3
Poland	26	24	23	21	23	22.3	3.7	1.7
Romania	28	31	32	26	26	28.0	0.0	3.0
Bulgaria	29	33	15	18	11	14.7	14.3	18.3
Albania	40	39	37	20	34	30.3	9.7	8.7
Cuba	43	41	35	46	35	38.7	4.3	2.3
Average	27.2	26.6	24.4	25.7	16.3	22.1	5.1	4.3

Source: Horvat (1974) p. 32.

cantly higher levels of basic welfare than the world average for countries with their GNP per capita.

Horvat's paper is interesting as a pioneering attempt to calculate standardised inter-system social indicators. It is also, as is natural with a pioneering work, rather crude. For example, its health service indicators are *partial* measures of *input*. They ignore some inputs, such as medicines and medical supplies, and fail to measure output, i.e. the good health of the population. For example, no hospital beds and one doctor in a country where oral contraceptives are available, may be at least as useful from a health point of view as twenty hospital beds used for abortions and ten doctors engaged in abortions and form filling. As a matter of fact, the Soviet death rate has been steadily rising since 1964. The infant mortality rate and virtually all the age-specific death rates have also been rising in the past decade. Table 8.8 shows that in 1970 Soviet life expectancy was six places behind the world average for a country with its GNP per capita, while its Horvat health service index was nineteen places ahead. This simply indicates that measuring the *output* of a health service by the *inputs* it uses, is wrong. Furthermore, a number of important social indicators (e.g. those relating to housing) are omitted. In addition, the Horvat calculations are vulnerable to Seers' (1976) criticism of the UN's SSDS (System of Social and Demographic

Statistics): it assumes that governments are benign. No attention, for example, is paid to statistics of the proportion of the population in detention. Although none of the state socialist countries publishes data on this awkward issue, it is well known that the number of detainees per thousand of the population is much higher in the USSR than in many capitalist countries.[9] Hence Horvat's calculations must be considered as a useful pioneering work in the calculation of standardised inter-system social indicators, but one to whose conclusions little significance can be attached.

CONCLUSION

The form which consumption planning has taken has varied very much over time and between countries depending on the concrete circumstances. A major method has been that of norms. This is a useful method, but has two weaknesses. These are, the arbitrary nature of many of the norms and the phenomenon of substitutability. The main method of balancing demand and supply is that of output increases. This can generate shortages and queues. These appear to be more significant in the CMEA countries than in China, where more emphasis is placed on formal rationing. Shortages and queues are not necessarily signs of macroeconomic disequilibrium. They may also result from disequilibrium relative prices, factors internal to the distribution system or popular attitudes.

One result of the inability of the offical Soviet economy to satisfy all consumer needs is the existence of a large and flourishing non-state, or parallel, market.

The general existence of sellers' market conditions has an important effect not only on consumer satisfaction but also on a wide range of economic phenomena, such as employment, job security, technical progress and information flows.

Experience has shown that the transition from capitalism to state socialism has both negative and positive effects on consumption. The calculation of standardised inter-system social indicators has not yet made much progress. Hence it is not yet possible to make well-based assertions about comparative welfare levels in the two systems.

[9] According to Shtromas (1977) the number of detainees in the USSR is about 2½–3 million, i.e. 1–1.2% of the population. Other authors give much lower figures.

SUGGESTIONS FOR FURTHER READING

P. Hanson, *The consumer in the Soviet economy* (London 1968).

P. Hanson, 'Acquisitive dissent', *New Society* (29 October 1970). This article is reprinted in P. Barker (ed.) *One for sorrow, Two for joy: Ten years of New Society* (London 1972).

Economic aspects of life in the USSR (Brussels 1975).

B. Mieczkowski, *Personal and social consumption in Eastern Europe* (New York 1975).

R. Portes, 'The control of inflation: Lessons from East European experience', *Economica* (May 1977).

P. Wiles, 'The control of inflation in Hungary', *Economie appliquée* vol. 27 (1974) pp. 119–48.

P. Wiles, 'La lotta contro l'inflazione nelle economie collectiviste: una valutazione', *Rivista di Politica Economica* (December 1974).

O. Sik, *The bureaucratic economy* (New York 1972) chapter 3.

A. Hegedus & M. Markus, 'The choice of alternatives and values in long-range planning of distribution and consumption', A. Hegedus et al., *The humanisation of socialism* (London 1976).

J. Robinson, *Economic management in China* (London 1976) pp. 4–6.

R. Huenemann, 'Urban rationing in Communist China', *China Quarterly* no. 26 (April–June 1966).

C. Howe, *China's economy* (London 1978) chapter 6.

9

PLANNING INTERNATIONAL TRADE

If the free traders cannot understand how one country can get rich at the expense of another, we should not be surprised since they themselves are also not prepared to understand how, within a single country, one class can get rich at the expense of another class.

K. Marx, *The poverty of philosophy*

A proletarian state's foreign trade organisation in capitalist encirclement must serve two basic goals: (a) to facilitate as much as possible and to stimulate the development of the productive forces of the country, and (b) to defend the socialist economy under construction from economic attack by the capitalist countries. The whole difficulty of the problem of foreign trade organisation lies in the fact that a proletarian state cannot for a single minute lose sight of both these goals and, depending on the foreign situation and the needs of domestic socialist construction, must choose the appropriate forms of foreign trade organisation. It is absolutely indisputable that the slightest breach in the foreign trade monopoly would bring with it an increase in capitalist pressure on our socialist forms of economy and the inevitable widening of this breach would lead to a subjugation of our entire national economy to the more technologically developed economy of the capitalist countries, i.e. to the downfall of socialist construction. On the other hand, the preservation of the pace of development of the national economy necessary for building socialism requires a certain development and modification of the existing forms of carrying out the foreign trade monopoly.

Extract from the resolution 'On Foreign Trade' of the Central Committee of the Russian Communist Party (bolsheviks) of 5 October 1925

THE CRITIQUE OF THE CAPITALIST INTERNATIONAL DIVISION OF LABOUR

The Marxist analysis of international trade is analogous to the Marxist analysis of the labour market. Where Western economists see fair exchange and mutual benefit, Marxists see unequal exchange and exploitation. From an analytical point of view, it is clear that each school considers a special case, for the Western

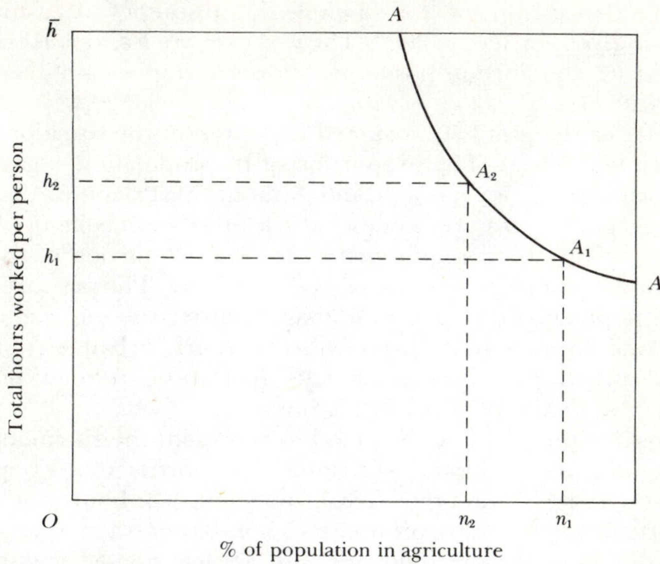

Figure 9.1 The pre-capitalist economy.

economists the non-constant sum game, and for the Marxists the constant sum game. From an empirical point of view, the real issue is what proportion of actual historical experience is accounted for by each of the models. A neat exposition of the view of capitalist international trade which underlies much second and third world trade practice has been provided by Hymer and Resnick (1971) and is reproduced below.

Consider the standard problem of the gains from trade. To make the question more specific, we will analyse the Mercantilist era (c. fifteenth–nineteenth centuries). The situation in the pre-capitalist countries with which Portugal, Spain, the Netherlands, England and France traded is assumed to be as depicted in figure 9.1.

The production possibility frontier is *AA* and is determined by the production function

$$\bar{d} = f(a, h, n) \qquad (1)$$

where $\bar{d}$ is food produced (and consumed) per head,
a is output per man hour in agriculture,
h is hours worked per man in agriculture, and
n is the % of the population in agriculture.

Assume that $\bar{d}$ is given (for example by subsistence or custom) and a is given (by technology). The variables are h and n. Hence, comparing equilibrium positions, a lower n implies a higher h, and vice versa.

Consider the point A_1, assumed to represent the situation in pre-colonial Africa. The proportion of the population engaged in agriculture (n_1) is very high, and the hours of agricultural work of these people (h_1) are modest. Much time is available ($\bar{h}-h_1$), after satisfying food requirements, for the production of rural household goods, for ceremonies and for leisure. The proportion of the population engaged in non-agriculture, $100-n_1$, e.g. the ruler and his family, the aristocrats, soldiers, urban servants, clerks, urban traders and artisans (i.e. those termed non-productive by the physiocrats), is small.

Consider the point A_2, assumed to represent the situation in pre-colonial Asia. The non-agricultural proportion of the population ($100-n_2$) is larger than that A_1, and hence the hours worked in agriculture per agriculturalist (h_2) is larger than that A_1, in order to provide food for the larger non-agricultural population.

Compare the welfare of the agricultural population (the great bulk of the total population) at A_1 and A_2. At both, food consumption per head is the same, but at A_2 hours of work in agriculture are higher than at A_1 because of the necessity of feeding the larger non-agricultural population. Except in the special case in which the agricultural population receives substantial benefits from the non-agricultural population (e.g. irrigation systems which raise productivity in agriculture, or consumer goods) it seems reasonable to suggest that the welfare of the masses was higher at A_1 than at A_2.

Introduce (Mercantilist) trade into the model. In the African case the state grew. A military group that succeeded in monopolising coercive power in a given area could establish law and order for traders and levy taxes. The strength of the state could also be used to enslave part of the population and use it for export, either directly (as slaves) or indirectly (as slave-produced commodities such as gold). It was thus possible to appropriate a surplus through exploitation of labour as well as through the taxation of trade. As far as welfare is concerned, there were three significant effects. First, the state grew. Secondly, a proportion of the population was enslaved. Thirdly, there was an inflow of manufactured goods (e.g. whisky and guns). The first and third benefited the elite. The first and second were losses for the masses.

In the Asian case the state shrank. The indigenous 'oriental despotisms' were shattered. This was a clear gain to the local agricultural population. This gain was reduced, or eliminated altogether, however, in those areas where the Mercantilist traders levied significant taxes which fell, directly or indirectly, on the agricultural population.

In the Latin American case, contact with the Mercantilists led to the complete collapse of the local societies. Almost all the inhabitants of Mexico and Peru (and North America) were killed.

The gains and losses from Mercantilist trade are summarised in equation (2) below.

$$\text{Gains from trade } (\equiv A) = \left[\begin{array}{l} \text{Gains to elites in Europe} \\ \qquad + \\ \text{Gains (or losses) to majority in} \\ \text{Europe} \\ \qquad + \\ \text{Gains to elites in underdeveloped} \\ \text{countries} \\ \qquad - \\ \text{Losses of exploited} \\ \qquad - \\ \text{Deadweight loss} \end{array}\right] \quad (2)$$

The question is, what is the sign of *A*? It is difficult to disagree with Hymer & Resnick's (1971 p. 482) view that, 'It is hard to imagine any reasonable set of calculations that would show that the value of the increase in world income during the 16th, 17th and 18th centuries could offset the tremendous costs associated with the murder and enslavement of Africans and Americans.'[1]

It is precisely to prevent the losses to the backward countries that, in the Marxist view, unrestricted trade between advanced capitalist countries and backward countries brings, while obtaining the benefits of international trade, that state socialist countries create a state monopoly of foreign trade. The advantages of the state monopoly of foreign trade are fivefold. First, it enables the country concerned to use scarce foreign currency

[1] The reasons why different conclusions follow in Western models is because the latter treat the population as homogeneous (rather than divided into classes), assume that welfare depends on marketed goods only, and assume that marketed output has two components, size and distribution, and that only the former is relevant for ascertaining 'efficiency'.

in the way that most facilitates rapid economic development (by cutting out imports of inessential goods and maximising imports of machinery). Secondly, it protects domestic industry. Thirdly, it insulates the economy from the law of value (e.g. it prevents capitalist recessions causing domestic unemployment). Fourthly, it allows the country to use its monopoly power (as a seller) or monopsony power (as a buyer). Fifthly, it restricts capitalist influence over the development of the economy to a minimum. The problems of the state monopoly of foreign trade are twofold, one technical and the other political. First, because the planners lack sufficient information and time to process it, they may make inefficient trading choices. Secondly, the possibility of private individuals obtaining commodities they want from abroad (e.g. travel, books) or selling abroad commodities that they have produced (e.g. books, songs or wheat) is reduced.

Summary

The characteristic feature of socialist foreign trade is the state monopoly. This is based on a theory of trade between advanced and backward countries which stresses the losses which unrestricted commercial intercourse can bring the latter. The state monopoly of foreign trade has both advantages and problems.

THE SOCIALIST INTERNATIONAL DIVISION OF LABOUR

The disintegration of the single, all-embracing world market must be regarded as the most important economic sequel of the Second World War...China and other, European, people's democracies broke away from the capitalist system and, together with the Soviet Union, formed a united and powerful socialist camp confronting the camp of capitalism. The economic consequence of the existence of two opposite camps was that the single all-embracing world market disintegrated, so that we now have two parallel world markets, also confronting one another.

J. Stalin, *Economic problems of socialism in the USSR* (1952)

Relations between socialist countries are international relations of a new type. Relations between socialist countries, whether large or small, and whether more developed or less developed economically, must be based on the principles of complete equality, respect for territorial integrity, sovereignty and independence, and non-interference in each other's internal affairs, and must also be based on the principles of mutual support and mutual assistance in accordance with proletarian internationalism...

> If, proceeding only from its own partial interests, any socialist country unilaterally demands that fraternal countries submit to its needs, and uses the pretext of opposing what they call 'going it alone' and 'nationalism' to prevent other fraternal countries from applying the principle of relying mainly on their own efforts in their construction and from developing their economies on the basis of independence, or even goes to the length of putting economic pressure on other fraternal countries – then these are pure manifestations of national egoism...
>
> In relations among socialist countries it would be preposterous to follow the practice of gaining profit for oneself at the expense of others, a practice characteristic of relations among capitalist countries, or to go so far as to take their 'economic integration' and the 'Common Market', which monopoly capitalist groups have instituted for the purpose of seizing markets and grabbing profits, as examples which socialist countries ought to follow in their economic cooperation and mutual assistance.
>
> Extract from a letter of the CC of the CCP to the CC of the CPSU (June 1963)

In this section five different models of socialist international trade will be considered. They are, the socialism in one country model, the socialist imperialism model, the international planning model, the socialist multilateralism model, and the economic integration model. Each model roughly corresponds to the actual historical experience of certain countries at certain times.

Socialism in one country

This model approximately corresponds to the experience of the USSR before 1945 and of China since 1960. In it the country concerned uses the state monopoly of foreign trade to ensure that scarce foreign exchange is used primarily to import machinery and thus accelerate economic growth. (An important difference between the foreign trade policies pursued by the USSR and China in the first twenty years after their collectivisation of agriculture, has been the imports of grain by China. These have resulted from the non-extractive nature of Chinese collectivisation combined with the disappointing rate of growth of grain output.) The country cuts itself off from the international labour and capital markets. The internal price level is insulated from world prices by the monopoly, the maximum possible volume of imports is acquired and the choice between possible imports is governed primarily by technological and political factors. Imports are paid for (apart from credits) by selling on the world market sufficient exports to generate the requisite foreign exchange, almost independently of domestic costs and profitability. The country regards the acquisition of technically advanced imports as the main object of foreign trade. In this it is unlike capitalist countries, which regard exports as the main desideratum in international trade. This is simply another example, analogous to those already encountered in chapters 6 and 8, of the general phenomenon that economic growth in the state socialist world is normally supply constrained. In the capitalist world, on the other hand, it is normally demand constrained.

One problem with this model is that it ignores the contradiction between the international nature of the productive forces and the nation state. This is not so serious for huge countries such as the USSR and China, but is very serious for smaller countries. Another problem with this model is that the state monopoly of foreign trade is an integral part of the statist model of economic and social development. In Yugoslavia in the 1950s, when there was a reaction against the statist model, the country reverted to a Western model of foreign trade. The state monopoly was abandoned and the free movement of labour restored.

Socialist imperialism

At the end of the Second World War Soviet troops occupied much of Eastern and Central Europe, China and Korea. The USSR used the dominant political position which she acquired in this way to benefit herself economically and to impose her ideas on economic organisation on some of her neighbours. She removed machinery from East Germany and Manchuria and imposed reparations on Finland, East Germany, Hungary and Romania.[2] She reoriented trade towards herself,[3] and established

[2] 'Stalin showed himself a vastly more efficient extractor and recipient of direct tribute in 1945–52 than France and Britain in 1919–31. Indeed, since Mercantilism there has been nothing like it. The very notion that there was some difficulty in absorbing tribute would have seemed utterly astonishing to him: an example of the "internal contradictions of capitalism" too comical to be true. His own problems, although they were grave and caused terrible waste, affected only his procurement machinery. Once he had reformed that, reparations paid off handsomely' (Wiles 1968 p. 488).

[3] She is also widely believed to have manipulated the terms of trade in her own favour. Firm evidence for this is sparse. The best known example is Polish coal, of which the USSR bought *c.* 50,000,000 tons in 1946–53 at very low prices. This, however, was part of a deal made in 1945, whereby Poland received all German assets in Poland plus a share of the reparations due to be received by the USSR from Germany. In 1956, the USSR cancelled Poland's outstanding debt to the USSR ($626 million) in compensation for the losses Poland had incurred through selling her coal very cheaply.

companies with joint Soviet-local ownership and Soviet management in East Germany, China, Bulgaria, Hungary, Romania, Yugoslavia and Czechoslovakia which partly produced goods for the USSR.[4] She imposed an oppressive and inefficient agricultural system, a high share of investment and defence in the national income, and an economic mechanism which disregarded personal consumption, throughout Eastern Europe. Soviet behaviour towards her dependants in this period was much less favourable to them than US behaviour towards her dependants.[5]

The main burden of socialist imperialism fell on what was first of all the Soviet occupation zone of Germany and then became the German Democratic Republic. According to one source (Marer 1974), in 1945–60 Soviet Zone/GDR net transfers to the USSR were about 19 milliard current US dollars. This huge sum represented between a fifth and a third of Soviet Zone/GDR GNP in 1946–53 and exceeded the total flow of Marshall Aid to all Western Europe. According to an estimate quoted in the same source, Soviet Zone transfers were about 3% of Soviet national income in 1950 and higher percentages in the immediate post-war years. The burden on the Soviet Zone/GDR was greater than the gain to the USSR because of the inefficient dismantling of machinery.

Economic relations between the USSR and Eastern Europe

[4] According to the Yugoslav Ministry of Foreign Affairs (*White book* 1951 pp. 37–8), in the Yugoslav case, as far as these companies were concerned, 'The formal parity [in ownership between the USSR and Yugoslavia]...was only a screen to conceal direct exploitation and appropriation of profits by the utilisation of Yugoslavia's natural resources and of the values created by the labour of the Yugoslav working people...The two following examples are sufficient to reveal the way these companies were operated to the detriment of Yugoslavia. The JUSPAD (Jugoslav–Soviet Danube Shipping Stock Company) transported Soviet cargo at the price of 12–18 para for one kilometer-ton, while the price was 42 para for Yugoslav cargo. The JUSTA (Jugoslav–Soviet Stock Company for Civil Air Transport) took over complete control of civil air navigation in Yugoslavia even refusing to give the Yugoslav state air transport authorities the data needed for their control work. The operation of these mixed companies at the expense of the Yugoslav economy is but a pale picture of the degree of exploitation that would have resulted from the establishment of a number of mixed manufacturing companies, which the Soviet Government had been proposing to Yugoslavia. In such companies undoubtedly, the exploiting tendencies would have been much greater.'

[5] At the end of the Second World War, during which the USSR had liberated all Eastern Europe from the Nazis, her economic situation was extremely grave. Much of her manpower had been killed in the war and her richest industrial and agricultural areas devastated. The USA, on the other hand, suffered relatively few casualties and greatly expanded her output during the war. In addition, the Marshall plan brought the USA major political and economic gains.

(especially the Soviet Zone of Germany) in this period, were analogous to those between the Soviet Government and Soviet collective farms under Stalin. In both cases coercion was used to collect tribute. In both cases the Soviet Government collected a substantial revenue in this way. In both cases, however, there was a substantial cost in terms of low rates of growth of labour productivity, high costs of production and poor development of quality and technical progress, and a sullen resentful attitude by the labour force. Because the collective farmers are geographically isolated, in their case the latter never led to any very strong resistance. In the foreign trade case, however, because of the existence of nation states and compact groups of workers in industrial cities, it led to the break with Yugoslavia in 1948, the demonstrations by the German workers in 1953 and the Polish workers in 1956.

In 1953–56 the USSR radically changed her policies. The legitimacy of varying roads to socialism was recognised. The Soviet shares of the mixed companies were returned to the host countries and reparations were ended. (The removal of machinery had already ended in 1946.)[6] The prices at which CMEA has traded since the early 1950s have persistently been more favourable for the exporters of finished products than for the exporters of raw materials. As a result the USSR, which mainly exports raw materials and imports machinery, has had worse terms of trade inside CMEA than those that prevailed on the world market (Marer 1972). In addition, the USSR extended (mainly by way of trade) substantial economic assistance towards China, notably by providing the designs, machinery and many of the specialists for the construction of the majority of the modern industrial plants, the building of which constituted the core of the Chinese First Five Year Plan (1953–57). These economic policy changes were part of the general attempt to replace coercion by cooperation in the relationship between the Soviet Government and its subjects which characterised 1953–56. (Another example is Soviet agricultural policy.) Similarly, during

[6] It was very inefficient. In Germany, the Soviet organisations concerned often 'failed to pack, label or despatch properly. Very many priceless assets were simply destroyed or lost. Meanwhile, the ministries quarrelled vehemently over who should have what, and the military government found it impossible to set any upper limit to dismantling. Hence a party arose within the military government and the Ministry of Foreign Trade... that favoured the better organised and less destructive process of taking reparations out of current production' (Wiles 1968 p. 488).

Table 9.1. *CMEA – population of members at the end of 1976 (millions)*

Member	Population
Bulgaria	8.8
Cuba	9.5
Czechoslovakia	15.0
GDR	16.8
Hungary	10.6
Mongolia	1.5
Poland	34.5
Romania	21.6
USSR	257.8
Vietnam	47.0

Source: *Statisticheskii* (1977) p. 9.

the 1960s and 1970s the USSR provided Cuba with designs, machinery and specialists for industrialisation, substantial credits, and relatively attractive export markets. In addition, in the 1970s the USSR has provided economic assistance to Vietnam.

Nevertheless, relations between the state socialist countries have continued to be characterised not only by cooperation but also by conflict. The deterioration in Sino-Soviet relations after 1958 led to the withdrawal of Soviet specialists in 1960 and a rapid decline in mutual trade, similar to the decline in trade which followed the Soviet–Yugoslav dispute in 1948. Within CMEA the USSR has always occupied a dominant position. CMEA was established on the initiative of the USSR. Its headquarters are in the capital of the USSR. Its policies are largely determined by the USSR. This is inevitable in view of the enormous disproportion in population and output between the USSR and the other members (see table 9.1.).

Table 9.1 shows that a single country, the USSR, accounts for about 60% of the entire population of CMEA. In this respect, CMEA is an organisation similar to the Zollverein. It is an economic organisation entirely dominated by one member, in the latter case Prussia, in the former the USSR. This has aroused considerable dissatisfaction in some of the other members. Since 1962, the Romanians have persistently counterposed national independence and national development to CMEA integration, which they have regarded as an expression of Soviet national interests and a threat to their rapid industrialisation and national sovereignty. Many people in the more advanced CMEA countries consider that the structure of foreign trade and production which CMEA has imposed on them are not in their own best interests. In 1965, E. Apel, the Chairman of the GDR planning commission, committed suicide, after prolonged trade negotiations with the USSR, allegedly in protest against the planned trade agreements between the GDR and USSR for 1966–70. In 1968 it was widely asserted in Czechoslovakia, that concentration on the import of Soviet raw materials, their processing and the export of the finished products to the USSR, was not in the best interest of Czechoslovakia. The country would be better off, it was often said, producing producer and consumer goods for export to Western Europe and for domestic use. This would have a beneficial effect on the technical level of production and on home consumption.

International planning

In the 1950s CMEA made the transition from the socialist imperialism model to the socialism in one country model, modified by bilateral trade. Each country planned its own development, its plans including a substantial and growing volume of bilateral trade with its CMEA partners. This, however, was insufficient to overcome the contradiction between the international nature of the productive forces and the nation state. The members of CMEA, with their existing institutions, were unable to capture all the gains that might have been available from specialisation and economies of scale. The rapid development of economic integration in the capitalist world, particularly in Western Europe, made them increasingly aware of this. In 1960 the Polish leader Gomulka observed of the relations between CMEA members, 'There is no cooperation whatsoever in the important sector of investment: everyone peels his own turnip – and loses by it.'

Accordingly, in 1962, Khrushchev suggested that CMEA should establish 'a unified planning organ, empowered to compile common plans and to decide organisational matters'. Marxists consider that within any nation the efficient allocation of resources requires national planning, as explained in chapter 1. Similarly, Khrushchev argued in 1962, the efficient allocation of resources within CMEA requires supranational, CMEA-wide, planning. This planning, it was suggested, should concern itself primarily with investment.

Nevertheless, CMEA was not transformed into a supranational planning organisation, for two reasons. First, Romania, as a less-developed country, objected on classical Listian[7] grounds to supranational investment planning based on current comparative costs. Secondly, in the early 1960s, it became increasingly realised within CMEA that there was a contradiction between seeking to raise efficiency and striving to increase still further the role of central planning. It was precisely at this time that there was widespread discussion of how, given the development of the productive forces and the techniques of planning, planning was hindering efficiency. Hence the focus of discussion within CMEA on measures to improve its *modus operandi* switched from strengthening the planning element to strengthening market relations.

Socialist multilateralism

According to standard Western theory, bilateralism in international trade is bound to lead to waste. It either constrains the volume of trade to the export potential of the country with the lesser export potential, or forces the country with a greater export potential to accept goods which it does not want very much. This argument has been applied to CMEA by van Brabant (1973, 1974) and Ausch (1972). Ausch's analysis is set out in figures 9.2, 9.3 and 9.4. In figure 9.2, the arrows indicate the direction of trade and the numbers the volume. For example, *A* imports 40 units from *B* and exports 80 units to *B*. Trade is multilateral and each country is in balance of trade equilibrium. Total trade volume is 240. Under conditions of bilateralism with the export constraint operative, trade will take place as in figure 9.3. Total trade volume is 120. Welfare is substantially less than in the multilateral case. In figure 9.4, *h* indicates hard commodities and *s* soft ones. In a situation of bilateralism with soft commodities, the volume of trade is 360. This is more than in the multilateral case, but one third of the trade consists of the import of soft commodities, i.e. goods that are not much wanted. Hence welfare may well be less than in the multilateral case. The softness of much of the trade taking place may be confirmed by the activities of capitalist import–export firms, re-exporting the soft goods and supplying hard ones in exchange, thus

[7] List was a nineteenth-century German economist. He argued that free trade is only in the interest of the advanced countries and that backward countries require protection if they are to industrialise.

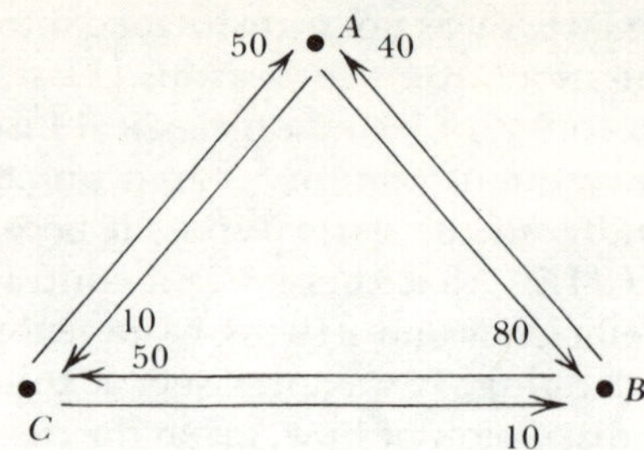

Figure 9.2 Multilateral trade.

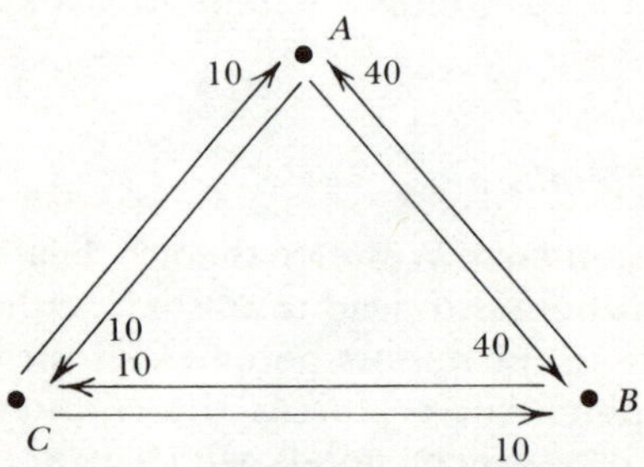

Figure 9.3 Bilateralism with the export constraint operative.

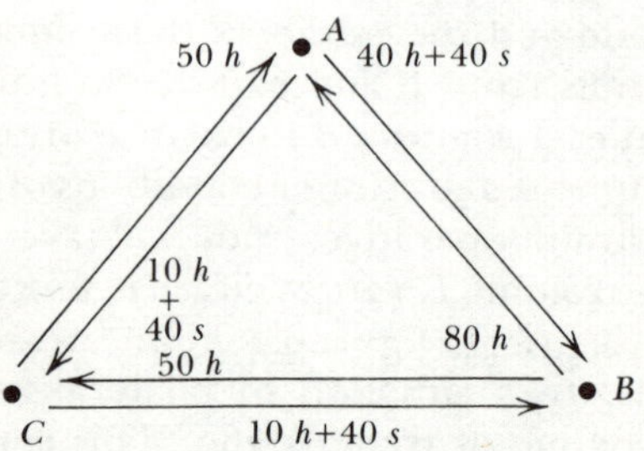

Figure 9.4 Bilateralism with soft commodities.

introducing elements of *de facto* multilateralism. Figure 9.4 also illustrates how the administrative economy can generate a discrepancy between output levels and welfare levels.

The merits of multilateralism have been recognised in CMEA circles since the mid 1950s. In 1957 and 1963 agreements were reached between the members on multilateral clearing. The 1963 agreement created a special organ for this purpose, the Bank for International Economic Cooperation, accounts with which are kept in transferable roubles. In the agreement setting up this bank it is stated that 'within one year from the foundation of the Bank...the Board will study ways of introducing into the scope of its operations transacted in transferable roubles, the possibility of a conversion into gold or freely convertible currencies'. Similarly, the Comprehensive Programme of integration adopted in 1971 stated the intention to 'study' the question of convertibility, with a view to working out the conditions and methods for it. Nevertheless, currencies remain inconvertible and trade bilateral. Each member of CMEA strives for strictly balanced bilateral trade with each of her CMEA partners and for each calendar year.[8] Why is this?

The fundamental reason concerns the internal economic arrangements of the USSR, the current Soviet economic model to use the Polish terminology, or economic mechanism to use the Hungarian terminology.

The current Soviet model can be described as an administrative economy (Ellman 1973). In general, economic decisions are made in accordance with instructions from above, as in any factory, army or civil service. This model has been rejected in Yugoslavia and China and substantially modified in Hungary, but remains essentially unaltered in the USSR, despite the economic reform announced in September 1965. Bilateralism in foreign trade is simply one specific example of the administrative economy in action.

In the bilateral case, trade is carried on in accordance with instructions. Prices, which are important for accounting and aggregation, are barely relevant for allocative purposes. In the multilateral case, the volume and composition of trade is largely determined by relative prices. The price system of the administrative economy, however, is most unsuitable for allocative purposes. For one thing, internal and external prices are separated. This means that an enterprise cannot realistically compare domestic and foreign prices with a view to making trade

[8] Strictly speaking, the trade is not even fully bilateral, since the members seek to balance their trade in hard and soft goods taken separately. (Multilateral negotiations take place at the end of each year to find a market for the softest commodities, i.e. those that could not be sold in bilateral trade. The volume of trade generated in this way is insignificant, c. 2–3% of the total.)

Table 9.2. *Price differences in Hungary's exports to CMEA countries*

Major commodity groups	Number of commodities exported to two or more countries	Number of commodities showing price differences exceeding 25 per cent (differences in per cent) 25–34	35–44	45–54	55–69	70–79	80–89	90–99	100 and over	Total
Machinery and equipment	608	42	25	10	21	11	2	8	20	139
Fuels and other materials (including metals)	52	3	8	3	6	2	—	—	3	25
Chemical products (including rubber)	18	1	—	1	1	1	—	—	1	5
Construction materials	10	—	—	—	—	—	—	—	—	—
Agricultural raw materials (excluding those used for food)	16	—	1	—	2	—	—	—	2	5
Live animals	—	—	—	—	—	—	—	—	—	—
Rawproducts for the foodindustry	2	—	—	—	—	—	—	—	—	—
Finished food products	66	5	5	3	6	3	1	1	3	27
Industrial consumer goods	248	20	11	13	13	7	6	6	16	92
Total	1,020	71	50	30	49	24	9	15	45	293

Source: Ausch (1972) p. 80.

decisions. For another, the price a country obtains for its exports varies very much between its export markets. An example is set out in table 9.2.

As can be seen from table 9.2, for many exports to CMEA countries, the same commodity can vary in price by more than 100% depending on which country it is sold to. In addition, the relative prices of primary and processed goods differ inside CMEA and on the world market. Furthermore, the CMEA countries operate a multiple exchange rate system.

Given all these price discrepancies, only administrative control over trade can preserve the present volume and structure of trade. The transition to multilateralism in foreign trade would require a reform of the price system so as to enable it to replace many of the administrative procedures which currently determine the volume and direction of foreign trade. The idea, however, of substantially replacing instructions by market relations in economic management, was rejected by the Soviet CC in December 1969. Hence, foreign trade has remained bilateral and currencies inconvertible.

Economic integration

Economic integration depends to a considerable extent on political factors. The success of integration measures, on a voluntary basis, can be ensured only on the condition of complete trust between socialist states, their close ideological and political unity.'

Sorokin & Alampiev (1970 p. 47)

The abandonment in the late 1960s in Czechoslovakia and the USSR of a reform of the economic mechanism both internally and within CMEA, led to the emergence of a new model of CMEA cooperation, that of economic integration. This was clearly embodied in the 'Comprehensive programme for the deepening and improvement of collaboration and the development of socialist economic integration of the CMEA countries' adopted in Bucharest in 1971. The objective of economic integration is to maximise the gains from economies of scale, specialisation and participation in the international division of labour. Economic integration takes such forms as trade, industrial cooperation, movement of labour, technical and scientific cooperation, energy integration, the financing of investment, the creation and operation of socialist common enterprises, and plan coordination.

A major aspect of CMEA integration is the coordination of the trade plans of the member states. This has facilitated a substantial increase in trade.[9] The magnitude of the increase in

[9] Some trade is discouraged by the plans. Foreign trade plans naturally tend to consist of the trade that took place in some base year, adjusted upwards by some percentage. Hence if a country wants to sell goods, e.g. the results of a good

Table 9.3. *Growth of CMEA trade (milliards of current US dollars)*

Year	Total exports by CMEA countries	of which, Exports by CMEA countries to their CMEA partners	Exports to other CMEA countries as percentage of total exports[a]
1948[b]	3.2	1.4	44
1950	4.2	2.5	60
1951	5.4	3.2	59
1952	6.1	3.8	62
1953	6.9	4.3	62
1954	7.5	4.7	63
1955	8.0	4.8	60
1956	8.6	4.8	56
1957	9.8	5.9	60
1958	10.3	6.1	59
1959	12.2	7.4	61
1960	13.2	8.1	61
1961	14.3	9.0	63
1962	16.0	10.2	64
1963	17.2	11.1	65
1964	18.7	12.0	64
1965	20.0	12.5	62
1966	21.4	12.6	59
1967	23.1	14.5	63
1968	25.2	16.0	63
1969	27.7	17.5	63
1970	30.9	19.3	62
1971	33.8	21.2	63
1972[c]	39.9	25.3	63
1973	48.1	28.8	58
1974	56.9	32.0	56

[a] Because of price differences between intra-CMEA trade and world market trade, for most of the period these figures exaggerate the share of intra trade in total trade.

[b] CMEA was founded in 1949.

[c] Cuba, which joined CMEA in 1972, and Vietnam which joined in 1978, are excluded throughout.

Source: Kaser (1967) p. 144 (for 1948–65 inc); UN *Yearbooks of international trade statistics* (for 1966–74 inc).

harvest, for one year only, and does not wish to enter into a commitment to supply increasing quantities of them indefinitely, it will strive either not to sell them within CMEA or to exclude them from the basis and sell them on a one-off 'outside the plan' framework. For example, in recent years Hungary has sold the USSR agricultural products, and bought from the USSR industrial raw materials, settlement being in US dollars. This trade took place outside the framework of the five year Hungarian–Soviet foreign trade plan so that it should not be included in the basis.

trade can be seen clearly from the data set out in table 9.3. In the 24 years 1950–74 the exports of CMEA rose fourteenfold (in current prices), and the proportion of their exports to each other in their total exports fluctuated between 56% and 65%. Of the members of CMEA, the USSR has by far the largest volume of foreign trade and the third largest (after Romania and Poland) proportion of trade with non-CMEA countries.

Integration is concerned not just with trade but primarily with the structure of production. The members of CMEA try to coordinate their medium- and long-term planning to cut out duplication of production and gain the maximum benefits from economies of scale and specialisation. This coordination takes various forms.

One is the specialisation of production of particular products in one country, with all CMEA providing a market, e.g. buses in Hungary. In this way the producer can hope to gain the maximum economies of scale and consumers the possibility of using their resources more efficiently elsewhere. This has not been very successful. As far as buses are concerned, some countries (such as Poland and the USSR) have started their own production of buses since they were unable to rely on adequate supplies of good quality buses from Hungary. The reason for this appears to be that good quality buses are a hard commodity and Hungary preferred selling them for hard currencies in Western countries. (The production of buses in Poland is based on a deal with a French firm.) The inability of Poland and the USSR to obtain from their partner the necessary quantity and quality of buses was an example of the costs of bilateralism and inconvertibility.

Another is joint production, where several members collaborate in the construction and operation of one plant or mining complex. Examples are the Kiyembayev asbestos project in the Urals, the Ust' Ilim cellulose plant in Eastern Siberia and a nickel–cobalt mine in Cuba. The countries supplying the investment resources receive in return some of the output when the project is functioning. In East–West trade such projects are known as compensation deals, and in West–South trade as foreign investment (by the West) and the export of raw materials (by the South).

Another is specialisation in components, where one country runs an assembly plant and others supply components. A good example is the Tol'yatti car plant on the Volga (constructed in collaboration with the Italian firm Fiat), which produces the Zhiguli car. Components for it are produced in Bulgaria, Hungary, Poland and Yugoslavia and these countries receive completed cars in return. In general, CMEA integration is noticeable for its lack of component specialisation. Specialisation appears to be largely confined to specialisation within the range of final products. This situation, which compares unfavourably with that in Western Europe, appears to be an example, on the international level, of the adverse effects on an economy of the rationing of producer goods (see chapter 3 above).

Another is the supply of labour by one member to another. By the mid 1970s there were probably about 150,000 workers from CMEA countries working in other CMEA countries. A large share of the foreign workers are employed in the GDR, where the labour shortage is most acute. There are also foreign workers in the USSR, working on big joint production projects such as the Orenburg gas pipeline and the Ust' Ilim cellulose plant. The provision of labour is one of the ways countries such as Bulgaria contribute their share to these projects. The movement of labour between CMEA countries (and from countries such as Yugoslavia to CMEA countries) is hindered by currency inconvertibility. Intra-CMEA movement of labour is distinguished from South–West labour movement by its small scale; its organised, inter-governmental character; and the fact that foreign workers do not seem to be employed mainly in unskilled poorly-paid jobs.

Another area of integration is the joint research and development programme. An example is the joint R & D programme carried out (under an agreement signed in 1972) in the field of numerically-controlled machine tools. Scientific and technical cooperation between CMEA members has a long history prior to the emergence of joint R & D programmes. In 1949–67 a major form which scientific and technical cooperation took was the free provision of scientific and technical documents, i.e. designs for new machines, products and processes. Some years ago a foreign observer noted (Kaser 1967 p. 153) that, 'The interchange of expertise has unquestionably been one of Comecon's most successful objectives.'

A well-known and very tangible example of integration is the Druzhba oil pipeline which carries Soviet oil to Hungary, Poland, GDR and Czechoslovakia. In 1974 it was agreed to build a gas pipeline from Orenburg in the USSR to Eastern Europe.

Hungary, GDR, Poland, Czechoslovakia and Bulgaria each agreed to build part of the pipeline, in exchange for gas deliveries from 1980 onwards. In addition, the Mir united power grid allows members to lend or borrow power during peak periods and also to export (or import) power. In fact, integration in the energy area (largely the import of Soviet oil and natural gas by the other CMEA members) has been one of the major achievements of CMEA. It provides the smaller CMEA countries with an essential raw material, and the USSR with a means of paying for imports from Eastern Europe and a potent political lever. Nevertheless, the East European countries are increasingly dependent on energy imports from non-CMEA sources. In determining export markets for oil and gas, the USSR has to balance its hard currency requirements against CMEA integration.

This latter fact illustrates the general proposition that the continued inconvertibility of the CMEA currencies is a serious problem for CMEA. It tends to ensure that the best quality goods go to the capitalist world and that it is only goods of lesser quality, or top quality goods in smaller quantities than are required, that go to other CMEA countries. This is simply an expression of one of the oldest propositions in economics, Gresham's Law. In effect, within CMEA two types of goods (and the corresponding forms of money) circulate, bad or soft goods (i.e. those that can be sold only in the CMEA countries) and good or hard goods (i.e. those that can be sold in the capitalist world for convertible currency). As Gresham's Law leads one to expect, bad drives out good, so that it is difficult to obtain from a CMEA partner as much as one wants of goods that are hard. CMEA trade expands, but so do the frustrations of its members, who are unable within CMEA to obtain in sufficient quantities the goods they most want, due to institutional limitations.

Since 1971, CMEA has had a bank, the International Investment Bank, which extends credits for investment, i.e. project loans. (The IIB is analogous to the EEC's European Investment Bank (EIB) or the World Bank (IBRD).) Also in the financial field, the members of CMEA are committed by the Comprehensive Programme to study, in 1976–79, the possibility and procedures for establishing single rates of exchange between their currencies. The intention is to make a decision on this matter in 1980.

In addition, within CMEA there are socialist common enterprises ('socialist multinationals'). An early example was Haldex, the Polish–Hungarian concern for processing coal dumps. Other examples are Interatomenergo, the huge organisation created in 1973 to develop and construct nuclear power stations for all CMEA, and the cotton mill 'Friendship', jointly owned by the GDR and Poland and founded in 1972. Most of the socialist common enterprises have a bilateral character. As a result of the growth and usefulness of socialist common enterprises, CMEA adopted in 1976 the 'Uniform principles for the creation and functioning of international economic organisations'. This document was intended to provide a legal framework for the socialist common enterprises. It put forward two main principles. First, that the activities of socialist common enterprises should be governed strictly by economic criteria. Secondly, that each socialist common enterprise should be governed by the economic and financial regulations of the country where its headquarters are.

An important aspect of CMEA integration is plan coordination. During the 1970s, the members of CMEA devoted increasing efforts to coordinating their medium- and long-term plans, and these plans formed the bases for their long-term trade agreements. An example of plan coordination, namely the five CMEA comprehensive programmes agreed in 1976, was given in chapter 2.

The CMEA integration programme has had two important results for planning in CMEA countries. First, it has transformed foreign trade from being merely a temporary way of obtaining useful goods, into a factor influencing the long-run structure of production. Now, when planning the development of particular industries and lines of production, the planners in each CMEA country have to consider whether it might not be more effective to import the good in question on a long-term basis and devote the investment resources elsewhere. Similarly, the development of the production of goods with substantial export potential has become an important factor in medium- and long-term planning. The relative importance of foreign trade considerations in medium- and long-term planning in the CMEA countries depends on the ratio of foreign trade to national income and the balance of payments situation. For example, for Hungary, which has both a high ratio of foreign trade to national income and which suffered an adverse movement of the terms of trade in 1973–75, the increased importance of foreign trade has meant that export potential now plays a major role in perspective planning. This is a sharp contrast with the practice of the period when socialist planning was introduced into Hungary. Secondly, integration has led to great efforts to determine, and apply, reliable methods for determining the efficiency of foreign trade. There is a considerable literature on the optimisation of foreign trade (Shagalov 1973, 'Optimization' 1965). There is also, however, a very substantial gulf between the scientific literature and the real problems of, and methods used in, foreign trade planning. In the USSR, a temporary official method for calculating foreign trade efficiency was issued in 1968. The integration programme led to its being supplemented in 1973 by another temporary method, that for determining the efficiency of specialisation and cooperation within CMEA. Work on developing these methods is proceeding.

According to Western calculations (Brada 1973a, 1973b) of the efficiency of CMEA trade with Western countries, it is characterised by substantial inefficiencies. These largely reflect the poor marketing of exports. Brada's calculations led to two interesting conclusions. First, bilateralism did not seem to be an important source of inefficiency. Secondly, the introduction of the NEM in Hungary appeared to lead to a *deterioration* in the efficiency of Hungary's trade with the West.

On the whole, the economic integration model can only be considered, at best, a partial success. It has been hindered by institutional problems (bilateralism and inconvertibility), political problems (the desire of the CMEA members to preserve their national individuality) and the attractiveness of trade with the West.

CONCLUSION

Given suitable institutions, the capitalist international division of labour normally leads to an enormous expansion of trade and rapid economic growth. It also leads to enormous income inequalities and substantial inefficiency (e.g. the waste of resources during periodic recessions). The state socialist countries have attempted to create a socialist form of cooperation which would capture the advantages, while avoiding the problems, of the capitalist international division of labour.

Up till now, however, the state socialist countries have been unable to create a rival, socialist, international division of labour which is clearly more equitable and efficient than the capitalist one. The socialism in one country model worked for the USSR before 1945 and has worked for China since 1960, but it is not a model for a group of countries. The socialist imperialism model came into existence in unique circumstances which have largely passed away. The international planning model foundered on the conflict between static comparative costs and the industrialisation of formerly backward countries, national rivalries and the imperfect socialisation of the productive forces. The socialist multilateralism model was not implemented due to the unwillingness of the USSR to abandon the administrative economy. The economic integration model, currently being implemented by CMEA, suffers from a number of limitations. It is a grouping round a hegemonic power which is unable to include a country – China – which is state socialist but hostile to the USSR. Hence, it lacks appeal to countries jealous of their national independence. Its inability to introduce multilateralism and convertibility restricts trade and technical progress. In trade with the West the marketing skills of the CMEA countries are poor.

The problem of establishing an international economic order which combines equity, efficiency and growth remains to be resolved.

SUGGESTIONS FOR FURTHER READING

I. Steedman, *Trade among growing economies* (Cambridge 1979).
A. G. Frank, *Capitalism and underdevelopment in Latin America* (2nd edn New York & London 1969).
S. Amin, *Accumulation on a world scale* (New York & London 1974).
J. Robinson, *The new mercantilism* (Cambridge 1966).
S. Gomulka & J. Sylestrowicz, 'Import led growth; theory and estimation', *On the measurement of factor productivities: theoretical problems and empirical results* F. L. Altmann, O. Kyn & H. J. Wagener (eds.) (Gottingen–Zurich 1976).
P. Marer, 'Soviet economic policy in Eastern Europe', *Reorientation and commercial relations of the economies of Eastern Europe* (JEC US Congress, Washington DC 1974).
M. Kaser, *Comecon* (2nd ed. Oxford 1967).
M. Lavigne, *Le comecon* (Paris 1973).
S. Ausch, *Theory and practice of CMEA cooperation* (Budapest 1972).
M. Senin, *Socialist integration* (Moscow 1973).
Comecon: Progress and prospects (Brussels 1977).

F. Levcik, 'Migration and employment of foreign workers in the CMEA countries and their problems', *East European economies post-Helsinki* (*JEC US Congress, Washington DC* 1977).

V. I. Kuznetsov, *Economic integration: two approaches* (Moscow 1976).

F. Holzman, *Foreign trade under central planning* (Cambridge, Mass. 1974).

C. T. Saunders (ed.), *East–West cooperation in business: Inter-firm studies* (Vienna & New York 1977).

J. Brada, 'The allocative efficiency of centrally planned foreign trade: A programming approach to the Czech case', *European Economic Review* no. 4 (1973).

J. Brada, 'The microallocative impact of the Hungarian economic reform of 1968: some evidence from the export sector', *Economics of Planning* nos. 1–2 (1973).

C. Howe, *China's economy* (London 1978) chapter 5.

10

RESULTS OF SOCIALIST PLANNING

The data on the East European societies show several disproportions and contradictions in economic, social and cultural growth. Basic among them is the contradiction between the growing economic and cultural sophistication of the population and the authoritarian structure of power relations. Even the private farmers in Poland are largely dependent on the state, not to speak of the rest of the population, which is employed in state-owned or state-controlled enterprises, offices and institutions.

A. Matejko (1974 p. xvii)

In China the decisive instrument embodying the new power was the People's Liberation Army, a military structure that was close to the masses but which was not under their control. In fact the political structures of the People's Republic shared one crucial feature with those of the Soviet Union after the rise of Stalin – all decisions, and indeed all real political discussion, were reserved for a tiny group of top Party leaders. Ordinary Party members, peasants and workers, were left with the task of implementing policies which they had not participated in formulating.

L. Maitan (1976 p. 9)

The consequences of state ownership and management of the economy can conveniently be considered under two heads, theoretical and empirical.

THEORETICAL CONSIDERATIONS

The theoretical issue raised by the historical experience of socialist planning is whether or not the state socialist countries have established a new, more advanced, mode of production. In order to examine this question, seven criteria will be used. They all derive from the Marxist critique of capitalism and are, efficiency, the labour process, the division of labour, democracy and the state, distribution, the social ownership of the means of production and economic planning.

Table 10.1. *Relative static efficiency in 1960 (USA = 100)*

	National income per employed worker		National income per unit of factor (labour and reproducible capital) inputs	
	Based on national price weights (1)	Based on US price weights (2)	Based on national price weights (3)	Based on US price weights (4)
United States	100	100	100	100
Northwest Europe	44	56	50	63
France	43	55	49	62
Germany	43	55	52	63
UK	44	56	50	63
Italy	22	37	28	45
USSR	22	38	28	45

Source: Bergson (1968) p. 22.

Efficiency

According to a Western interpretation, experience has shown that capitalism is more efficient than socialism. According to a Soviet interpretation, it has shown that socialism is superior to capitalism. Consider each view in turn.

A Western interpretation. The chief Western researcher in this area is Bergson. He has asserted two propositions. The first, which will be termed 'the weak Bergson inference', is that there is no evidence for the Marxist view that socialism is more efficient than capitalism (Bergson 1968). The second, which will be termed 'the strong Bergson inference', is that 'Socialism...is markedly less efficient than capitalism' (Eckstein 1971 p. 239). These conclusions are drawn from consideration of data of the type set out in tables 10.1 and 10.2.

Inspection of tables 10.1 and 10.2 suggests (to Bergson) that there is nothing special about the Soviet experience, i.e. the weak Bergson inference. After all, the dynamic efficiency of the Soviet economy (using column 2 of table 10.2), while better than that of the UK and USA, is worse than that of Italy, Germany and France. Similarly, the static efficiency of the Soviet economy (table

Table 10.2. *Relative dynamic efficiency (1950–62)*

	Average annual rate of growth of national income per employed worker (%) (1)	Average annual rate of growth of national income per unit of factor (labour and reproducible capital) inputs (%) (2)
United States	2.4	2.0
Northwest Europe	4.1	3.4
France	4.8	4.1
Germany	5.6	4.6
UK	1.9	1.4
Italy	5.3	4.7
USSR	4.7	2.8

Source: Bergson (1968) p. 53.

10.1 column 3) is worse than that of the United States, France, Germany and the UK and on a par with Italy.[1] This latter fact suggests that (Eckstein 1971 p. 239), 'socialism, as exemplified by the USSR, is markedly less efficient than capitalism, as exemplified by the USA, though perhaps about as efficient as capitalism as exemplifed by Italy'.

Bergson's inferences can be expressed as follows. Consider table 10.1 column 3. The observation is that

$$\frac{\Sigma P_{USA}\, X_{USA}}{(L,\, K)_{USA}} > \frac{\Sigma P_{USSR}\, X_{USSR}}{(L,\, K)_{USSR}}$$

Assume that each side of the inequality is a point on a production function that has the following properties:
(a) constant or decreasing returns to scale
(b) identical technology
(c) homogeneous labour and capital
(d) the only difference between the economies is 'the system'.
These assumptions enable us to write

$$Y_{USA} = f(K,\, L,\, t,\, e)_{USA}$$

[1] By 'static efficiency' Bergson understands output per unit of inputs at a given time. By 'dynamic efficiency' he understands the rate of change of output per unit of inputs.

(where Y is output, K is capital, L is labour, t is technology and e is the system efficiency)
and

$$Y_{USSR} = f(K, L, t, e)_{USSR}$$

The observation is that

$$\frac{Y_{USA}}{(L, K)_{USA}} > \frac{Y_{USSR}}{(L, K)_{USSR}}$$

$$\therefore e_{USA} > e_{USSR} \qquad (1)$$

The last step follows from the assumption that L, K and t are the same in both functions and increasing returns insignificant. Hence only differences in e can cause differences in $Y/(L, K)$.

$$\therefore e_{cap} > e_{soc} \qquad (2)$$

(where e_{cap} is the efficiency of capitalism and e_{soc} is the efficiency of socialism.) (2) follows directly from (1) combined with assumption (d).

Hence, it follows that Bergson's conclusions are theory impregnated and are not necessarily valid if one or more of the four assumptions are false. For example, if assumption (b) were false and the USA used more advanced technology than the USSR, as much recent empiricial work suggests, then it might be that the Soviet system was much more efficient than the USA one but that this was more than offset by the technology gap. The effect of dropping implausible assumption (b) is considered below in the section 'Dynamic efficiency reconsidered'. Similarly, as Berliner (1964) and Hanson (1971) have pointed out, if assumption (d) were false it might be that the observed differences in productivity levels simply reflected the well-known cultural and historical differences between the USA and the USSR, differences that would persist even if the USA were socialist and the USSR capitalist.

Because of the obvious and very important non-system differences between the USA and the USSR, it would clearly be desirable to make comparisons between two countries that really are alike in all respects except 'the system'. Fortunately, there are two countries that come close to this requirement, i.e. for which assumption (d) is actually close to being valid, the German Federal Republic and the German Democratic Republic. Several authors (Schnitzer 1972, Obst 1973, Gregory & Leptin 1977) have attempted to measure their relative efficiency.

The work of these authors shows that in the post-war period the level of productivity in the Federal Republic has consistently been above that of the Democratic Republic. It also shows that comparisons of the growth rates of productivity of the two countries are sensitive to the data used and the years chosen. The main reasons for the data problems are that the two systems have different national accounting systems (material product system (MPS) and system of national accounts (SNA)) and use different methods for calculating industrial production. In Bergsonian terminology one can say that, (a) the static efficiency of the Federal Republic throughout the post-war period has been higher, and (b) comparisons of dynamic efficiency are sensitive to the data used and the years compared. In 1950–58 the rate of growth of aggregate labour productivity, according to Western calculations (Gregory & Leptin 1977 p. 529), was ⅓ greater in the Democratic Republic than in the Federal Republic. On the other hand, also using Western data (Gregory & Leptin 1977 table 1), in the period 1960–73 the rates of growth of industrial labour productivity, overall labour productivity and total factor productivity were virtually equal in the two countries. (The biggest difference between the data for the two countries for this period is the greater variability of the series for the Federal Republic resulting from the greater instability of a capitalist economy.) Extending the comparison forward to include the recession of 1974–75 would probably improve the relative position of the Democratic Republic. It seems likely that a comparison for the whole period 1950–78 (not all the data for which is yet to hand) would show higher rates for the Democratic Republic than for the Federal Republic. Hence, as far as Bergsonian dynamic efficiency is concerned, the GDR is a counterexample both to the strong Bergson inference (certainly) and to the weak Bergson inference (probably). On the other hand, as far as Bergsonian static efficiency is concerned, the GDR is an example for both inferences.

What explains finding (a)? Is it a result of the system and hence corroboration of the strong Bergson inference, or is it a result of exogenous factors (differential war-time destruction and differing policies by the occupying countries)? Gregory & Leptin incline to the first answer, and the author to the second. The gap appears to have arisen in the years 1944–50 and can hardly be considered independently of the military and political events of those years (e.g. the economic relations between the USSR and the Soviet Zone, as discussed in the previous chapter).

Table 10.3. *Capitalist inefficiency. (1) Total economic surplus and its major components (USA, selected years, milliards of dollars)*

	1948	1953	1958	1963
Total property income	51.4	59.3	75.9	104.6
Waste in distribution	14.5	20.1	24.2	29.7
Corporate advertising other than by trade corporations	2.3	3.8	5.6	7.7
Surplus employee compensation				
Finance, insurance and real estate	5.3	8.0	11.9	16.8
Legal services	0.2	0.4	0.5	0.9
Surplus absorbed by government	51.0	102.0	126.6	168.0
Total surplus (i.e. total of above)	124.7	193.6	244.8	327.7
Total surplus as % of GNP	48.1	53.0	55.1	56.1

Source: Baran & Sweezy (1968) p. 374.

In order to see the importance of assumption (d), let us take two countries, Czechoslovakia and India, not in table 10.1, and apply assumption (d) to them. Because productivity levels in Czechoslovakia are much higher than in India, by applying the Bergson method to them we 'observe' that 'capitalism, as exemplified by India, is markedly less efficient than socialism, as exemplified by Czechoslovakia', i.e. we 'observe' a counter-example to the static version of both Bergson inferences.

It is important to note that Bergson's work, although purporting to test the Marxist hypothesis of the superior efficiency of socialism, in fact only tests the neoclassical hypothesis about the superior efficiency of capitalism and fails completely to test the Marxist hypothesis. The reason for this is that the Marxist hypothesis is not about the relationship between utilised inputs and the market value of output (which are what Bergson measures and what the neoclassical hypothesis is about). It is about the relationship between available inputs and the social utility of output. Marxists do not doubt the technical efficiency of capitalist industry. They simply consider that capitalism is an inefficient economic system which fails to utilise many of the available resources (unemployment, idle capacity) and produces many commodities which are either bads (e.g. hard drugs, weapons) or wasteful (e.g. consumption of parasitic groups). If one sets out to measure what Marxists regard as the inefficiencies of capitalism, it is easy to see that they are a very large proportion of the national income. Two American Marxists, in their well-known study of the US economy (Baran & Sweezy

Table 10.4. *Capitalist inefficiency* (2)

	Capacity utilization (1959 = 100)	Full employment unemployment rate[a]
1953	98	5.7
1954	87	7.6
1955	92	4.9
1956	89	4.8
1957	85	6.9
1958	76	8.6
1959	81	7.8
1960	81	8.5
1961	80	10.0
1962	83	10.3
1963	83	10.4

[a] The 'full employment unemployment rate' is the actual unemployment rate, adjusted for the fact that the labour force when there is unemployment, is less than the labour force that would be available at full employment, as marginal workers leave the labour force.

Source: Baran & Sweezy (1968) p. 242.

1968), give numerous examples of waste in the USA. They estimate, for example (Baran & Sweezy 1968 p. 141) that car model changes in the late 1950s were costing the country about 2.5% of its GNP each year. According to their calculations, in each of the years 1951–63, more than half of the US GNP was 'surplus', most of which (e.g. income of parasitic groups; waste in distribution; advertising; financial, insurance, real estate and legal services; military expenditure) constituted waste. In addition the USA is always characterised by substantial unutilised labour and capacity. Some data is set out in tables 10.3 and 10.4.

Conclusion. On the basis of comparing efficiency levels in a number of countries, Bergson came to two conclusions:

(1) (the weak Bergson inference). There is no evidence for the superior efficiency of socialism.

(2) (the strong Bergson inference). Socialism is less efficient than capitalism.

The conclusions are only valid inferences from the data if four assumptions are simultaneously valid. The most implausible of the Bergson assumptions is (b). The effects of dropping it are considered below. The dynamic efficiency of the German

Table 10.5. *Average growth rates in the EEC and CMEA (in % p.a.)*

	National income		Industrial production	
Years	CMEA	EEC	CMEA	EEC
1961–65	6.1	4.7	8.3	5.3
1966–70	7.3	4.5	8.4	4.8
1971–74	6.6	3.6	8.1	3.4
1975	6.4	−2.5	8.5	−7.6

Source: Kudrov (1976) p. 21.

Democratic Republic is certainly a counterexample to the dynamic version of the strong Bergson inference, and possibly also to the dynamic version of the weak Bergson inference. If assumption (d) is applied to countries excluded from the Bergson sample (e.g. Czechoslovakia and India) there is a counterexample which refutes the static version of both conclusions. The Bergson analysis does not in fact test the Marxist hypothesis.

A Soviet interpretation. The leading Soviet specialist on the relative efficiency of the two systems is V. M. Kudrov (1972, 1973, 1976). He has argued that, as far as growth is concerned, the socialist countries have definitely established their superiority. 'In the course of economic competition, socialism as a world system has proved its decisive superiority over capitalism with respect to the rate of growth' (Kudrov 1972 p. 7). This proposition will be termed 'Kudrov's first inference'. It is asserted on the basis of data of the type set out in tables 10.5 and 10.6.

As far as efficiency is concerned, Kudrov argues that with respect to a number of indices (the proportion of the population employed, the early peaceful utilisation of atomic energy, the early development of supersonic passenger airliners), the USSR is ahead of the USA. Nevertheless, he recognises that in general the USA is still more efficient than the USSR. This proposition will be termed 'Kudrov's second inference'. Kudrov argues that this gap is being narrowed and that in due course the USSR will establish the superiority of socialism in the field of efficiency as it already has done in the field of economic growth. In the last twenty-five years industrial labour productivity, the decisive

Table 10.6. *A dynamic comparison of the Soviet and US economies (USSR as % of USA)*

	1950	1957	1965	1975
National income	31	50	59	> 66
Industrial output	30	47	62	> 80
Agricultural output	55	70	*c.* 75	85
Labour productivity				
in industry	30–40	40–50	40–50	> 55
in agriculture	20	20–25	20–25	20–25
Output in physical units				
oil	14	28	63	120
steel	30	49	75	128
mineral fertilisers	31	42	69	125
cement	26	58	111	188

Source: Kudrov (1976) p. 22.

synthetic index of efficiency, has already risen sharply in the USSR relative to the USA (see table 10.6), and in due course will exceed it, thereby definitely establishing the superiority of socialism and the reactionary nature of capitalism.

From Kudrov's analysis, it seems likely that he would accept Bergson's 'paradoxical' conclusion that 'efficiency depends predominantly on the stage of development, and so is in reality little affected by the social system' (Eckstein 1971 p. 238), subject to two crucial provisos. First, capitalism generates significant types of waste (e.g. unemployment). Secondly, the 'stage of development' itself is not independent of the social system.

Kudrov's inferences, like Bergson's, rely on assumption (d) of the list on page 248. If (d) were not valid, it might be that the data in tables 10.5 and 10.6 simply show that the possibilities open to backward countries are greater than those open to advanced ones ('the advantages of a late start'). Similarly, if (d) were not valid, it might be that Kudrov's first inference simply reflects the non-system differences between the countries selected. After all, if table 10.6 'proves' the 'decisive superiority of socialism over capitalism', a comparison of the USSR and Japan would 'prove' the 'decisive superiority of capitalism over socialism'. What is required for a serious consideration of this question is adequate data and plausible assumptions. The data should be from one country (such as Germany) in which both systems are functioning, or from all the countries of both systems. The assumptions

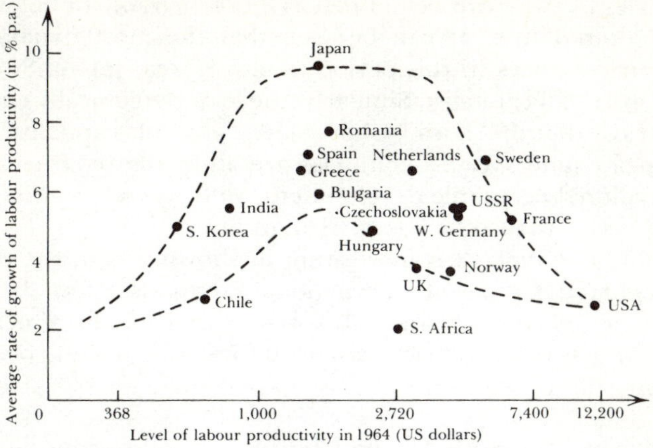

Figure 10.1 International dynamic efficiency 1958–68.
Source: Gomulka (1971) p. 73.

should form the basis of a theory aimed at explaining differences in growth rates between countries.

Dynamic efficiency reconsidered. Drawing inferences from statistical data about the dynamic efficiency of the systems is inevitably theory impregnated. Bergson's conclusions are only valid inferences (about the neoclassical hypothesis) if all four of his assumptions are true. Kudrov's first inference is only true if the fourth of the Bergson assumptions is true. It is interesting to reconsider this question in the light of the Gomulka growth model and of the data for a large number of countries. This is done in figure 10.1.

Figure 10.1 shows the rate of growth of labour productivity plotted against a proxy for the level of development of the economy (the independent factor determining the rate of growth according to the Gomulka growth theory). The international mainstream falls within the upper and lower dotted lines. The upper dotted line shows the approximate upper rate of growth of labour productivity statistically recorded for various given levels of labour productivity. The lower dotted line shows the approximate minimum rate of growth of labour productivity statistically recorded for various levels of labour productivity. The dynamically efficient countries can be defined as those near, on, or outside, the upper dotted line. The dynamically inefficient countries likewise can be defined as those near, on, or below, the lower dotted line. It can be seen that the most dynamically efficient countries in this period (South Korea, Japan, Sweden, France) are all capitalist. Similarly, the least dynamically efficient countries (South Africa, Chile, UK) are all capitalist. The European state socialist countries are all in the mainstream of international economic development, with some (e.g. Romania) doing better than others (e.g. Hungary).

Gomulka's analysis is interesting in showing both the theory impregnated nature of international comparisons of dynamic economic efficiency,[2] and also that the capitalism/socialism dichotomy is not a sufficient criterion for distinguishing between efficiency and inefficiency.

Conclusion. (1) Both US and Soviet specialists consider that experience so far has demonstrated the superior quality of their system.

(2) Both US and Soviet specialists consider that, in general, the USA is the more efficient economy.

(3) Both systems have characteristic types of waste. The USA fails to utilise a significant proportion of the available resources (hence, e.g. unemployment, unutilised capacity) and devotes substantial resources to the production and distribution of bads (e.g. guns and hard drugs) and goods destined for parasitic groups. The USSR wastes substantial amounts of labour and material resources within the production process and also produces both bads (e.g. vodka) and goods destined for parasitic groups (e.g. censorship officials).

(4) Comparisons of efficiency are inevitably theory impregnated. Bergson's inferences depend on four assumptions, all of which are of dubious validity. Kudrov's depend on the fourth of them. If the Gomulka theory is utilised, it can be seen that the socialism/capitalism dichotomy is not a sufficient criterion for distinguishing between dynamically efficient and inefficient economies. For example, in 1958–68 all the European state socialist countries fall in the international mainstream, whereas the capitalist countries show a very wide dispersion, some being exceptionally efficient (e.g. Sweden) and others being exceptionally inefficient (e.g. South Africa).

[2] Similarly, the application of Kaldor's growth theory raises the UK's performance in the growth league to β?+ (Kaldor 1966 p. 15).

(5) Neither the neoclassical hypothesis nor the Marxist hypothesis are corroborated by the evidence. Whether or not both, either, or neither, are considered to be definitely refuted depends on how precisely the hypotheses are formulated (e.g. do the hypotheses refer to some measure of central tendency or can they be refuted by a single observation?), which theory of economic growth one utilises, which time period one considers, what proportion of the output of each system one judges to be waste, and on what the level of waste of resources outside and inside production is judged to be.

(6) The two systems are equally good at producing tendentious arguments.

The labour process

As far as the labour process is concerned, the only notable differences between the CMEA countries and the advanced capitalist countries are twofold. First, that in the former the organisation of work typically copies, with a lag, that in the latter. Secondly, the pace of work is typically slower in the former than in the latter. In general, it seems reasonable to say that the CMEA countries have made no progress whatsoever towards organising the labour process so as to end the division between the scientist and the process worker. This is scarcely surprising, both in view of the Bolshevik attitude to Taylorism (see chapter 6 above) and in view of Marx's own thesis that a society in which the labour process had been fundamentally transformed would be one in which technical progress had eliminated dreary, repetitive, work. Such a state of affairs has not yet been reached in even the most advanced countries. It was argued in chapter 6 that, pace Bettelheim, the situation is not fundamentally dissimilar in China.

As far as labour conditions are concerned, it was pointed out in chapter 6 that there are a large number of important differences between the state socialist and capitalist countries. The state socialist countries normally provide full employment, security of employment, and social security, sometimes make significant use of coerced labour, lack independent trade unions and probably have a poor record in industrial safety.

The division of labour

As far as the technical division of labour is concerned, the Soviet model is to follow the capitalist countries in increasing the division of labour, in subdividing ever more finely the labour process between an ever increasing variety of specialists. As far as the division of society into rulers and ruled is concerned, no progress has been made here either. During the revolutionary period itself, and during subsequent occasional dramatic upheavals, e.g. the mass promotion of the pushed up ones in the USSR in the 1930s,[3] numerous individuals have changed their position in society. Nevertheless, this has nowhere prevented the crystallisation of a privileged ruling stratum and the division of society into rulers and ruled.

Is this a result of the malevolence of the party leadership, the political institutions of state socialism, the technical backwardness of the countries concerned, or the inevitable result of the development of modern technology? This question was long ago considered by Gramsci, who posed the question, 'Does one start from the premise of a perpetual division of the human race [into rulers and ruled], or does one believe that this is only a historical fact answering to certain conditions?' He argued (Gramsci 1957 pp. 143–4) that 'this division is a product of the [technical] division of labour, that it is a technical fact'. This view, that even under socialism there is a technical need for the division of society into rulers and ruled, is orthodox in all the CMEA countries. Hence, the orthodox view is that the Marxist aspiration to overcome this must be postponed to the higher stage of communism.

In Yugoslavia, on the other hand, the Soviet–Yugoslav split led, from 1950 onwards, to the development of a new variant of state socialism. It aims to substitute a self-managed model of economic life, for the statist model of the Soviet type. It stresses the need to reduce the role of the state in economic life and expand that of self-managed collectives, such as enterprises. According to Yugoslav theory, state ownership of the means of production is not yet social ownership but only a stage towards it. This is

[3] The 'pushed up ones' (*vydvizhentsy*) were people from working class or peasant backgrounds who, despite their lack of conventional academic qualifications, received an accelerated higher education in c. 1928–34 and were 'pushed up' into responsible positions. They took over the jobs of the liquidated Old Bolsheviks in 1937–38 and formed the social basis of the Stalinist regime. A typical pushed up one was Khrushchev.

because control is not directly in the hands of society. According to the Ljubljana programme (*Programme* 1958 p. 112):

with the development of the socialist democratic system there is a reduction in the role of the state government in the direct management of the economy, in the sphere of cultural and educational activities, health, social policy, etc. Management functions in these fields pass to a growing extent to the various self-management organs, either independent or linked in an appropriate organising mechanism.

The economic institutions of Yugoslavia have evolved substantially from 1950 to the present day. Yugoslavia has, furthermore, experienced serious problems resulting from Soviet hostility (in 1948–55), her own national divisions, and her backwardness. As far as Yugoslavia herself is concerned, perhaps the most relevant question about self-management concerns its success, or lack of it, in the role of a legitimising ideology for a Communist Party which both holds a monopoly of power and has been attacked by the Soviet Union (and others) for 'betraying socialism' and 'restoring capitalism'. We are concerned here, however, less with Yugoslavia herself than with the 'Yugoslav model'. From this standpoint the crucial question is, does the Yugoslav model exhibit new relations of production that are clearly superior to those of capitalism?

Two conclusions can be drawn about the Yugoslav model. First, that self-management has important advantages relative both to capitalism and to statist socialism. It reduces inequality within work units, and gives their members greater control over their working lives. This, of course, is not a Yugoslav discovery, but is the reason for the widespread development of producer cooperatives throughout the world, a well-known example being the Israeli kibbutz. A group of sociologists who compared industrial plants in five countries, kibbutz plants in Israel, self-managed factories in Yugoslavia, and capitalist plants in Austria, Italy and the United States, came to the conclusion that (Tannenbaum 1974 pp. 225–6),

Radically different organisational forms are possible and viable. An organisation in which policy is decided by top personnel is quite workable, and so is one in which policy is decided by the membership as a whole. Factories in which workers receive remuneration equal to that of managers can function effectively, just as can factories with substantial differences in reward between those at the top and those at the bottom. But the success of a sytem, however success may be defined, depends on 'conditions', and ultimately on the definition of success itself; and the preference that we as observers may feel for one system or another will depend on our own values. For those of us who place great value on equality, the kibbutz system, and perhaps the Yugoslav, is the model of success. The American model looks better to those who value individual achievement.

Secondly, as Brus (1975 p. 95) has noted, self-management, at any rate in the form adopted by Yugoslavia in the 1960s, can easily go beyond the 'limits defined by the economic and social rationality of central planning, by the growing need in the modern world for the internalisation of external costs and benefits, by the requirements of maintaining the supremacy of the point of view of the "system" as a whole over that of "sub-systems" '. If one considers the Yugoslav experience from the standpoint of such criteria as inflation, unemployment, the distribution of income, regional policy and the allocation of investment, it is difficult to disagree with Brus. This has been recognised not only by outside observers but also by the Yugoslav authorities. Accordingly, in Yugoslavia in the 1970s there were further institutional changes which 'shifted back to some of the more traditional features of socialism: income distribution, the role of planning, solidarity of the working class, and the leading role of the party' (Milenkovitch 1977 p. 57).

When, from 1957 onwards, the Chinese increasingly diverged from the Soviet model of development, one of the areas in which they diverged was the alleged technical need for the division of society into rulers and ruled. The Maoist stress on the need, here and now and not in the distant future, to develop new, socialist, relations of production, led to three major innovations. They were, the obligation of all managerial personnel to perform manual labour, the elected revolutionary committee which was responsible for executive management in Chinese factories, and the possibility of criticising officials.

In 1958 participation by managers in physical labour became compulsory throughout China. All enterprise managers were required to spend at least one or two days in physical labour each week. Managers and experts above the enterprise level were required to spend at least one month each year in manual labour in factories or farms, unless exempted by age or health. Furthermore, according to Richman (1969 pp. 804–5), it is common in Chinese industrial plants for the best paid workers to earn more than any of the managerial staff. Participation by managers in manual labour can be useful in reducing social differentiation.

It has undoubtedly served to break down the traditional negative attitude towards labour on the part of intellectuals, managers and experts. It probably has provided for a better insight into grass-roots operating conditions and problems, including the needs, behaviour, attitudes, and problems of workers. It probably has often contributed to greater organizational solidarity and identification, more effective communication, and a reduction in the information gap at different levels of the enterprise (Richman 1969 p. 233).

It can also, however, have negative aspects. It is often used as a punishment. This reveals that the traditional attitude to manual labour continues. Furthermore, some top people have tried to recreate their usual conditions of comfort in the places to which they are transferred, reducing the amount of work they do to a token contribution, and using their influence to obtain state assistance for 'their' commune. In addition, the peasants are often sceptical about the usefulness of the work done by those who are not experienced in agricultural work. Where the time of scarce qualified people is more productive employed in their specialisms than in physical labour, the practice is wasteful.[4] The participation by cadres in manual labour has both pros and cons, but it has not prevented the crystallisation of a privileged leading stratum (Maitan 1976 pp. 245–6).

As a result of the Cultural Revolution, the management system in Chinese factories was changed. The appointed director was replaced by an elected revolutionary committee with a chairman and vice-chairman. The revolutionary committee, which normally consisted of production workers, cadres and military personnel, was responsible for the management of the enterprise. To the extent that this was an application of self-management, the first of the conclusions drawn above about the Yugoslav model apply. Richman (1969 p. 256), however, reports that for the 'election' for managerial staff there was generally only one candidate. This means that what actually happened was not self-management but was simply a device to legitimise appointments from above. In February 1978, in his speech to the Fifth National People's Congress, Chairman Hua announced the replacement of the revolutionary committees by the old system of appointed directors.

[4] 'According to a Chinese regulation, persons outside certain large urban centres are – heavens knows why – not allowed to maintain any correspondence with persons in foreign countries. One Chinese chemist was forced to interrupt a professional correspondence with a Soviet colleague while he was sent out of Peking for a year' (Klochko 1964 p. 79).

The possibility of, and indeed official encouragement for, the criticism of cadres at all levels has been an important feature of Chinese life during campaigns such as the Hundred Flowers (1957) and the Cultural Revolution (1966–68). The outcome of these campaigns, however, was not the massive replacement of the authoritarian and arrogant cadres and the development of intellectual freedom, but the suppression of the most radical critics and the re-emergence in positions of authority of most of the old cadres. It is scarcely surprising that the outcome of Maoism was popular cynicism about official campaigns and widespread depoliticisation (Maitan 1976 pp. 307–8). As one team leader said in the early stages of the Socialist Education Movement when explaining the poor response to an invitation to criticise cadres (Chen 1969 p. 218), 'If we make criticisms we are afraid that we will be sentenced to labour reform like those who made criticisms in 1958.'

The view that new, socialist, relations of production are being created in China (or were being created prior to the 11th Congress) simply repeats some of the errors of War Communism. Take, for example, the Chinese policy of sending educated young people into the countryside to work on the land. In the Chinese press one can read that this is a 'brilliant policy for building the new socialist countryside, an important measure for narrowing and eliminating the differences between mental and manual labour'. In other words, the official interpretation of this policy is that it is a step towards the Marxist goal of overcoming the division of labour and is a move towards socialism or communism. In fact, however, it is simply the compulsory allocation of the labour (and persons) of educated youngsters, resulting from the inability of the authorities to generate enough urban jobs to employ the growing labour force and the fact that discontented youngsters are less of a political threat in the countryside than as urban unemployed. This may well be a necessary policy under difficult circumstances, but one should be careful not to confuse ideology with reality.

Democracy and the state

In chapter 1 it was suggested that there are theoretical and historical reasons for distinguishing between two types of democracy, liberal democracy and totalitarian democracy. Both make the value judgement that social choices ought to be determined by the wishes of all members of society, and in this sense both are 'democratic'. Liberal democracy assumes, however, that individual choices are both unconcerned with, and independent of, the choices of other individuals. Totalitarian democracy, on the other hand, assumes that the decision-making process normally corresponds to the 'Prisoners' Dilemma' situation. How do the two groups of countries, to which these two theoretical categories are intended to relate, compare, from a political point of view?

The Marxist–Leninist view is that the state socialist countries are far more democratic than capitalist ones. In capitalist countries, although the people appear to choose the rulers, in fact the rulers are chosen by, and represent the interests of, a small group of monopoly capitalists. Although formal freedom exists, the workers are unable to take advantage of it because they lack the possibility of turning their formal freedom into real freedom. Everyone is free to own newspapers, but in fact they are owned by, and used to disseminate the views of, a tiny group of millionaires. The votes cast at elections simply reflect the views and interests of the capitalists, which are pumped into the population by the media and the whole indoctrination system (schools, churches, advertising, television etc.). In state socialist countries, on the other hand, power is exercised by leaders who are responsible to the population through the state electoral system and inner party democracy. In addition, the workers have not formal freedom but real freedom, since meeting places and means of communication are at the disposal of workers' organisations and the state provides employment, social security and free educational and medical services for all.

Experience has shown that this thesis does contain important elements of the truth. In capitalist countries the means of communication are often owned by tiny cliques, the state socialist countries do generally provide full employment, social security and free or cheap educational and medical services. But, it also excludes important elements of the truth. It ignores the possibilities open to the labour movement for using liberal democracy to advance both working-class interests and the interests of individual members of the working class. In particular, experience has shown that the political freedoms offered by liberal democracy (the right to free movement of people and ideas, absence of censorship, independent social organisations, an independent judiciary and the right to strike) are of great benefit to all sections of society. In chapter 6, the negative effects of the absence of independent worker organisations in the state socialist countries, on industrial accidents and diseases, on labour morale and on the use of coerced labour, were briefly surveyed.

It is because of this important lesson of experience, that in 1964, Togliatti, the leader of the Italian Communist Party, a party with mass working-class support in an advanced capitalist country, clearly stated in his so-called Testament that, in assessing the political system in the state socialist countries, 'The problem attracting most attention, both in the USSR and in the other socialist countries is, however, the problem of overcoming the regime of restriction and suppression of democratic and personal freedoms.' Similarly, in China at the end of 1974 three young revolutionaries posted on the walls of a busy street in Canton what came to be known as the Li Yi-che manifesto. This urged that the human rights and civic freedoms, which in the past, though guaranteed by the 1954 constitution, were constantly violated (arbitrary arrests, torture, executions for political crimes), should be reaffirmed and effectively enforced. Most important of all, it argued, is the freedom of opinion. Without free criticism from the people there can be no true political life, no participation of the masses, no socialist democracy. It is not an accident that in the country where for sixty years the doctrine of the irrelevance of the political freedoms offered by liberal democracy has been orthodox, a liberal movement has re-emerged. Up till now, no state socialist country has provided political freedom, although its absence is much less extreme now than in 1952. The progress in liberalisation that has been made throughout Eastern Europe since 1952, is a striking demonstration of the capacity of state socialism for self-renewal.[5]

Considered from the standpoint of classical Marxism, it makes most sense to regard the state socialist countries as countries in which the Communist Party has substituted itself for the national bourgeoisie as the main engine of economic develop-

[5] Since 1953 much progress in this area has been made throughout Eastern Europe. In the USSR, substantial steps forward are the reestablishment of a partial labour market (i.e. closing the camps, permitting workers to change their jobs freely but not permitting firms to fire workers, and issuing passports to villagers), the toleration of active oppositionists such as Sakharov, the ending of jamming some radio stations broadcasting to the USSR, and allowing political opponents and a substantial proportion of one ethnic minority to leave the country. In some state socialist countries, e.g. Poland, the censorship has been quite liberal for many years. Furthermore, some state socialist countries, e.g. Hungary, allow substantial travel to capitalist countries by their citizens.

ment. Hence its intolerance of independent social and political organisations, and its own internal organisation (the determination of policy by a small group of leaders or a single leader) takes on a decisive weight in the overall characterisation of these societies. It is characteristic of ruling Communist Parties that supreme power is concentrated in a single pair of hands for decades (e.g. USSR 1929–53, China 1949–76), in violation of all democratic principles but in a way familiar in the Roman Empire or Oriental Despotisms.

It is because of the use that these dictators have made of their power, that the crucial issue for Marxism–Leninism today concerns the development of the political system. As Hegedus (1970 p. 30) has put it, 'the fundamental problem of Marxism today concerns the position to be taken regarding the theoretical or practical alternatives within the political structure, the power structure, the state – or closer to reality – the administration of society. This problem can be avoided for a while as a so-called delicate question but social reality requires an answer more and more urgently'. This fundamental question has been posed theoretically by Hegedus (1976a), Carrillo (1977) and Miliband (1977), and practically by Mao, Dubcek and Brezhnev, and remains the fundamental problem of the further development of state socialism. This fundamental problem has two aspects. The first concerns the evolution of the role of the party leadership within the party ('inner party democracy'). The second concerns the role of the state in state socialist society.

As far as the first is concerned, the general position throughout the international Communist movement remains as established by Lenin. That is, the leader has enormous power, remains in office till death and cannot be removed by the membership. Organisation of party members round political positions at variance with the leadership is banned, and has been since the resolution on fractions adopted at the 10th Congress of the Russian Communist Party in 1921. The nearest the state socialist countries have moved to a Schumpeterian conception of democracy (rotation of elites) is in Poland, where both in 1956 and in 1970 the leadership changed in response to popular pressure. 'Democracy by riot and strike', like the 'collective bargaining by riot' which existed in late-eighteenth- and early-nineteenth-century Britain, is undoubtedly relatively progressive. While progressive relative to autocracy, however, it is scarcely a regular process for rotation of elites in response to popular wishes. In the USSR there has been a move, if not towards democracy, then at least towards oligarchy, as shown by the dismissal of Khrushchev in 1964. Oligarchy too is relatively progressive, relative that is to autocracy. How the relative importance of the autocratic, oligarchic and democratic elements in the Soviet political system will evolve, remains to be seen.

As far as the second is concerned, perhaps the most important difference between the role of the state in capitalism and in state socialism concerns the existence of organisations independent of the state apparatus. As a Hungarian writer has put it (Rakovski 1977 p. 89),

> In capitalism in general, a considerable part of social practice and social interests is hived off from the totality of multifunctional institutions and constitutes itself as a group of specialised and formally autonomous organisations.
>
> This formal autonomy does not exclude a real dependence. It is hard to resist the temptation to consider these formal relations as nothing more than a mystification of the real relations. However, there is a basic difference between societies in which some at least of the specialised institutions are formally independent from the others, and those in which everything is subordinated to a single administrative hierarchy. It is this institutional difference which separates capitalist societies from soviet societies.

It is difficult to regard the subordination of the whole of society to a single administrative hierarchy as a characteristic of a higher type of social organisation than liberal democratic capitalism.

Experience so far has shown that Trotsky's argument, referred to in chapter 1, is correct in that there are indeed circumstances in which 'the democratic tasks of backward bourgeois nations in our epoch lead to the dictatorship of the proletariat'. It is possible to establish dictatorships in backward countries that create a proletariat and solve problems (such as industrialisation and the build up of defence capacity) that other regimes may be unable to resolve. Experience has also shown, however, that it is not true that under these circumstances 'the road to democracy leads through the dictatorship of the proletariat'. The dictatorship appears to be a road leading to rapid industrialisation, the rapid development of military power and permanent dictatorship. As far as the responsibility of the governors to the governed is concerned, and this is an important aspect of democracy, the dictatorship has not led to it anywhere. The Indian people had an opportunity of passing judgement on Mrs Gandhi, but no such opportunity was available to the Chinese people during Mao's rule. Mao's own attitude to democracy was clearly explained in 1973 when he told the visiting French leader Pompidou that (Benton 1977 p. 102), 'Napoleon's methods were best – he dissolved all the parliaments and nominated those he wanted to rule.' This autocratic, pre-democratic, attitude is normal, but not universal, throughout the state socialist world. In Brecht's well-known words, the attitude of some of the governments of the state socialist countries to popular dissatisfaction is that 'if the government has lost the confidence of the people it is necessary to dissolve the people and elect a new one', an attitude illustrated once more by events in Cambodia in 1975–76. In Poland and Hungary, on the other hand, the Governments are much more responsive to popular feelings. For example, in Poland agriculture is still mainly in private hands.

It would seem that the state socialist countries apply a decision-making procedure appropriate to one particular situation (the Prisoners' Dilemma) to a wide variety of situations. What is common to all the situations is the authoritarian character of the decision-making process. What is characteristic of only one of them (the Prisoners' Dilemma) is that this leads to a result more favourable for the individuals concerned than the one they themselves would have chosen. Only in this one case is there a sense in which the outcome can be considered democratic. The unwarranted extension of a decision-making process entirely justified in a special case, results in general and permanent authoritarianism. This authoritarianism is more extreme than in traditional authoritarian regimes, since it is part of a violent and revolutionary transformation of the entire society.

Distribution

As far as the distribution of income is concerned, it was argued in chapter 7 that the available evidence is inadequate to make satisfactory comparisons between state socialism and capitalism, largely because of the absence of data for China. It seems very probable, however, that the distribution of income in the state socialist countries is significantly more equal than in capitalist countries at comparable levels of development. Furthermore, countries with state ownership of the means of production naturally do not have the small minority of individuals with huge holdings of means of production normal under capitalism. In addition, the elite in the state socialist countries is significantly worse off than the elite in capitalist countries. State socialism is neither a necessary, nor a sufficient, condition to ensure a more equal distribution of income than any capitalist country. It does, however, seem to be one of the factors, along with level of development and smallness of the population, associated with greater equality.

As far as the distribution of power is concerned, it would seem that the result of the combination of a permanent dictatorship with the absence of independent social organisations, is inequalities of power much greater than in liberal democratic capitalist countries. The inequality between those who organised, and those whose lives were transformed by, collectivisation and the Gulag Archipelago in the USSR; collectivisation, the Great Leap Forward and the Great Proletarian Cultural Revolution in China; and sending down the entire urban population in Cambodia; were all enormous. On the other hand, in both capitalist and state socialist countries, the long-run tendency appears to be for inequalities of power to diminish. Capitalism no longer sports the slave-worked plantations of the eighteenth and nineteenth centuries, nor the great differences between the masters and servants of the early factories. In the state socialist world, Stalin was officially criticised at the 20th and 22nd Congresses and the chances of a repetition in China of episodes such as the Great Leap Forward and the Great Proletarian Cultural Revolution appear to be low.

The social ownership of the means of production

An important phenomenon distinguishing all the state socialist countries from the capitalist ones is the state ownership of all, or virtually all, of the means of production. Is this sufficient for a higher mode of production? The Marxist–Leninist answer is positive, but, in addition to the points made above about the political differences between capitalism and state socialism, the following points are relevant.

What happens when the means of production are nationalised in an economy which is too backward for the emancipation of the proletariat? This question was long ago considered by the founder of the Russian Marxist movement, G. V. Plekhanov. Writing in the 1880s and polemicising against the Narodnik view that it would be possible to organise a socialist revolution in Russia in the near future, he argued that this was absurd. Russia, he wrote in *Socialism and the political struggle* (1883), lacked the necessary conditions for this. These conditions were both objective (huge development of the productive forces, need for full socialisation for further economic development, working class as bulk of the population) and subjective (general acceptance of socialist ideas). Were revolutionary socialists to take power under these conditions and attempt to establish socialism, they 'would have to seek salvation in the ideals of "patriarchal and authoritarian communism", introducing into these ideals only the change that a socialist caste would manage national production instead of the Peruvian Children of the Sun [i.e. the Incas] and their officials.' Such a regime would be unable to attain the goals of the socialist movement.

This view was general in the Russian Marxist movement, and was endorsed two decades later by Lenin. In *Two tactics of Socialdemocracy in the democratic revolution* (1905), he argued against

> the absurd, semi-anarchist view that the maximum programme, the conquest of power for a socialist revolution, can be achieved immediately. The present degree of economic development of Russia – an objective condition – and the degree of class consciousness and organisation of the broad masses of the proletariat – a subjective condition indissolubly linked with the objective condition – make the immediate, complete emancipation of the working class impossible. Only the most ignorant people can ignore the bourgeois character of the present democratic revolution. Only the most naive optimists can forget how little as yet the masses of the workers are informed of the aims of socialism and of the methods of achieving it. And we are all convinced that the emancipation of the workers can only be brought about by the workers themselves; a socialist revolution is out of the question unless the masses become class-conscious, organised, trained and educated by open class struggle against the entire bourgeoisie. In answer to the anarchist objections that we are delaying the socialist revolution, we shall say: we are not delaying it, but are taking the first steps in its direction, using the only means that are possible along the only right path, namely the path of a democratic republic. Whoever wants to approach socialism by any other path than that of political democracy will inevitably arrive at absurd and reactionary conclusions both economic and political.

It can be seen that the classical Marxist attitude to premature attempts to build socialism is not that this will lead to a higher mode of production, but that it can only lead to a 'patriarchal and authoritarian communism' with a socialist caste substituting itself for the Incas, i.e. what Lenin termed 'absurd and reactionary conclusions both economic and political'.

Despite this classical Marxist position, the means of production have in fact been nationalised in countries which, from a classical Marxist perspective, lack the possibilities of constructing a socialist society. How should one evaluate the social relations resulting from this? This question was considered by Lange (1962 p. 12), who argued that state ownership was necessary, but not sufficient, for social ownership. It was not sufficient because state ownership might experience either anarcho-syndicalist degeneration or bureaucratic degeneration. Anarcho-syndicalist degeneration (as in Yugoslavia) turns state ownership into group ownership. This emphasises one half of the socialist objective (use by society) at the expense of the other (use for society). Bureaucratic degeneration (as in the USSR) turns state ownership into bureaucratic control. This emphasises use for society at the expense of use by society. This argument has been developed by Brus (1975), who has argued that the socialisation of the means of production is a *process* which begins with nationalisation and continues with democratisation.[6] By this criterion none of the state socialist countries have yet achieved the social ownership of the means of production because they have not yet established democracy. Hence, it follows that the state socialist countries are not characterised by a higher mode of production than the capitalist ones (because they have not established the social ownership of the means of production), although it is possible that they are on a road that will lead there.

Economic planning

All the state socialist countries have national economic plans. Is this sufficient to characterise them as forming part of a higher mode of production? The Marxist–Leninist answer is positive, provided there is also social ownership of the means of production. It is necessary to bear in mind, however, that the reason for this positive answer is the theory according to which

(a) a planned economy is bound to be more efficient than an anarchic one, and

(b) planning and the market are two mutually exclusive categories, so that an economy can be either planned or market but not both.

[6] Similarly, the Soviet sociologist Arutiunian, whose argument about socialisation as a process was quoted in chapter 6, concluded that (Arutiunian 1973 p. 114), 'The social task of the day comes down to the need for further democratisation of the functions involved in the disposition of property.'

As far as (a) is concerned, sixty years after the October Revolution it is possible to consider this theory as an empirical proposition. This was done above. The main conclusion reached was that the socialism/capitalism dichotomy is not a sufficient condition for distinguishing between efficient and inefficient economies. Indeed, if the Gomulka theory is utilised and efficiency understood as the rate of growth of labour productivity relative to the level of labour productivity, (a) is refuted in 1958–68 by four counterexamples (South Korea, Japan, Sweden and France).

As far as (b) is concerned, experience has shown that it is simply not true. What actually exists, both in the state socialist and in the capitalist countries, is planning *and* the market (Katsenelinboigen 1977a, 1977b, Meade 1968, Galbraith 1968).[7] When attempts have been made to eliminate market relations in the state socialist countries (the USSR in 1918–20 and 1930, China in 1958–59, Cuba in the 1960s) the results have always been adverse and it has always been necessary to reintroduce some market relations.

In view of these important lessons of experience, Sweezy (1977) for one has concluded that,

> I used to think that important principles were involved in the market vs plan question, but I no longer do. The concept of a pure market economy is of course an extreme and I think not very useful abstraction... Nevertheless, the notion of an opposition between market and plan, while by no means inherent in the concepts as such, *may* refer to a reality. Markets tend not only to reproduce but also to intensify and strengthen the social relations which they embody. They favour the rich over the poor, the skilled over the unskilled, the knowledgeable over the ignorant. If these tendencies agree with the biases of the planners, or if planners want at most to moderate excesses in the processes and results of market behaviour, there is no conflict. On the other hand, if planners aim to achieve results seriously at odds with the natural tendency of markets, or rather a system of markets, then indeed there is real opposition which may result in a struggle with several possible outcomes. But it will not be a struggle of market against plan or vice versa, but rather an essentially political struggle between the beneficiaries of the status quo and those who wish to change the status quo.

[7] Important market relations existing in the USSR at the present time include, the free market in agricultural products; the labour market; the legal consumer goods market; the black market in state provided goods and services unobtainable through official channels, in privately produced goods and imported goods; the legal market in artisan produced goods and services (e.g. medical and educational services); and the illegal market in scarce goods between state enterprises unable to obtain the necessary goods through official channels.

Conclusions

(1) The CMEA countries do not differ fundamentally from the capitalist countries with respect to the labour process, the division of labour, and the social ownership of the means of production. In both groups of countries, most of the population is forced to engage in dreary labour in a stratified, unequal society in which the means of production are not in social ownership.

(2) The CMEA countries have eliminated the enormous inequalities in ownership of the means of production normal under capitalism. In addition, they have a more equal distribution of income than comparable capitalist countries. In these two important respects, they are a higher form of socioeconomic organisation than capitalism. Their distribution of power, however, is more *un*equal.

(3) The situation in China is difficult to assess in the absence of reliable information and in the presence of frequent changes in economic policy. It seems, however, especially since the 11th Congress, basically similar in the above respects to the other state socialist countries.

An important feature of Chinese institutions in 1958–76 was the attempt to transform the relations of production in a communist direction before a society of material abundance was reached. The purpose of this was to avoid the bureaucratic degeneration (i.e. conclusion (1) above) alleged to have befallen the other state socialist countries. It had both negative results (e.g. the economic crisis of 1959–61) and positive results (e.g. the relatively egalitarian income distribution and the requirement for managers and officials to perform manual labour). Implicit in the actions of the post-Mao Chinese leadership has been the orthodox Marxist–Leninist view that it is necessary to achieve a society of material abundance before the relations of production can be transformed in a communist direction.

(4) The most significant political differences between the state socialist and capitalist countries are threefold. First, the former lack any regular process for rotation of elites in response to popular wishes. Secondly, in the former the whole of society is subordinated to a single administrative hierarchy. Thirdly, all the former but only some of the latter, lack the traditional liberal political freedoms. In these three important respects, state socialism is a lower form of socioeconomic organisation than liberal democratic capitalism.

(5) Experience has shown that the classical Marxist attitude to revolutions by socialists in backward countries was partially correct. Such revolutions have all led to what Plekhanov termed a 'patriarchal and authoritarian communism' with a socialist caste substituting itself for the Incas, i.e. what Lenin termed 'absurd and reactionary conclusions both economic and political'. Although the Parvus–Trotsky–Lenin theory of permanent revolution was correct in stressing the possibility of making revolutions in backward countries in the name of socialism, it was wrong, at any rate up till now, in supposing that the outcome would be democracy, understood as responsible government. The classical Marxist attitude was, however, also partially incorrect, because it ignored the possibility of such revolutions leading to rapid industrialisation. This is considered below under 'Empirical Considerations'.

(6) Self-management exists only in producer cooperatives in capitalist countries and in Yugoslavia. While it has important advantages, it does not eliminate the need for national economic planning and, in its Yugoslav form, its macroeconomic results are poor.

(7) All the state socialist countries have state ownership of the means of production. However, the premature introduction of state ownership can have very negative effects and the state ownership of the means of production is not necessarily social ownership.

(8) All the state socialist countries have national economic planning. All attempts to establish purely non-market economies, however, have led to adverse effects and had to be withdrawn. All existing state socialist economies (like the capitalist ones) have *both* planning *and* the market. As far as the relative efficiency of the capitalist and state socialist mixtures of planning and the market are concerned, this question was considered on pp. 247–257 above. It was concluded (conclusion (4), p. 256 above), inter alia, that 'the socialism/capitalism dichotomy is not a sufficient criterion for distinguishing between dynamically efficient and inefficient economies'.

EMPIRICAL CONSIDERATIONS

The main empirical issue raised by the historical experience of the state socialist countries is their success, or otherwise, in catching up with, and overtaking, the most advanced capitalist countries.

It can be seen from table 10.6 that the USSR has made substantial progress in overtaking and surpassing the United States. It already exceeds it in the production of a number of basic industrial commodities (e.g. oil, steel and mineral fertilisers) and in twenty-five years its national income has more than doubled relative to that of the United States. Similarly, whereas in 1941–45 the Soviet war with Germany, not the strongest capitalist country, was very even and nearly resulted in a German victory, at the present time the USSR has achieved military parity with the strongest capitalist country. Similarly, China has made rapid industrial and military progress since 1949. Although catching up with the advanced countries in labour productivity is still a matter for the distant future, the country has made substantial industrial progress[8] and does have its own nuclear weapons and delivery systems. Stalin and his successors have been successful in achieving the objectives he posed. Future years may well see further progress in catching up and overtaking, both in the economic and military fields. Nevertheless, although Soviet progress in *catching up* is clear, the apparent lack of technological creativity displayed by the USSR, raises doubts as to whether the country will ever *overtake* the United States.

Considered from this angle, Marxism–Leninism and Marxism–Leninism–Mao Tse-tung Thought appear as the ideologies of state-directed industrialisation in backward countries. They correspond, mutatis mutandis, to liberalism in Victorian Britain. Liberalism in Victorian Britain emphasised some genuine features of reality, the existence of political freedom and the ability of the new technology combined with capitalist social relations to generate new fortunes. It ignored, however, other aspects of reality, the grotesque inequalities, the lack of democracy, and the dependence of British prosperity on the fact that the British Navy and British temporary technological leadership enabled Britain to dominate the seas and markets of the world. Similarly, Marxism–Leninism and Marxism–Leninism–Mao Tse-tung Thought emphasise the very real phenomena of rapid industrialisation, the build-up of defence capacity, full employment, job security, social security and relative equality of income and ownership of the means of production. They ignore,

[8] In 1978, after a year's trials, China began exporting machine tools to the UK, the first industrial country. Although the machines were sold primarily on price, nevertheless this was a significant indication of the extent of Chinese industrialisation.

however, the equally real phenomena of the lack of any regular process for rotation of elites in response to popular wishes, the lack of liberal political freedoms, the authoritarian nature of power relations and the strongly hierarchical nature of the socio-political system. In addition, Marxism–Leninism ignores the lack of national independence in countries such as the GDR, Poland, Czechoslovakia and Hungary (where the situation is similar, in this respect, to that in much of Latin America).

Liberalism was undermined by the rise of democracy and the labour movement. The labour movement, committed to socialism, was able to use liberal democratic institutions to reduce inequalities substantially (by taxation, transfer payments and free or subsidised state provision of education, medical care and housing). Nevertheless, the labour movement has been unable to eliminate inequality, to establish permanent full employment, or to solve the chronic problem of Britain's low rate of economic growth. Where the labour movement is not committed to socialism (as in the United States) its social achievements have been even less impressive.

Marxism–Leninism has been undermined both by the growth of a white collar intelligentsia committed to pluralism and greater differentiation, and by movements striving for national independence. It has survived up till now in the USSR, however, because of the autocratic traditions of the Russian state, the service mentality of the white collar intelligentsia, the overwhelming importance in the USSR of the national question, and the continued success up till now of the Soviet state in maintaining economic growth, raising living standards, expanding Soviet world political influence, and preserving national independence. Where the social and national movements point in the same direction (as in Czechoslovakia) only external military force can maintain the veneer of Marxism–Leninism and the institutions of state socialism. Where the white collar intelligentsia is quantitatively insignificant, and the state socialist countries have supported the struggle against colonialism and semi-colonialism or Communist Parties have guided that struggle (e.g. the Caribbean, South East Asia, Southern Africa), then Marxism–Leninism and Marxism–Leninism–Mao Tse-tung Thought have spread.

Summary

This chapter considered the experience of socialist planning from the standpoint of the two issues raised in the first chapter, the creation of a higher mode of production and the need for backward countries to catch up. The first issue was considered from the standpoint of seven criteria, the conclusions on all the criteria being summarised above. As far as catching up is concerned, it was suggested that the USSR and China have both made substantial progress in this direction, the USSR much more so than China. Although the USSR still has many years to go before it is likely to catch up with the USA in the crucial synthetic efficiency index, labour productivity, it has already caught up in the decisive military field.

SUGGESTIONS FOR FURTHER READING

G. Lichtheim, *A short history of socialism* (London 1970).

S. Gomulka, *Inventive activity, diffusion and the stages of economic growth* (Aarhus 1971).

P. Berger, *Pyramids of sacrifice* (London 1976).

S. Gomulka, 'Economic factors in the democratization of socialism and the socialization of capitalism', *Journal of Comparative Economics* vol. 1 no. 4 (December 1977).

R. L. Carson, *Comparative economic systems* (New York 1973).

J. Vanek (ed.), *Self-management: Economic liberation of man* (London 1975).

E. L. Wheelright & B. McFarlane, *The Chinese road to socialism* (New York 1971).

L. Goodstadt, *China's search for plenty* (New York 1973).

R. Baum, *Prelude to revolution* (New York 1975).

R. Baum, Technology, economic organisation, and social change: Maoism and the Chinese industrial revolution, *China in the seventies* (Wiesbaden 1975) pp. 131–91.

E. F. Vogel, *Canton under Communism* (Cambridge, Mass. 1969).

E. H. Carr, 'Some random reflection on Soviet industrialisation', C. H. Feinstein (ed.), *Socialism, capitalism and economic growth* (the Dobb Festschrift) (Cambridge 1967).

R. Selucky, *Economic reforms in Eastern Europe* (New York 1972).

R. Medvedev, *Socialist democracy* (London 1975).

BIBLIOGRAPHY

This is a selective bibliography which includes only those works referred to in the text, listed at the end of the chapters or found particularly useful by the author.

NOTES

(1) Books in Russian are published in Moscow unless otherwise stated. Books in English are published in London unless otherwise stated.
(2) Russian words are transliterated into English according to the *Soviet Studies* transliteration system, with the exception that when proper names end in 'ii' the last two letters are sometimes transliterated by a 'y'.

Abdel-Fadil, M. (1973). 'Note sur les différents modes de développement dans les conditions du socialisme', *Cultures et développement* (1973).

(1976). *Development, income distribution and social change in rural Egypt (1952–1970)* (Cambridge 1976).

Abouchar, A. (1971). *Soviet planning and spatial efficiency* (Bloomington 1971).

(1972). 'The new standard methodology for investment allocation', *Soviet Studies* vol. 24.

Adler-Karlsson, G. (1968). *Western economic warfare 1947–1967* (Uppsala 1968).

(1976). *The political economy of East–West–South cooperation* (Vienna & New York 1976).

Amann, R. (1977). R. Amann, J. M.Cooper & R. W. Davies (eds.), *The technological level of Soviet industry* (New Haven 1977).

'American' (1977). 'The American rural small-scale industry delegation', *Rural small-scale industry in the People's Republic of China* (Berkeley 1977).

Amin, S. (1974). *Accumulation on a world scale* (New York & London 1974).

Andrle, V. (1976). *Managerial power in the Soviet Union* (1976).

Arrow, K. & Hahn, F. (1971). *General competitive analysis* (San Francisco & Edinburgh 1971).

Arutiunian, Yu. V. (1973). 'The distribution of decision-making among the rural population of the USSR', M. Yanowitch & W. A. Fisher (eds.) *Social stratification and mobility in the USSR* (New York 1973). Italics added to text quotation.

Ashbrook, A. G. Jr. (1975). 'China: Economic overview, 1975'; *China* (1975) q.v.

Ausch, S. (1972). *Theory and practice of CMEA cooperation* (Budapest 1972).

Avtomatika (1975). *Avtomatika i telemekhanika* No. 4 (1975) p. 190.

Avtomatizirovannaya (1972). *Avtomatizirovannaya sistema upravleniya* (1972).

Bachurin, A. (1969). 'V. I. Lenin i sovremennye problemy planirovaniya narodnogo khozyaistva', *Planovoe khozyaistvo* no. 11 (1969).

Bagchi, A. K. (1978). 'On the political economy of technological choice and development', *Cambridge Journal of Economics* vol. 2 no. 2 June 1978.

Bailes, K. E. (1977). 'Alexei Gastev and the Soviet controversy over Taylorism, 1918–24', *Soviet Studies* vol. XXIX no. 3 (July 1977).

Bajt, A. (1971). 'Investment cycles in European socialist economies: a review article', *Journal of Economic Literature* (1971).

Bandyopadhyaya, K. (1976). *Agricultural development in China and India* (New Delhi 1976).

Baran, P. & Sweezy, P. (1968). *Monopoly capital* (Penguin edn 1968).

Barsov, A. A. (1969). *Balans stoimostnykh obmenov mezhdu gorodom i derevnei* (1969).

(1974). 'Nep i vyravnivanie ekonomicheskikh otnoshenii mezhdu gorodom i derevnei', *Novaya ekonomicheskaya politika: Voprosy teorii i istorii* (1974).

Basic (1965). *Basic principles and experiences of industrial planning in the Soviet Union* (UN New York 1965).

Bastid, M. (1973). 'Levels of decision-making', Schram (1973) q.v.

Baum, R. (1975a). *Prelude to Revolution* (New York 1975).

(1975b). Technology, economic organisation and social change: Maoism and the Chinese industrial revolution, *China in the seventies* (Wiesbaden 1975) pp. 131–91.

Baumol. W. J. (1952). *Welfare economics and the theory of the state* (1952).

Beer, S. (1969). 'The aborting corporate plan: a cybernetic account of the interface between planning and action', E. Jantsch (ed.) *Perspectives of planning* (Paris 1969).

Bek, A. (1971). *Novoe naznachenie* (Frankfurt 1971).

Belkin, V. D. & Birman, I. Ya. (1964). Article in *Izvestiya* 4 December 1964.

Belyaev, V. (1968). 'Kakoi y tonny ves?' *Pravda* 6 December 1968.

Benton, G. (1976). 'China since the Cultural Revolution', *Critique* no. 6.

(1977). 'The factional struggle in the Chinese Communist Party', *Critique* no. 8.

Bergson, A. (1964). *The economics of Soviet planning* (New Haven & London 1964).

(1968). *Planning and productivity under Soviet socialism* (New York 1968).

Berliner, J. (1957). *Factory and manager in the USSR* (Cambridge, Mass. 1957).

(1964). 'The static efficiency of the Soviet economy', *American Economic Review* supplement (May 1964).
(1966). 'The economics of overtaking and surpassing', H. Rosovsky (ed.) *Industrialisation in two systems* (New York 1966).
(1976). *The innovation decision in Soviet industry* (Cambridge, Mass. 1976).
Bernstein, T. P. (1967). 'Leadership and mass mobilisation in the Soviet and Chinese collectivisation campaigns of 1929–30 and 1955–56: A comparison', *China Quarterly* no. 31 (July–September 1967).
Bettelheim, C. (1974a). *Les luttes de classes en URSS 1ère periode 1917–23* (Paris 1974).
(1974b). *Cultural revolution and industrial organisation in China* (New York 1974).
(1976). *Economic calculation and forms of property* (1976).
Bhaduri, A. (1977). 'On the formation of usurious interest rates in backward agriculture', *Cambridge Journal of Economics* vol. 1 no. 4 (December 1977).
Bliss, C. (1972). 'Prices, Markets and Planning', *Economic Journal* March 1972.
Bor, M. Z. (1971). *Osnovy planirovaniya narodnogo khozyaistva SSSR* (1971).
Bornstein, M. & Fusfeld, D. R. (1974). *The Soviet economy: a book of readings* (4th edn Homewood, Illinois 1974).
Brabant, J. M. P. van (1973). *Bilateralism and structural bilateralism in intra-CMEA trade* (Rotterdam 1973).
(1974). *Essays on planning, trade and integration in Eastern Europe* (Rotterdam 1974).
Brada, J. (1973a). 'The microallocative impact of the Hungarian economic reform of 1968: some evidence from the export sector', *Economics of Planning* vol. 13 nos. 1–2 (1973).
(1973b). 'The allocative efficiency of centrally planned foreign trade: a programming approach to the Czech case', *European Economic Review* no. 4 (1973).
Braverman, H. (1974). *Labour and monopoly capital. The degradation of work in the twentieth century* (New York 1974).
Brus, W. (1961). *Ogólne problemy funkcjonowanie gospodarki socjalistycznej* (Warsaw 1961).
(1973). *The economics and politics of socialism* (1973).
(1974). 'Income distribution and economic reforms in Poland', *Il Politico* vol. XXXIX no. 1 (1974).
(1975). *Socialist ownership and political systems* (1975).
Bufetova, L. P. & Golland, E. B. (1977). 'Narodnokhozyaistvenaya otsenka tekhnicheskogo progressa v otrasli', *Ekonomika i organizatsiya promyshlennogo proizvodstva* no. 2 (1977).
Bukharin, N. I. (1920). *Ekonomika perekhodnogo perioda* (1920).
Bukharin, N. I. & Preobrazhensky, E. (1969). *The ABC of Communism* (Penguin 1969 edn). This is a translation of a book first published in Russian in 1920.
Buzlyakov, N. I. (1969). *Metody planirovaniya povysheniya urovnya zhizni* (1969).

Byres, T. J. (1974). 'Land reform, industrialisation and the marketed surplus in India: An essay on the power of rural bias', D. Lehmann (ed.) *Agrarian reform and agrarian reformism* (1974).

Campbell, R. (1976). 'Technology levels in the Soviet energy sector', *East–West technological cooperation* (Brussels 1976).

Carr, E. H. (1939). *The 20 years' crisis* (1939).

(1945). *The Soviet impact on the Western World* (1945).

(1967). 'Some random reflections on Soviet industrialisation', C. H. Feinstein (ed.), *Socialism, capitalism and economic development* (the Dobb festschrift) (Cambridge 1967).

Carillo, S. (1977). *Eurocommunism and the State* (1977). There is a review in *New Times* no. 26 (1977).

Carson, R. L. (1973). *Comparative economic systems* (New York 1973).

Chao, K. (1970). *Agricultural production in Communist China 1949–1965* (Madison, Wis. 1970).

Chen, C. S. (1969). C. S. Chen (ed.), *Rural people's communes in Lien-chiang* (Stanford 1969).

Chen, J. (1973). *A year in upper felicity* (New York 1973).

Chen, Nai-Ruenn (1967). *Chinese economic statistics* (Chicago 1967).

Chertopolokhov, S. P. (1975). 'Ob ekonomicheskom zakone vozvysheniya potrebnostei v usloviyakh razvitogo sotsializme', *Lichnoe potreblenie pri sotsializme* N. D. Kolesov et al. (ed.) (Leningrad 1975) pp. 45–9. The text quotation is from p. 49. In the text I have altered the dates of his five periods slightly.

Chilosi, A. (1971). 'The theory of growth of a socialist economy of M. Kalecki', *Economics of Planning* no. 3 (1971).

China (1975). *China: A reassessment of the economy* (Joint Economic Committee US Congress Washington DC 1975).

CIA (1976). *People's Republic of China: Handbook of Economic Indicators* (Washington DC 1976).

Cipolla, C. (1965). *Guns and sails in the early phase of European expansion* (1965).

Clark, C. (1976). 'Economic development in Communist China', *Journal of Political Economy* vol. 84 no. 2 (1976).

Clecak, P. (1969). 'Moral vs material incentives', R. Miliband & J. Saville (eds.) *The Socialist Register 1969* (1969).

Crossland, C. A. R. (1956). *The future of socialism* (1956).

Crozier, M. (1964). *The bureaucratic phenomenon* (Chicago 1964).

Davies, R. W. (1967). 'Aspects of Soviet investment policy in the 1920s', C. H. Feinstein (ed.), *Socialism, capitalism and economic growth* (Cambridge 1967).

(1974). 'Economic planning in the USSR', M. Bornstein & D. Fusfeld (eds.), *The Soviet economy: a book of readings* (4th edn Homewood, Illinois 1974).

Davin, D. (1976). *Women-work: Women and the party in revolutionary China* (Oxford 1976).

Dido, M. (1971). Article in *L'espresso* (Rome) 26 September 71. The quote in the text is taken from *Critique* no. 4 p. 23.

Djilas, M. (1962). *Conversations with Stalin* (New York 1962).

Dmitriev, V. K. (1898). *Ekonomicheskie ocherki* (1898). The English translation of all three essays is V. K. Dmitriev, *Economic essays on value, competition and utility* (Cambridge 1974).

Dobb, M. (1955). *On economic theory and socialism* (1955).

(1960). *An essay on economic growth and planning* (1960).

(1967). *Papers on capitalism, development and planning* (1967).

Dodge, N. T. & Wilber, C. K. (1970). 'The relevance of Soviet industrial experience for less developed countries', *Soviet Studies* vol. 21 (1970).

Domar, E. (1957). 'A Soviet model of growth', E. Domar, *Essays in the theory of economic growth* (New York 1957).

Donnithorne, A. (1967). *China's economic system* (1967).

Dorner, P. (1972). *Land reform and economic development* (1972).

Dorofeyev, V. (1976). Article in *Literaturnaya Gazeta* 31 March 1976 p. 13.

Dovgan', L. I. (1965). *O tempakh rosta dvukh podrazdeleniya obshchestvennogo proizvodstva* (1965).

Downs, A. (1967). *Inside bureaucracy* (Boston 1967).

Draft (1956). *The draft programme for agricultural development in the People's Republic of China* (Peking 1956).

Drogichinsky (1971). N. E. Drogichinskii & V. G. Starodubrovskii (eds.), *Osnovy i praktika khozyaistvennoi reformy v SSSR* (1971).

Eason, W. W. (1963). 'Labour force', A. Bergson & S. Kuzmets (eds.), *Economic trends in the Soviet Union* (Cambridge, Mass. 1963).

East European (1977). *East European economies post-Helsinki* (Joint Economic Committee US Congress, Washington DC 1977).

Eckstein, A. (1968a). 'Economic fluctuations in Communist China's economic development', Ping-ti Ho & Tang Tsou (eds.) *China in Crisis* vol. 1 book 2 (Chicago 1968). This paper is reprinted in Eckstein (1975).

(1968b). A. Eckstein et al. (eds.) *Economic trends in Communist China* (Chicago 1968).

(1971). A. Eckstein (ed.) *Comparison of economic systems* (Berkeley, California 1971).

(1975). *China's economic development* (Ann Arbor 1975).

(1977). *China's economic revolution* (Cambridge 1977).

Economic (1965). *Economic Planning in Europe* (UN Geneva 1965).

Eighth (1956). *The Eighth National Congress of the Communist Party of China* (Peking 1956).

Ekonomicheskaya (1974). *Ekonomicheskaya Gazeta* no. 27 (1974).

Ekonomika (1975). *Ekonomika i organizatsiya promyshlennogo proizvodstva* no. 6 (1975).

Ekonomika KNR (1976). *Ekonomika KNR: vozmozhnosti i real'nost'* (1976).

Eleventh (1977). *The eleventh national congress of the Communist Party of China (documents)* (Peking 1977).

Ellman, M. J. (1966). 'Individual preferences and the market', *Economics of Planning* no. 3 (1966).

(1969a). 'Aggregation as a cause of inconsistent plans', *Economica* (February 1969).

(1969b). *Economic reform in the Soviet Union* (1969).

(1973). *Planning problems in the USSR* (Cambridge 1973).

(1975). 'Did the agricultural surplus provide the resources for the increase in investment in the USSR during the First Five Year Plan?' *Economic Journal* (December 1975).

(1977). 'Seven theses on Kosyginism', *De Economist* no. 1 (1977).

(1978). 'On a mistake of Preobrazhensky and Stalin', *Journal of Development Studies* (April 1978).

Engels, F. (1894). 'The peasant question in France and Germany'. Reprinted in K. Marks i F. Engel's, *Sochineniya* 2nd ed, vol. 22 (1962).

Feiwel, G. R. (1975). *The intellectual capital of Michal Kalecki* (Knoxville, Tenn. 1975).

Feldman, G. A. (1964). 'On the theory of growth rates of national income', pp. 174–99 & 304–31 of N. Spulber (ed.) *Foundations of Soviet strategy for economic growth* (Bloomington, Indiana 1964). This is a translation of a work originally published in 1928.

Fletcher, M. D. (1974). *Workers and Commissars: trade union policy in the People's Republic of China* (Bellingham Washington 1974).

Frank, A. G. (1969). *Capitalism and underdevelopment in Latin America* (2nd edn New York & London 1969).

Friss, I. (1971). 'On long term national economic planning', I. Friss, *Economic laws, policy, planning* (Budapest 1971) pp. 112–39.

Galbraith, J. (1968). *The new industrial state* (New York 1968).

Garnsey, E. (1975). 'Occupational structure in industrialised society: Some notes on the convergence thesis in the light of Soviet experience', *Sociology* vol. 9 no. 3 (September 1975).

Goldmann, J. (1964). 'Fluctuations and trends in the rate of economic growth in some socialist countries', *Economics of Planning* vol. 4 no. 2 (1964).

Goldmann, J. & Flek, J. (1967). 'Vlnovitý pohyb v tempu dynamice zásov', *Plánované Hospodarství* vol. 20 no. 9 (1967).

Gomulka, S. (1971). *Inventive activity, diffusion and the stages of economic growth* (Aarhus 1971).

(1977). 'Economic factors in the democratization of socialism and the socialization of capitalism', *Journal of Comparative Economics* vol. 1 no. 4 (December 1977).

(1978). 'Growth and the import of technology: Poland 1971–1980', *Cambridge Journal of Economics* vol. 2 no. 1 (March 1978).

Gomulka, S. & Sylestrowicz, J. (1976). 'Import led growth: theory and estimation', *On the measurement of factor productivities: theoretical problems and empirical results* F. L. Altmann, O. Kyn & H. J. Wagener (eds.) (Gottingen–Zurich 1976).

Goodstadt, L. (1973). *China's search for plenty* (New York 1973).

Goreux, L. M. & Manne, A. S. (1973). *Multi-level planning* (Amsterdam 1973).

Gorlin, A. C. (1974). 'Socialist corporations: the wave of the future in the USSR?', M. Bornstein & D. Fusfeld (eds.) *The Soviet economy: a book of readings* 4th edn (Homewood, Illinois 1974).

Gosudarstvennyi (1972). *Gosudarstvennyi pyatletnyi plan razvitiya narodnogo khozyaistva SSSR na 1971–1975 gody* (1972).

Gramsci, A. (1957). *The modern prince* (1957 edn).

Granick, D. (1967). *Soviet metal fabricating and economic development* (Madison, Milwaukee & London 1967).

(1976). *Enterprise guidance in Eastern Europe* (Princeton 1976).

Gray, J. (1972). 'The Chinese model: some characteristics of Maoist policies for social and economic growth', A. Nove & D. M. Nuti (eds.) *Socialist economics* (1972).

(1973). 'The two roads: Alternative strategies of social change and economic growth in China', S. Schram (ed), *Authority, Participation and Cultural Change in China* (Cambridge 1973).

Gregory, P. & Leptin, G. (1977). 'Similar societies under differing economic systems: the case of the two Germanys', *Soviet Studies* (October 1977).

Guidelines (1972). *Guidelines for project evaluation* (UNIDO 1972).

Habr, J. (1967). 'From central planning to socialist marketing: problems of information systems', *Bulletin of the International Statistical Institute* vol. 42 (1967) pp. 979–88.

Hahn, F. (1973). 'The Winter of our Discontent', *Economica* (August 1973).

(1974). 'Back to square one', *Cambridge Review* (November 1974).

Hamermesh, D. & Portes, R. (1972). 'The labour market under central planning', *Oxford Economic Papers* vol. 24 (1972).

Handy, L. J. (1971). 'National job evaluation: the Soviet Union and Poland', mimeo (DAE Cambridge 1971).

Hanson, P. (1968). *The consumer in the Soviet economy* (1968).

(1970). 'Acquisitive dissent', *New Society* 29 October 1970. This article is reprinted in P. Barker (ed.) *One for sorrow, Two for joy: Ten years of New Society* (1972).

(1971). 'East-West comparisons and comparative economic systems', *Soviet Studies* vol. 22 (1971).

(1974). *Advertising and socialism* (1974).

Haraszi, M. (1975). 'I have heard the iron cry', *New Left Review* no. 91.

Hayden, E. W. (1976). *Technology transfer to East Europe. US corporate experience* (New York 1976).

Hayek, F. (1935). F. Hayek (ed.) *Collectivist economic planning* (1935).

Heal, G. (1973). *The theory of economic planning* (Amsterdam 1973).

Hegedus, A. (1970). 'Marxist theories of leadership and bureaucracy', R. B. Farrell (ed.) *Political leadership in Eastern Europe and the Soviet Union* (1970).

(1976a). *Socialism and bureaucracy* (1976).

(1976b). A. Hegedus, M. Markus, A. Heller & M. Vajda, *The humanisation of socialism* (1976).

Hitch, C. J. & McKean, R. N. (1960). *The economics of defence in the nuclear age* (Cambridge, Mass. 1960).

Hoffman, C. (1967). *Work incentive practices and policies in the People's Republic of China* (New York 1967).

(1974). *The Chinese worker* (Albany 1974).

Holesovsky, V. (1968). 'Planning reforms in Czechoslovakia', *Soviet Studies* (April 1968).

Holzman, F. (1960). 'Soviet inflationary pressures 1928–57: causes and cures', *Quarterly Journal of Economics* (1960).

(1974). *Foreign trade under central planning* (Cambridge, Mass. 1974).

Horvat, B. (1958). 'The optimum rate of investment', *Economic Journal* (1958).

(1964). *Towards a theory of planned economy* (Belgrade 1964).

(1965). 'The optimum rate of investment reconsidered', *Economic Journal* (1965).

(1974). 'Welfare of the common man in various countries', *World Development* vol. 2 no. 7 (1974).

Howe, C. (1973a). *Wage patterns and wage policy in modern China 1919–1972* (Cambridge 1973).

(1973b). 'Labour organisation and incentives in industry, before and after the cultural revolution', Schram (1973) q.v.

(1977). C. Howe & K. R. Walker, 'The economist', D. Wilson (ed.) *Mao Tse-tung in the scales of history* (Cambridge 1977).

(1978) *China's economy* (1978).

Hsiao, K. H. (1971). *Money and monetary policy in Communist China* (New York 1971).

Huberman, L. & Sweezy, P. M. (1969). *Socialism in Cuba* (New York & London 1969).

Huenemann, R. (1966). 'Urban rationing in Communist China', *China Quarterly* no. 26 (April–June 1966).

Hymer, S. & Resnick, S. (1971). 'International trade and uneven development', J. N. Bhagwati, R. W. Jones, R. A. Mundell & J. Vanek (eds.), *Trade, balance of payments and growth* (Amsterdam 1971).

Incomes (1967). *Incomes in postwar Europe* (UN ECE *Economic Survey of Europe in 1965:* Part II chapters 7–11, Geneva 1967).

Investment (1965). *Investment appraisal* (National Economic Development Office) 1st edn 1965, 2nd edn 1967.

Ishikawa, S. (1967). *Economic development in Asian perspective* (Tokyo 1967).

(1972). 'A note on the choice of technology in China', *Journal of Development Studies* vol. 9 (1972).

Jánossy, F. (1970). 'The origins of contradictions in our economy and the path to their solution', *Eastern European Economics* vol. VIII no. 4 (Summer 1970). This is a translation of an article published in Hungary in 1969.

Kaldor, N. (1966). *Causes of the slow rate of economic growth of the United Kingdom* (Cambridge 1966).

Kalecki, M. (1943). 'Political aspects of full employment', *Political Quarterly* (1943).

(1972). *Selected essays on the economic growth of the socialist and the mixed economy* (Cambridge 1972).

Kaser, M. (1967). *Comecon* (2nd edn Oxford 1967).

Katsenelinboigen, A. (1977a). 'Coloured markets in the Soviet Union', *Soviet Studies* (January 1977).

(1977b). A. Katsenelinboigen & H. S. Levine, 'The Soviet case', *American Economic Review* Papers and Proceedings (February 1977).

Keren, M. (1976). 'The GDR's "Economic Miracle"', *Problems of Communism* (January–February 1976).

Keynes, J. M. (1937). 'The general theory of employment', *Quarterly Journal of Economics* vol. 51 (1937).

Khan, A. R. (1976). *The distribution of income in rural China* (mimeo ILO Geneva 1976).

Khanin, G. I. (1967). 'Ekonomicheskii rost i vybor', *Novyi Mir* no. 12 (1967).

Khozyaistvennaya (1968). *Khozyaistvennaya reforma i problemy realizatsii* (1968).

Kirichenko, V. N. (1974a). *Dolgosrochnyi plan razvitiya narodnogo khozyaistva SSSR* (1974).

(1974b). V. N. Kirichenko (ed.) *Kompleksnye programmy v sisteme perspektivnogo narodnokhozyaistvennogo planirovaniya* (1974).

Kiser, J. W. III (1976). 'Technology is not a one-way street', *Foreign Policy* no. 23 (Summer 1976).

Klochko, M. A. (1964). *Soviet scientist in China* (1964).

Kornai, J. (1959). *Overcentralization in economic administration* (1959).

(1967). *Mathematical planning of structural decisions* (Amsterdam 1967). There is a 2nd edn Amsterdam 1975.

(1970). 'A general descriptive model of planning processes', *Economics of Planning* nos. 1–2 (1970).

(1971). *Anti-equilibrium: On economic systems theory and the tasks of research* (Amsterdam & London 1971).

(1972). *Rush versus harmonic growth* (Amsterdam 1972).

Kostakov, V. G. & Litvyakov, P. P. (1970). *Balans truda* (2nd edn 1970).

Kovalevskii, A. M. (1973). *Perspektivnoe planirovanie na promyshlennykh predpriyatiyakh i v proizvodstvennykh ob"edineniyakh* (1973).

Krasovsky, V. P. (1967). *Problemy ekonomiki kapital'nykh vlozhenii* (1967).

Kritsman, L. (1921). *O edinom khozyaistvennom plane* (1921).

(1924). *Geroicheskii period Velikoi Russkoi Revolyutsii* (1924).

Krylov, P. (1969). 'Tsentralizovannoe planirovanie v novykh usloviyakh', *Ekonomicheskaya Gazeta* no. 45 (1969).

Kudrov, V. M. (1972). 'Pyatidesyatiletie SSSR i ekonomicheskoe sorevnovanie dvukh sistem', *Mirovaya Ekonomika i Mezhdunharodnye Otnosheniya* no. 10 (1972).

(1973). 'Sovremennyi etap v ekonomicheskom sorevnovanii SSSR i SShA', *Sorevnovanie dvukh sistem* vol. 6 (1973).

(1976). 'Sovremennyi etap ekonomicheskogo sorevnovaniya dvukh mirovykh sistem', *Izvestiya Akademii nauk SSSR: Seriya Ekonomicheskaya* no. 4 (1976).

Kuron, J. & Modzelewski, K. (1968). *An open letter to the party* (English translation, n.d. 1968?).

Kuznetsov, V. L. (1976). *Economic integration: two approaches* (Moscow 1976).

Lane, D. (1971). *The end of inequality?* (1971).

Lane, D. & O'Dell, F. (1978). *Soviet industrial workers* (1978).

Lange, O. (1937). 'On the economic theory of socialism', *Review of Economic Studies* (February 1937).

(1961). *Teorija reprodukcji i akumulacji* (Warsaw 1961).

(1962). O. Lange (ed.) *Problems of political economy of socialism* (New Delhi 1962).

Lardy, N. R. (1975). *China* (1975) q.v. pp. 94–115.

Lavigne, M. (1973). *Le comecon* (Paris 1973).

Lehmann, D. (1974). 'Agrarian reform in Chile, 1965–1972: An essay in contradictions', D. Lehmann (ed.) *Agrarian reform and agrarian reformism* (1974).

Lenin, V. I. (1921). Speech at the 3rd all-Russian food conference, reprinted in *Pol'noe sobranie sochinenii* 5th edn vol. 43 (1963). The quotation is from p. 359.

(1956 edn). *The development of capitalism in Russia* (Moscow 1956 edn).

Leontief, W. (1966). *Input–output economics* (New York 1966).

(1971). 'The trouble with Cuban socialism', *New York Review of Books* 7 January 1971.

Leptin, G. & Melzer, M. (1977). *Economic reform in East German industry* (Oxford 1977).

Lerner, A. Ya. (1975). *Fundamentals of cybernetics* (New York 1975). This is a translation of *Nachala Kibernetiki* (1967).

Levcik, F. (1977). 'Migration and employment of foreign workers in the CMEA countries and their problems', *East European economies post-Helsinki* (JEC US Congress, Washington DC 1977).

Levin, A. I. & Yarkin, A. P. (1976). *Platezhesposobnyi spros naseleniya* (1976).

Lewin, M. (1974). '"Taking grain": Soviet policies of agricultural procurements before the War, C. Abramsky (ed.) *Essays in honour of E. H. Carr* (1974).

Li, Choh-Ming (1962). *The statistical system of Communist China* (Chicago 1962).

Liberman, E. G. (1950). *Khozyaistvennyi raschet mashinostroitel'nogo zovoda* (1950).

(1970). *Ekonomicheskie metody povysheniya effektivnosti proizvodstva* (1970). The English translation is *Economic methods and the effectiveness of production* (New York 1972).

Lichtheim, G. (1961). *Marxism* (1961).

(1970). *A short history of socialism* (1970).

Lippit, V. D. (1975). *Land reform and economic development in China* (New York 1975).

Lipton, M. (1974). 'Towards a theory of land reform', D. Lehmann (ed.), *Agrarian reform and agrarian reformism* (1974).

Litvyakov, P. P. (1969). *Nauchnye osnovy ispol'zovaniya trudovykh resursov* (1969).

Loasby, B. J. (1976). *Choice, complexity and ignorance* (Cambridge 1976).

Lyovin, A. I. (1967). *Ekonomicheskoe regulirovanie vnutrennogo rynka* (1967).

Mack, R. P. (1971). *Planning on uncertainty* (New York 1971).

Macpherson, C. B. (1973). *Democratic theory: essays in retrieval* (Oxford 1973).

Mahalanobis, P. C. (1953). 'Some observations on the process of growth of national income', *Sankhya* 1953.

Maitan, L. (1976). *Party, army and masses in China* (1976). (This is a translation from the Italian.)

Mandeville, B. (1724). *The fable of the bees* (1724). There is a Penguin 1970 edn.

Mannheim, K. (1936). *Ideology and utopia* (1936).

Manual (1968–69). Little, I. & Mirrlees, J., *Manual of industrial project analysis in developing countries* 2 vols. (OECD Paris 1968–69).

Mao Tse-tung (1954–61). *Selected Works* 4 vols (Peking 1954–61).

(1974a). S. Schram (ed.), *Mao Tse Tung unrehearsed* (1974).

(1974b). *Miscellany of Mao Tse Tung thought* (Joint Publications Research Service, Arlington, Virginia USA 1974).

(1977a). *On the ten major relationships* (Peking 1977).

(1977b). *Selected Works* vol. 5 (Peking 1977).

Marer, P. (1972). *Postwar pricing and price patterns in socialist foreign trade 1946–1971* (Indiana 1972).

(1974). 'Soviet economic policy in Eastern Europe', *Reorientation and commercial relations of the economies of Eastern Europe* (JEC US Congress, Washington DC USA 1974).

Marx, K. (1961). *Capital* vol. 1 (Moscow 1961).

Marx, K. & Engels, F. (1973 ed). *Feuerbach: Opposition of the Materialist and Idealist Outlooks* (the first part of *The German ideology*) (1973). This is a translation of the Soviet 1965–66 edition.

Matejko, A. (1974). *Social change and stratification in Eastern Europe* (New York 1974).

Matthews, M. (1975). 'Top incomes in the USSR: towards a definition of the Soviet elite', *Survey* vol. 21 no. 3 (1975).

(1978). *Privilege in the Soviet Union* (1978).

McAuley, A. (1977). 'The distribution of earnings and incomes in the Soviet Union', *Soviet Studies* (April 1977).

McAuley, M. (1969). *Settling labour disputes in Soviet Russia* (Oxford 1969).

Meade, J. E. (1968). 'Is the New Industrial State Inevitable?' *Economic Journal* (June 1968).

Medvedev, R. (1975). *Socialist democracy* (1975).

Mesa-Lago, C. (1968). *The labour sector and socialist distribution in Cuba* (New York 1968).

Metodicheskie (1969). *Metodicheskie ukazaniya k sostavleniyu gosudarstvennogo plana razvitiya narodnogo khozyaistva SSSR* (1969). The second edition is *Metodicheskie* (1974).

(1974). *Metodicheskie ukazaniya k razrabotke gosudarstvennykh planov razvitiya narodnogo khozyaistva SSSR* (1974).

Mieczkowski, B. (1975). *Personal and social consumption in Eastern Europe* (New York 1975).

Milenkovitch, D. D. (1977). 'The case of Yugoslavia', *American Economic Review* Papers & Proceedings (February 1977) pp. 55–60.

Miliband, R. (1975). 'Bettelheim and Soviet experience', *New Left Review* 91.

(1977). *Marxism and politics* (Oxford 1977).
Mill, J. S. (1891). *Principles of political economy* (1891). Book I chapter 9 and Book II chapters 6 & 7.
Millar, J. R. (1977). 'The prospects for Soviet agriculture', *Problems of Communism* (May–June 1977).
Mises, L. von (1920). 'Economic calculation in the socialist commonwealth', in Hayek (1935). This essay is a translation of a work first published in 1920.
National (1960). *National programme for agricultural development 1956–1967* (Peking 1960).
Neumann, J. von & Morgenstern, O. (1944). *Theory of games and economic behaviour* (1st edn Princeton 1944).
Nolan, P. (1976). 'Collectivisation in China – some comparisons with the USSR', *Journal of Peasant Studies* vol. 3 no. 2 (January 1976).
Nove, A. (1958). 'The problem of success indicators in Soviet industry', *Economica* (1958).
(1964). 'Occupational patterns in the USSR and Great Britain', chapter 15 of A. Nove, *Was Stalin really necessary?* (1964).
(1968). *The Soviet economy* (3rd edn 1968).
(1977). *The Soviet economic system* (1977).
Nove, A. & Nuti, D. M. (1972). *Socialist economics* (Penguin 1972).
Novozhilov, V. V. (1926). 'Nedostatok tovarov', *Vestnik Finansov* no. 2 (1926).
(1959). 'Izmerenie zatrat i ikh rezul'tatov v sotsialisticheskom khozyaistve', V. S. Nemchinov (ed.) *Primenenie matematiki v ekonomicheskikh issledovaniyakh* (1959). The English translation is A. Nove (ed.) *The use of mathematics in economics* (Edinburgh 1964).
Nuti, D. M. (1971). 'Social choice and the Polish consumer', *Cambridge Review* 28 May 1971.
(1977). 'Large corporations and the reform of Polish industry', *Jahrbuch der Wirtschaft Osteuropas* vol. 7 (Munich 1977).
Obst, W. (1973). *DDR Wirtschaft, Modell und Wirklichkeit* (Hamburg 1973).
Oksenberg, M. (1975). 'Communications within the Chinese bureaucracy', *China in the seventies* (Wiesbaden 1975) pp. 87–129.
Olivera, J. (1960). 'Cyclical growth under collectivism', *Kyklos* vol. 13 no. 2 (1960).
'Optimization' (1965). 'Optimization methods in planning foreign trade', *Economic Planning in Europe* (Geneva 1965). Part 2 of *Economic Survey of Europe in 1962*.
Padoul, G. (1975). 'China 1974: Problems not models', *New Left Review* no. 89 (January–February 1975).
Paine, S. (1976a). 'Balanced development: Maoist conception and Chinese practice', *World Development* vol. 4 no. 4.
(1976b). 'Development with growth: A quarter century of socialist transformation in China', *Economic and Political Weekly* special issue (August 1976).
Parkin, F. (1972). *Class Inequality and political order* (1972).
Pasqualini, J. (1975). J. Pasqualini & R. Chelminski, *Prisoner of Mao* (1975).

Patel, S. J. (1961). 'Rates of industrial growth in the last century, 1860–1958', *Economic Development and cultural change* (1961).

Perakh, M. (1977). 'Utilization of Western technological advances in Soviet industry', *East–West technological co-operation* (Brussels 1977).

Perlmutter, H. V. (1969). 'Emerging East–West ventures: The transideological enterprise', *Columbia Journal of World Business* (September–October 1969).

(1972). 'Towards research on and development of nations, unions and firms as worldwide institutions', H. Günter (ed.) *Transnational industrial relations* (1972).

Planning (1975). *Planning of manpower in the Soviet Union* (Moscow 1975).

Plekhanov, G. V. (1883). *Sotzializm i politicheskaya borba* (Geneva 1883). This is reprinted in *Sochineniya* 3rd edn (n.d.) vol. 2. The passage quoted in the text is on p. 81.

Political Economy (1957). *Political Economy. A textbook issued by the Institute of Economics of the Academy of Sciences of the USSR* (Moscow 1957). This is an English translation of the second Russian edition, published in 1956.

Pollitt, B. (1971). 'Some notes on Soviet economic debate in the 1920s', Discussion Paper No. 129, Economic Growth Centre, Yale University, USA, Appendix A.

Ponchaud, F. (1978). *Cambodia year zero* (1978).

Portes, R. (1974). *Macroeconomic equilibrium under central planning*, Seminar Paper 40, Institute for International Studies, Stockholm.

(1976a). 'The control of inflation: Lessons from East European experience', Birkbeck College discussion paper no. 44.

(1976b). 'Macroeconomic equilibrium and disequilibrium in centrally planned economies', Birkbeck College discussion paper no. 45.

(1977). 'The control of inflation: Lessons from East European experience', *Economica* (May 1977).

Programme (1958). *Programme of the League of Communists of Yugoslavia* (Belgrade 1958).

Pryor, F. L. (1973). *Property and industrial organization in communist and capitalist nations* (Bloomington, Indiana 1973).

(1977). 'Some costs and benefits of markets: An empirical study', *Quarterly Journal of Economics* (February 1977).

Raj, K. N. (1967). 'Role of the "machine-tools" sector in economic growth', C. H. Feinstein (ed.), *Socialism, capitalism and economic growth* (Cambridge 1967).

Raj, K. N. & Sen, A. K. (1961). 'Alternative patterns of growth under conditions of stagnant export earnings', *Oxford Economic Papers* (1961).

Rakovski, M. (1977). 'Marxism and Soviet societies', *Capital and Class* no. 1 (Spring 1977).

Ramsey, F. (1928). 'A mathematical theory of saving', *Economic Journal* (1928).

Rawski, T. G. (1975). 'China's industrial system', *China* (1975) q.v. pp. 175–98.

Reforma (1968). *Reforma stavit problemy* compilers Yu. V. Yakovlets & L. S. Blyakhman (1968).

Reshaping (1974). *Reshaping Britain* (PEP broadsheet No. 548 1974).

Richman, B. (1969). *Industrial society in Communist China* (New York 1969).

Riskin, C. (1973). 'Maoism and motivation: work incentives in China', *Bulletin of Concerned Asian Scholars* vol. 5 no. 1 (1973).

(1975). 'Workers' incentives in Chinese industry', *China* (1975) q.v.

Roberts, P. C. (1970). 'War Communism: A Re-examination', *Slavic Review* (June 1970).

(1971). *Alienation and the Soviet economy* (Albuquerque, N. Mex. USA 1971).

Robinson, J. (1960). *Exercises in economic analysis* (1960).

(1964a). 'Chinese agricultural communes', *Coexistence* (May 1964).

(1964b). 'Consumer's sovereignty in a planned economy, *On political economy and econometrics* (Warsaw 1964).

(1966). *The new mercantilism* (Cambridge 1966).

(1975). *Economic management in China* (1975). 2nd edn 1976.

(1977). 'Employment and the Choice of Technique', K. S. Krishnaswamy, A. Mitra, I. G. Patel, K. N. Raj, M. N. Srinavas (eds.), *Society and Change* (Bombay 1977).

Runciman, W. G. & Sen, A. K. (1965). 'Games, Justice and the General Will', *Mind* (1965).

Rweyemamu, J. (1973). *Underdevelopment and industrialization in Tanzania* (Nairobi 1973).

Sakharov, A. (1969). *Reflections on progress, peaceful coexistence and intellectual freedom* (1969).

Saunders, C. T. (1977). C. T. Saunders (ed.), *East–West cooperation in business: Inter-firm studies* (Vienna & New York 1977).

Schnitzer, M. (1972). *East and West Germany: A Comparative Economic Analysis* (New York & London 1972).

Schram, S. (1973). S. Schram (ed.) *Authority, participation and cultural change in China* (Cambridge 1973).

Schran, P. (1969). *The development of Chinese agriculture* (Illinois 1969).

Scott, H. (1974). *Does socialism liberate women?* (Boston 1974).

Seers, D. (1976). 'A system of Social and Demographic statistics: A review note', *Economic Journal* (September 1976).

Selucky, R. (1972). *Economic reforms in Eastern Europe* (New York 1972).

Selyunin, V. (1968). 'Vedomstvennyi bar'er', *Ekonomicheskaya Gazeta* no. 25 (1968).

Sen, A. K. (1961). 'On optimising the rate of saving', *Economic Journal* (1961).

(1968). *Choice of technique* (3rd edn Oxford 1968).

Senin, M. (1973). *Socialist integration* (Moscow 1973).

Shagalov, G. L. (1973). *Problemy optimal'nogo planirovaniya vneshnyeekonomicheskikh svyazei* (Moscow 1973).

Shanin, T. (1972). *The awkward class* (Oxford 1972).

Shtromas, A. (1977). 'Crime, law and penal practice in the USSR', *Review of socialist law* vol. 3 issue 3 (September 1977).
Sigurdson, J. (1977). *Rural industrialisation in China* (Cambridge, Mass. 1977).
Sik, O. (1972). *The bureaucratic economy* (New York 1972).
Silverman, B. (1971). *Man and Socialism in Cuba: The Great Debate* (New York 1971).
Simes, D. K. (1975). 'The Soviet parallel market', *Survey*, Vol. 21, No. 3 (Summer 1975).
Singh, A. (1973). 'Political economy of socialist development in China since 1949', *Economic and Political Weekly*, Vol. VIII, no. 47 (November 24 1973).
Sinha, R. P. (1974). 'Chinese economic performance', *The World Today* no. 1 (1974).
(1975). 'Chinese agriculture: A quantitative look', *Journal of Development Studies*, Vol. 11 (April 1975).
(1976). *Food and poverty* (1976).
Skurski, R. (1972). 'The buyers' market and Soviet consumer goods distribution', *Slavic Review* (December 1972).
Smekhov, B. M. (1968). 'Khozyaistvennaya reforma i stabil'nost' planov', B. M. Smekhov (ed.) *Problemy sovershenstvovaniya planirovaniya* (1968).
Solzhenitsyn, A. (1970 ed.). *The first circle* (1970).
Soos, K. A. (1976). 'Causes of investment fluctuations in the Hungarian economy', *Eastern European Economics* Vol. XIV, No. 2 (1976).
Sorokin, G. M. & Alampiev, P. M. (1970). G. M. Sorokin & P. M. Alampiev (eds.) *Problemy ekonomicheskoi integratsii stran – chlenov SEV* (1970).
Soviet (1972). *Soviet planning: principles and techniques* (Moscow 1972).
Spulber, N. (1964). *Foundations of Soviet strategy for economic growth* (Bloomington, Indiana USA 1964).
Stalin, J. (1929). 'On the right deviation in the AUCP(b)', printed in full in Stalin (1955a).
(1931). 'New circumstances – new tasks of economic construction', speech of 23 June 1931, reprinted in *Sochineniya* vol. 13.
(1954). *Works* vol. 11 (Moscow 1954).
(1955a). *Works* vol. 12 (Moscow 1955).
(1955b). *Works* vol. 13 (Moscow 1955).
(1972). *Economic problems of socialism in the USSR* (Peking 1972). The first edition was published in Moscow in 1952.
'Standard' (1960). 'The standard method for determining the economic efficiency of investment and new technology in the national economy', *Problems of economics* vol. III no. 6.
(1970). 'The standard method for determining the economic efficiency of investment', *Matekon* vol. VIII no. 1 (1970).
Statisticheskii (1977). *Statisticheskii ezhegodnik stran chlenov Soveta Ekonomicheskoi Vzaimopomoschi* (1977).
Steedman, I. (1979). *Trade among growing economies* (Cambridge 1979).

Steinbruner, J. D. (1974). *The cybernetic theory of decisions* (Princeton 1974).
Strauss, E. (1969). *Soviet agriculture in perspective* (1969).
Sutton, A. C. (1968). *Western technology and Soviet economic development 1917 to 1930* (Stanford, California 1968).
(1971). *Western technology and Soviet economic development 1930 to 1945* (Stanford, California 1971).
(1973). *Western technology and Soviet economic development 1945 to 1965* (Stanford, California 1973).
(1974). *Wall Street and the Bolshevik revolution* (New York 1974).
Sweezy, P. (1977). *American Economic Review*, Papers and Proceedings (February 1977) pp. 67–8.
Swianiewicz, S. (1965). *Forced labour and economic development* (Oxford 1965).
Szamuely, L. (1974). *First models of socialist economic systems* (Budapest 1974).
Talmon, J. L. (1952). *The origins of totalitarian democracy* (1952).
(1957). *Utopianism and politics* (1957).
(1960). *Political Messianism: the romantic phase* (1960).
Tannenbaum, A. S. et al (1974). *Hierarchy in organisations* (San Francisco 1974).
Ticktin, H. (1975). 'The current crisis and the decline of a superpower', *Critique* no. 5.
(1976a). 'The contradictions of Soviet society and Professor Bettelheim', *Critique* no. 6.
(1976b). 'The USSR: the beginning of the end', *Critique* no. 7.
Timar, J. (1966). *Planning the labour force in Hungary* (New York 1966).
Togliyatti, P. (1964). 'Pamyatnaya zapiska Pal'miro Tol'yatti', *Pravda* 10 September 1964.
Trotsky, L. D. (1930). *Permanentnaya revolyutsiya* (Berlin 1930). Italics added.
Turcan, J. R. (1977). 'Some observations on retail distribution in Poland', *Soviet Studies* vol. XXIX no. 1 (January 1977).
Use (1975). *Use of systems of models in planning* (UN New York 1975).
Vainshtein, A. L. (1969). *Narodnyi dokhod rossii i SSSR* (1969).
Val'tukh, K. K. (1977). 'Intensifikatsiya proizvodstva i sovershenstvovanie planirovaniya', *Ekonomika i organizatsiya promyshlennogo proizvodstva* no. 2 (1977).
Vanek, J. (1975). J. Vanek (ed.) *Self-management: Economic liberation of man* (1975).
Vogel, E. F. (1969). *Canton under Communism* (Cambridge, Mass. 1969).
Warriner, D. (1969). *Land reform in principle and practice* (1969).
Watanbe, S. (1974). 'Reflections on current policies for promoting small enterprises and sub-contracting', *International Labour Review* (November 1974).
Watson, A. (1975). *Living in China* (1975).
Weitzman, P. (1974). 'Soviet long term consumption planning: distribution according to rational need', *Soviet Studies* (July 1974).
Weitzmann, M. (1974). 'Prices versus quantities', *Review of Economic Studies* (1974).

Wheelwright, E. L. & McFarlane, B. (1970). *The Chinese road to socialism* (1970).
White book (1951). *White book on aggressive activities by the Governments of the USSR, Poland, Czechoslovakia, Hungary, Rumania, Bulgaria and Albania towards Yugoslavia* (Belgrade 1951).
Whyte, M. K. (1975). 'Inequality and stratification in China', *The China Quarterly* (December 1975).
Wilczynski, J. (1976). *The multinationals and East–West relations* (1976).
Wiles, P. (1962). *The political economy of Communism* (Oxford 1962).
(1968). *Communist international economics* (Oxford 1968).
(1972). 'Soviet unemployment on US definitions' *Soviet Studies* vol. 23 (April 1972).
(1974a). *Distribution of income: East and West* (Amsterdam 1974).
(1974b). 'La lotta contro l'inflazione nelle economie collectiviste: una valutazione', *Rivista di Politica Economica* (December 1974).
(1974c). 'The control of inflation in Hungary', *Economie appliquée* vol. 27 (1974) pp. 119–48.
Yuan-li Wu. (1967). 'Planning, management and economic development in Communist China', *An economic profile of Mainland China* (Joint Economic Committee US Congress Washington DC 1967).
Zielinski, J. (1967). 'On the theory of success indicators', *Economics of Planning* no. 1 (1967).
(1970). 'Planification et gestion au niveau de la branche industrielle en Europe de l'Est', *Revue de l'Est* vol. 1, no. 1 (1970).
(1973). *Economic reforms in Polish industry* (1973).

INDEX